BBC BASIC
Reference Manual

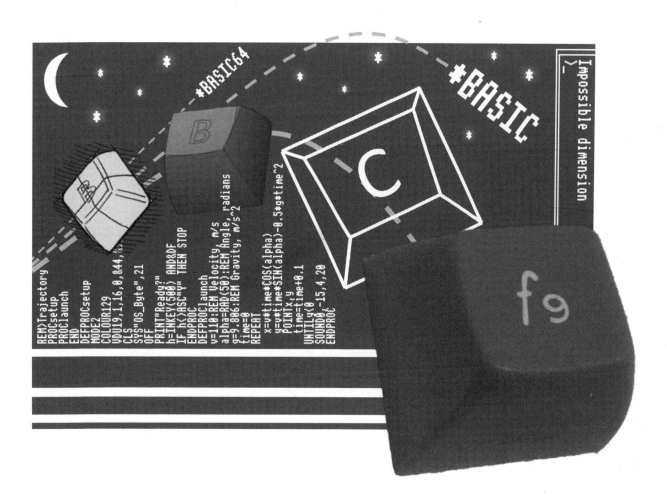

Copyright © 1992 Acorn Computers Limited. All rights reserved.

Updates and changes copyright © 2017 RISC OS Open Ltd. All rights reserved.

Issue 1 published by Acorn Computers Technical Publications Department.

Issue 2 published by RISC OS Open Ltd.

No part of this publication may be reproduced or transmitted, in any form or by any means, electronic, mechanical, photocopying, recording or otherwise, or stored in any retrieval system of any nature, without the written permission of the copyright holder and the publisher, application for which shall be made to the publisher.

The product described in this manual is not intended for use as a critical component in life support devices or any system in which failure could be expected to result in personal injury.

The product described in this manual is subject to continuous development and improvement. All information of a technical nature and particulars of the product and its use (including the information and particulars in this manual) are given by the publisher in good faith. However, the publisher cannot accept any liability for any loss or damage arising from the use of any information or particulars in this manual.

If you have any comments on this manual, please complete the form at the back of the manual and send it to the address given there.

Within this publication, the term 'BBC' is used as an abbreviation for 'British Broadcasting Corporation', however the BBC is not affiliated in any way with this manual.

All trademarks are acknowledged as belonging to their respective owners.

Published by RISC OS Open Ltd.

Issue 1, October 1992 (Acorn part number 0470,280).
Issue 2, October 2017 (updates by RISC OS Open Ltd).

Contents

Part 1 – Overview 1

About the BBC BASIC Reference Manual 3
Intended readership 3
Structure of the manual 3
Conventions used in this manual 4

About BBC BASIC 5
The BASIC interpreter 5
BASIC V and BASIC VI 5
BASIC versions 6
Window managed programs 7

Part 2 – Programming techniques 9

Command mode 11
Entering BASIC 11
Leaving BASIC 12
Command mode 12

Simple programming 15
Entering a program 15
Altering a program 16
Deleting whole programs 19
Numbering lines in a program 20
Listing long programs 21
Comments 22
Multiple statements 23
Saving and recalling programs 24

Variables 27
Types of variables 27
Naming variables 27

Numeric expressions 29
Integers and floating point numbers 29
Special integer variables 31
Arithmetic operators 31

Binary and logic 33
Binary numbers and bits 33
Hexadecimal numbers 33
Shift operators 34
AND, OR and EOR 36
TRUE and FALSE 37

String expressions 39
Assigning values to string variables 39
Joining strings together 40
Splitting strings 40
How characters are represented 43
Converting between strings and numbers 43

Arrays 47
The DIM statement 47
Two dimensional arrays 47
Finding the size of an array 49
Operating on whole arrays 49
Array operations 52

Outputting text 55
Print formatting 55
The text cursor 58
Defining your own characters 60

Inputting data 63
Inputting data from the keyboard 63
Including data as part of a program 65
Programming the keyboard 67
Using the mouse in programs 69
Programming function keys 71

Control statements 73
IF... THEN... ELSE 73
Operators 74
IF... THEN... ELSE... ENDIF 75
FOR... NEXT 77
REPEAT... UNTIL 80
WHILE... ENDWHILE 81
CASE... OF... WHEN... OTHERWISE... ENDCASE 82
GOTO 84
GOSUB... RETURN 84
ON... GOTO/GOSUB 85

Procedures and functions 87
Defining and calling procedures 87
Parameters and local variables 88
ON... PROC 92
Recursive procedures 93
Functions 94
Function and procedure libraries 95

Data and command files 101
Data files 101
Writing or reading single bytes 102
Writing or reading ASCII strings 103
Command files 104

Screen modes 107
Changing screen modes 107
Numbered screen modes 108
Text size 109
Colour modes 110
Changing colours 111
Changing the colour palette 112
VIDC1-style 256-colour modes 113
Using the screen under the Wimp 115

Simple graphics 117
The graphics screen 117
The point command 118
The line command 119
Rectangle and rectangle fill 120
Circle and circle fill 121
Ellipse and ellipse fill 121
Graphics colours 122
The graphics cursor 124
Relative coordinates and BY 124
Printing text at the graphics cursor 125

Complex graphics 127
Plotting simple lines 129
Ellipses 133
Arcs 134
Sectors 135
Segments 136
Flood-fills 136
Copying and moving 137

Graphic patterns 139
Default patterns 139
Plotting using pattern fills 140
Defining your own patterns 140
Native mode patterns 141
BBC Master mode patterns 143
Giant patterns 144
Simple patterns 145

Viewports 147
Text viewports 147
Graphics viewports 149

Sprites 151
Loading a user sprite 151
Plotting a user sprite 152

Teletext mode 153
    Coloured text 153
    Making text flash 154
    Double-height text 154
    Changing the background colour 154
    Concealing and revealing text 155
    Teletext graphics 155

Sound 159
    Activating the sound system 159
    Selecting sound channels 159
    Allocating a wave-form to each channel 159
    Setting the stereo position 160
    Creating a note 161
    Synchronising the channels 162
    Finding the value of the current beat 163
    Finding the current tempo 163
    Executing a sound on a beat 164

Accessing memory locations 165
    Reserving a block of memory 165
    The '?' indirection operator 166
    The '!' indirection operator 166
    The '|' indirection operator 167
    The '$' indirection operator 167

Error handling and debugging 169
    Trapping an error 169
    Generating errors 171
    External errors 171
    Local error handling 172
    Debugging 174

VDU control 177

Editing BASIC files 191
    Editing BASIC files with Edit 191
    Editing BASIC files with the BASIC screen editor 193

Part 3 – Reference 213

Keywords 215

* Commands 435

ARM assembler 441
Using the BASIC assembler 441
Saving machine code to file 445
Executing a machine code program 445
Format of assembly language statements 446
Recommended Books 447

Part 4 – Appendices 449

Appendix A – Numeric implementation 451
Numeric types 451
Effects of storage size 453
What is floating point arithmetic? 455
Implementation 455

Appendix B – Minimum abbreviations 459

Appendix C – Error messages 465

Appendix D – INKEY values 469
INKEY values by functional group 469
INKEY values by number 473

Appendix E – Specifying screen modes 477
Mode Strings 477
Mode Variables 479

Appendix F – Default palettes 481

Appendix G – Plot codes 483

Appendix H – VDU variables 485

Appendix I – BBC BASIC's history 489

Index 503

Part 1 – Overview

1 About the BBC BASIC Reference Manual

BBC BASIC is one of the most popular and widely-used versions of the BASIC programming language. This manual provides a complete description of BBC BASIC for users of computers running RISC OS version 3.10 or later.

Intended readership

You should read this manual if you are

- a computer user who has never used BBC BASIC before, who wants an introduction to a new computer language;
- an experienced programmer in other computer languages, who wants an insight into BBC BASIC's features without having to resort to a lengthy tutorial-type manual;
- an experienced BBC BASIC programmer, who needs specific information about the structure of BBC BASIC, and the use of its commands.

Structure of the manual

The manual is divided into the following parts:

Part 1 – Overview — includes this chapter, and the chapter entitled *About* BBC BASIC, which gives an introduction to BASIC VI. It compares BASIC VI with BASIC V, and describes the benefits and effects of using both versions.

Part 2 – Programming techniques — explains how to program in BBC BASIC, and introduces many of the commands (or keywords) provided by the language. The last chapter in this section describes the BASIC screen editor.

Part 3 – Reference — contains a complete list of BBC BASIC keywords, in alphabetical order. It defines the syntax of all the keywords, and gives you examples of how to use them.

Part 4 – Appendices — contains the appendices, which have useful reference material, such as numeric representation, error messages, keyword abbreviations and VDU variables. A brief history of BBC BASIC is also included.

Conventions used in this manual

The following conventions are applied throughout this manual:

- Specific keys to press are denoted as Ctrl, Delete and so on.
- Instructions which require you to press a combination of keys are shown thus: Shift-Home means hold down the Shift key and press and release the Home key.
- Text you type on the keyboard and text that is displayed on the screen appears as follows:
  ```
  PRINT "Hello"
  ```
- Classes of item are shown in *italics*: For example, in the descriptions of BASIC keywords, you might see something like:
  ```
  LET var = expression
  ```
  where *var* and *expression* are items you need to supply, for example:
  ```
  LET a$="hello"
  ```
- Items within square brackets [ ] are optional. For example,
  ```
  GCOL [expression2,] expression1
  ```
  means that you must supply at least one expression. If you supply two, you must separate them with a comma.
- All interactive commands are entered by pressing the Return key. However, this is not actually shown in the examples or syntax of commands.
- Extra spaces are inserted into program listings to aid clarity, but need not be typed in.
- Program listings are indented to illustrate the structure of the programs.

If at any time you wish to interrupt a program the computer is executing you can do so safely by pressing Esc.

Feel free to experiment. Try modifying the programs listed in this manual and writing new ones of your own.

2   About BBC BASIC

BBC BASIC consists of special keywords with which you create sequences of instructions, called programs, to be carried out by the computer. You can use programs to perform complicated tasks involving the computer and the devices connected to it, such as:

- performing calculations
- creating graphics on the screen
- manipulating data.

Several of the applications provided with RISC OS are themselves written in BBC BASIC.

The BASIC language operates within an environment provided by the computer's operating system. The operating system is responsible for controlling the devices available to the computer, such as:

- the keyboard
- the screen
- the filing system.

For example, it is the operating system which reads each key you press and displays the appropriate character on the screen. You can enter operating system commands directly from within BASIC, by prefixing them with an asterisk (*). These commands are described in the RISC OS *User Guide*.

The BASIC interpreter

When you run a BASIC program, the operating system passes it to the BASIC *interpreter*. This translates your instructions into a form that the computer can understand called machine code.

BASIC V and BASIC VI

RISC OS computers come with two different variants of the BASIC interpreter. The main difference between these is how they handle real (floating point) numbers internally.

5

- BASIC V is the most commonly used interpreter. Each real number is stored using 5 bytes of memory, and all real arithmetic is performed in software. This version of BASIC is provided by the "BASIC" module.
- BASIC VI is an alternative interpreter that performs calculations involving real numbers with greater accuracy. Real numbers are stored using 8 bytes of memory, and arithmetic is performed in accordance with the IEEE 754 floating point standard. Apart from increased accuracy, this also makes for easier data interchange with other languages like C. There are in fact two different variants of the BASIC VI interpreter, to cater for the two main floating point instruction sets which ARM processors have supported over the years:
    - The first variant of BASIC VI, provided by the "BASIC64" module, was released with RISC OS 3.10 and is designed around the FPA instruction set.
    - The second variant of BASIC VI, provided by the "BASICVFP" module, was released with RISC OS 5.24 and is designed around the VFP instruction set.

If you do need to know more about real numbers, *Appendix A – Numeric implementation* explains in detail how they are stored and manipulated, and gives details of the differences between the FPA and VFP variants of BASIC VI.

BASIC versions

Different versions of the BBC BASIC interpreter provide different features. This manual describes the features present in version 1.73 of the interpreter.

If you have an older version than this then you will need to obtain the latest version from the RISC OS Open web site (http://www.riscosopen.org) as part of the "System resources" archive. Open the archive and follow the instructions in the ReadMe file to merge these updates with your !System.

To load the newer version of the BASIC V interpreter in place of the one in the RISC OS ROM you will need to execute the following * Command:

```
RMEnsure BASIC 1.73 RMLoad System:Modules.BASIC
```

This should only be done once after the machine has started, and before entering the desktop, because BASIC programs that run inside the desktop will stop working if the BASIC interpreter changes whilst they are using it.

The recommended method for doing this is to create a file containing this command, set its file type to 'Obey', and add it to the `Choices:Boot.PreDesk` directory. Further information on the !Boot application and the PreDesk directory can be found in the RISC OS *User Guide*.

About BBC BASIC

You will find a list of the differences between each released version of the BASIC interpreter in *Appendix I – BBC BASIC's history*.

Window managed programs

If you wish to write programs that work in the desktop windowing environment you must read *The Window Manager* chapter in the RISC OS *Programmer's Reference Manual*. The Window Manager provides:

- a simple to use graphical interface
- the facilities to allow programs to run in a multitasking environment, so that they can interact with each other, and with other software.

The Window Manager is usually referred to as the Wimp (**W**indows, **I**cons, **M**enus and **P**ointer) and it simplifies the task of producing programs that conform to the notion of a 'desktop', where the windows represent documents on a desk. An example of a BASIC program written under the window environment is !Patience.

Instructions to avoid

If you do decide to write a window managed program you must be careful to avoid instructions in BASIC which will either interfere with the running of other programs under the Wimp, or simply not work at all. These include:

Avoid	Described in	Reason
GET, INKEY, INPUT	*Inputting data*	These commands work under the Wimp, but can cause problems.
*FX commands	*Inputting data*	Some *FX commands should be avoided under the Wimp; for example, using the Tab and cursor keys to get ASCII codes.

COLOUR, GCOL, MODE	*Screen modes*	These commands will interfere with other programs – use the facilities provided by the Wimp instead. For example:
		`SYS "ColourTrans_SetGCOL"`
		`SYS "Wimp_SetColour",0`

Flood-filling	*Complex graphics*	Flood-filling is not usable under the Wimp.
Viewports	*Viewports*	The Wimp uses its own viewports.
CLOSE#0	*Keywords*	This will close files opened by other programs.

Window managed programs

CLS, CLG	*Keywords*	These affect the whole screen.
TIME = *expression*	*Keywords*	This will change the clock for other programs, which they may not expect.

Part 2 – Programming techniques

3 Command mode

This chapter describes how to enter and leave BASIC, and how command mode works while within BASIC.

Entering BASIC

BASIC V

To start BASIC V, press F12 to access the command line and type the following:

```
BASIC
```

Press Return, and BASIC will start with a message of the form:

```
ARM BBC BASIC V (C) Acorn 1989
Starting with 651516 bytes free
```

BASIC VI

RISC OS 5 includes BASIC VI in ROM, whereas previous versions of RISC OS supplied it on disc. This is in contrast to BASIC V which has always been supplied in ROM.

To start BASIC VI, press F12 to access the command line and then type `BASIC64`. Press Return, and BASIC will start with a message similar to:

```
ARM BBC BASIC VI (FPA) (C) Acorn 1989
Starting with 581628 bytes free.
```

If you get the error message `Module BASIC64 not found` or `Module BASICVFP not found` on RISC OS 5 it suggests that the named module has been unplugged from ROM; consult the RISC OS *User Guide* for details on how to correct this.

On versions of RISC OS where BASIC VI is not in ROM, you will get the following error message if BASIC VI is not loaded and you are using a version of BASIC V older than version 1.73:

```
File 'BASIC64' not found
```

Leaving BASIC

If you get this message then you should download and install the latest version of !System from the RISC OS Open web site (http://www.riscosopen.org) and ensure that the updated BASIC module is loaded before the desktop starts, as described in the section entitled BASIC *versions* on page 6.

If you get the error message

```
File 'System:Modules.BASIC64' not found
```

then your !System does not contain a copy of BASIC64 and in this case too you should update to the latest version of !System.

BASIC files saved from both BASIC V and BASIC VI are the same and can be run using either BASIC, although the difference in arithmetic precision may give slightly different results for calculations using real numbers. Note also that differences in the lower-level interfaces to BASIC may cause compatibility issues for some advanced programs; consult the later chapters for details.

Leaving BASIC

To leave BASIC, type QUIT, then press Return twice to get back to the desktop.

Command mode

When you enter BASIC it is in *command* or *interactive* mode (sometimes this is termed *immediate* mode). This means that you can type commands and the computer responds straight away. For example, if you type

```
PRINT "Hello"
```

the computer displays the following on the screen:

```
Hello
```

PRINT is an example of a keyword which the computer recognises. It instructs the computer to display on the screen whatever follows the PRINT statement enclosed in quotation marks. Keywords are always written in upper case letters (capitals).

If you make a mistake, the computer may not be able to make sense of what you have typed. For example, if you type:

```
PRINT "Hello
```

the computer responds with the message:

```
Missing "
```

This is an error message. It indicates that the computer cannot obey your command because it does not follow the rules of BASIC (in this case because the computer could not find a second quotation mark).

If PRINT is followed by any series of characters enclosed in quotation marks, then these characters are displayed on the screen exactly as you typed them. Thus:

```
PRINT "12 - 3"
```

produces the output:

```
12 - 3
```

PRINT, however, can also be used to give the result of a calculation. For example, typing

```
PRINT 12 - 3
```

produces the output:

```
         9
```

In this case, because the sum was not enclosed in quotation marks, the computer performed the calculation and displayed the result.

Similarly, multiplication and division can be performed using the symbols * and /. For example:

```
PRINT 12 * 13
PRINT 111 / 11
```

Some commands, although they have an effect on the computer, do not give evidence that anything has changed. If, for example, you type

```
LET FRED = 12
```

nothing obvious happens. Nevertheless, the computer now knows about the existence of a variable called FRED which has the value 12. A variable is a name which can have different values assigned to it. It is described in more detail later in this manual.

Now if you type

```
PRINT FRED / 3
```

the computer responds by displaying the number 4.

The program below illustrates how you can give commands to produce some graphics on the screen:

```
CLS
CIRCLE FILL 600,500,100
```

Command mode

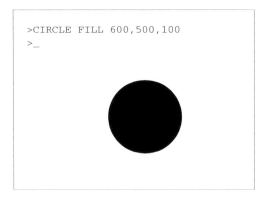

The CLS command clears the screen.

The CIRCLE FILL command tells the computer to draw a circle at a position 600 units across from the left of the screen and 500 units up from the bottom. The third number tells the computer how big the circle should be, in this case giving a radius of 100 units. Note that the units used by drawing commands ("OS units") often do not directly equate to pixels on the screen. In most cases, there are two OS units per pixel.

4 Simple programming

A program is a list of instructions to be carried out by the computer. These instructions are stored in memory and are only executed when you tell the computer to do so.

Entering a program

Once you have entered BASIC you can begin to type in programs. Each line of a program is numbered so that it can be referred to more easily. Note that you must press Return at the end of each line you type in. For example, type the following:

```
10 PRINT "Hello"
```

Note that nothing happens (but all must be well as no error message was printed). Now type

```
RUN
```

The Hello message is displayed on the screen. The number 10 at the start of the line is called the line number, and identifies the text after it as a program statement to be stored in memory, rather than as a command to be executed immediately.

You can type spaces either between the start of the line and the line number, or between the line number and the instruction without affecting the execution of the program.

```
     10        PRINT "Hello"
```

and

```
10PRINT "Hello"
```

are equally valid.

One of the advantages of programs is that they can be executed repeatedly: Typing RUN again here causes `Hello` to be displayed a second time – there is no need to type the complete `PRINT "Hello"` statement again.

The following is a simple program demonstrating the use of a variable and the INPUT statement:

```
10 PRINT "Can you give me a number ";
20 INPUT number
30 PRINT "The number you typed was ";number
```

The line numbers determine the order in which the computer executes these instructions. They can take any whole value between 0 and 65279. You can type line numbers in any order you like; BASIC will sort them into ascending order and obey them in this order.

Now RUN this program. The computer obeys line 10 and displays the message:

```
Can you give me a number ?
```

The question mark is added automatically by the execution of line 20. It will appear on a new line if you miss off the semicolon at the end of line 10.

The keyword INPUT instructs the computer to wait for you to type something, in this case a number. Type the following (followed by Return):

```
6
```

Line 30 is now obeyed, and the following message is displayed:

```
The number you typed was 6
```

Altering a program

Once you have entered a program, you may wish to make changes to it.

You can of course type in a whole new version of the program, but there are quicker methods available.

To see the program which is currently stored in memory, type

```
LIST
```

Lines 10, 20 and 30 are listed on the screen.

Replacing and adding lines

To add extra lines to the program, type in the new line with an appropriate line number:

```
5 PRINT "Hello"
40 PRINT "Twice ";number " is ";2*number
```

and then:

```
LIST
```

Note that these two extra lines are added to the program in such a way that the line numbers are listed in numerical order:

```
 5 PRINT "Hello"
10 PRINT "Can you give me a number ";
20 INPUT number
30 PRINT "The number you typed was ";number
40 PRINT "Twice "; number " is "; 2*number
```

To replace lines, enter the new line with the line number of the one which is to be replaced. For example:

```
40 PRINT number;" squared is ";number*number
```

Now when you type

```
LIST
```

the following is displayed:

```
 5 PRINT "Hello"
10 PRINT "Can you give me a number ";
20 INPUT number
30 PRINT "The number you typed was ";number
40 PRINT number;" squared is "; number*number
```

Altering a single line in a program

If you wish to alter only part of a line, for example, to correct a single spelling mistake, you can do so using the cursor edit keys. These are the arrow keys to the right of the main keyboard.

Suppose you want to change the word typed to entered on line 30. Begin by pressing the ↑ arrow key twice. The original cursor position which was under line 40 becomes a square and the cursor moves up to the start of line 30.

Press End a few times (this key was labelled Copy on older Acorn computers). The cursor editing moves along line 30, the square moves along as well, and line 30 is copied underneath line 40. Keep on pressing End until the word typed is copied and then stop.

If you hold the End key down, the repeat action allows you to move the cursor quickly across the screen. A quick press and release gives you precise control, moving one character position. The following is displayed on your screen:

Altering a program

```
 5 PRINT "Hello"
10 PRINT "Can you give me a number ";
20 INPUT number
30 PRINT "The number you typed_was ";number
40 PRINT number;" squared is "; number*number
30 PRINT "The number you typed
```

Press Backspace until the word `typed` is deleted from the new line 30. The cursor on the old line 30 does not move:

```
 5 PRINT "Hello"
10 PRINT "Can you give me a number ";
20 INPUT number
30 PRINT "The number you typed_was ";number
40 PRINT number;" squared is "; number*number
30 PRINT "The number you
```

Type the word

`entered`

and press End to copy the rest of line 30 to your new version.

Press Return. The square disappears and the cursor moves to the start of a new line. Now type

`LIST`

to produce the following:

```
 5 PRINT "Hello"
10 PRINT "Can you give me a number ";
20 INPUT number
30 PRINT "The number you entered was ";number
40 PRINT number;" squared is "; number*number
```

There are no restrictions on how much you move the cursor around when you are copying. Note when the cursor reaches the end of the screen it will wrap-around to the other side of the screen. You can use the right and left arrow keys to miss out parts of lines or to repeat them. You can also copy from several different lines on to your new line as you go.

Deleting lines

You can either delete lines one at a time, or delete a group of lines at once using the DELETE command.

Simple programming

To delete a single line, you just type the line number followed by Return. To delete line number 5, for example, type

5

To check that line 5 is deleted, type

LIST

and the computer displays the following:

```
10 PRINT "Can you give me a number ";
20 INPUT number
30 PRINT "The number you entered was ";number
40 PRINT number;" squared is "; number*number
```

The DELETE command allows you to delete a number of consecutive lines in three different ways:

- By deleting a block of lines. To delete all line numbers between 10 and 30 inclusive, type

    DELETE 10,30

- By deleting from the beginning of a program. To delete all lines from the beginning of the program to line 30, type

    DELETE 0,30

    The number zero is the minimum line number that can be used in a program. Therefore, all lines from the start of the program to line 30 are deleted.

- By deleting from a line to the end of the program. To delete all lines from line 20 to the end of the program, for example, type

    DELETE 20,65279

    The number 65279 is the maximum line number that can be used in a program, so in this case all lines from line 20 to the end of the program are deleted. Of course, you can use any other number which is higher than the last line of the program, so something like 60000 will usually work just as well, and is somewhat quicker to type!

Deleting whole programs

Before you enter a new program, make sure no program currently exists in memory. If it does, the lines of the new program you enter will get mixed up with the lines of the existing program, and this could produce strange results!

To delete any existing program, you can use the DELETE command described above, but an easier method is to type

NEW

This tells the computer to forget about any existing program, and to be ready to accept a new one.

Although the DELETE and LIST commands combined with cursor editing are fine for making small changes to a BASIC program, it is usually easier to edit programs using the desktop Edit application. In addition, the BASIC Editor provides an alternative way to edit BASIC programs outside of the desktop environment. See the chapter entitled *Editing BASIC files* on page 191 for details of using this program.

Numbering lines in a program

There may be occasions when you want to change the line numbers of a program without changing their order. The command to use is RENUMBER. This facility is particularly useful when you want to insert a large number of lines between two existing ones.

You can specify two numbers after typing the RENUMBER command. The first number tells the computer what you want the new first program line number to be. The second number tells the computer how much to add to each line number to get the next one.

For example,

```
RENUMBER 100,20
```

makes the first line into line 100 and numbers the remaining lines 120, 140, 160, and so on.

If you leave out the second number in the RENUMBER command, the computer automatically increments the line numbers in steps of 10. So, for example, you might want to renumber the following program:

```
23 PRINT "This demonstrates"
24 PRINT "the use of"
48 PRINT "the very useful"
67 PRINT "RENUMBER command"
```

Typing

```
RENUMBER 100
LIST
```

produces the following display:

```
100 PRINT "This demonstrates"
110 PRINT "the use of"
120 PRINT "the very useful"
130 PRINT "RENUMBER command"
```

Typing

RENUMBER

without including a number after the command, means that your program lines are renumbered 10, 20, 30, 40 and so on.

Automatic line numbering

You do not have to type line numbers at the beginning of each new program line. The computer does it automatically when given the AUTO command. For example, type

AUTO

The computer displays the number 10 on the line below. If you type the first program line and press Return, the number 20 appears on the next line, and so on. To leave this automatic line numbering mode, press Esc.

Starting a program from a particular line

You can start a program at a line other than line 10 by following the AUTO command with the first line number you wish to use. Thus,

AUTO 250

generates lines which are numbered 250, 260, 270, and so on.

You can also specify the number of spare lines between each of your program lines by adding a second number, separated from the first by a comma. Thus,

AUTO 250,15

starts at line number 250 and subsequently increases the line numbers in steps of 15, generating lines numbered 250, 265, 280, and so on.

Listing long programs

The LIST command, used above to display the current program on the screen, can be used to look at part of a program. This is particularly useful if the program is very big and you want to concentrate on one part of it.

Listing sections of programs

To look at one particular line type, for example

LIST 40

To look at a number of consecutive lines type, for example,

```
LIST 20,40
```

To see from the beginning of the program up to a particular line type, for example,

```
LIST ,30
```

To display from a particular line to the end of the program type, for example,

```
LIST 20,
```

Halting listings from the command line

If you list more of a program than can fit on the screen all at once, the beginning of the listing disappears off the top of the screen before you have time to read it. If you are running BASIC from the command line there are three ways of getting round this problem:

- Pressing the Scroll Lock halts the listing; pressing it again allows the listing to continue. This enables you to step through chunks of the listing.
- Holding down Ctrl and Shift together after typing LIST halts the displayed listing on the screen. To continue the listing, take your finger off either Ctrl or Shift.
- Putting the computer into paged mode. This is the most reliable method. To enter this mode press Ctrl-N, then type LIST. The listing stops as soon as the whole screen is filled. To display the next screenful of listing, press Scroll Lock twice. This method ensures that you will not miss any of the listing. To cancel the effect of Ctrl-N, type Ctrl-O when the listing is finished.

In addition to the methods described for halting listings, you can also slow the listing down by pressing Ctrl. This makes the screen halt for the auto-repeat rate time (typically about 1/25th of a second) between each new line. Thus it takes a second to scroll one screenful in a 25-line text mode.

Comments

When writing programs, especially long or complex ones, you should insert comments to remind you what each part of the program is doing. This is done by using the REM keyword which is short for 'remark'.

REM tells the computer to ignore the rest of the line when it executes the program. For example, to add comments to the following program:

```
10 PRINT "Can you give me a number ";
20 INPUT number
30 PRINT "The number you typed was ";number
40 PRINT number;" squared is "; number*number
```

type

Simple programming

```
 5 REM Read in a value and assign it to number
25 REM Now print out the number given.
35 REM And its square
```

and then

```
LIST
```

to display the complete program:

```
 5 REM Read in a value and assign it to number
10 PRINT "Can you give me a number ";
20 INPUT number
25 REM Now print out the number given.
30 PRINT "The number you typed was ";number
35 REM And its square
40 PRINT number;" squared is "; number*number
```

You may like to add further REM statements to underline comments or leave space above them to make them clearer:

```
 5 REM Read in a value and assign it to number
 6 REM ---------------------------------------
10 PRINT "Can you give me a number ";
20 INPUT number
24 REM
25 REM Now print out the number given
26 REM ------------------------------
30 PRINT "The number you typed was ";number
34 REM
35 REM And its square
36 REM --------------
40 PRINT number;" squared is "; number*number
```

Multiple statements

A line of BASIC can contain up to 238 characters and can be spread over several lines on the screen. In all the programs given so far, each line of BASIC contains a single statement. Several statements, however, may be placed on one line separated by colons (:). For example:

```
10 PRINT "Can you give me a number ";:INPUT number
30 PRINT "The number you typed was ";number: REM print out
the number
40 PRINT number;" squared is "; number*number: REM and its
square
```

Note that REM statements must only be placed at the end of a line since the whole of the rest of the line is ignored. If you alter the program so that line 30 reads as follows:

```
30 REM print out the number: PRINT "the number you typed was ";number
```

you will prevent the PRINT statement being executed.

The lines above illustrate that lines with more than one statement can overflow onto the next screen line very easily, making the program hard to read. You should therefore try to avoid too many multi-statement lines.

Saving and recalling programs

You can save a copy of the current program to disc at any time. This allows you to recall (load) it at a later date, without having to retype all the instructions.

Saving a program from the command line

To save a program from the command line, type

```
SAVE "program_name"
```

The program will be saved to the currently-selected directory, with the name *program_name*. At this stage, you should confine your names to numbers and upper- and lower-case letters. Other characters may be used but some have special meanings. See the RISC OS *User Guide* for further information on file naming.

After using SAVE, your program remains in memory and is unaltered in any way. You can still edit, LIST, RUN, and so on.

Another capability of the REM statement is that it allows you to give the program name for use by the SAVE command. The filename must be preceded by a > character, and the REM containing it must be the first line of the program. Thus, if the first line of the program is

```
10 REM >prog1
```

all you need to do is type the SAVE command (or its abbreviation SA.) on its own, and the name `prog1` will be used to save the program.

Loading a program from the command line

To load a program which you have previously saved, in this case prog1, type

```
LOAD "prog1"
```

Simple programming

The LOAD operation replaces the current program with the one from the disc (so you should be sure that you don't mind losing the current program before you load a new one). You can check this by listing the program currently in memory.

In addition to loading a program, you can add a program to the end of the current one using the APPEND command. The appended program is renumbered to ensure that its line numbers start after those of the initial program. The statements LIBRARY and OVERLAY may be used to add libraries of procedures and functions to the current program (see the chapter entitled *Procedures and functions* on page 87 for details).

Saving and loading a program from Edit

Programs can also be loaded, edited and saved with the desktop Edit program. See the chapter entitled *Editing BASIC files* on page 191 for further information.

Saving and recalling programs

5 Variables

A variable has a name and a value associated with it. The name, for example, FRED or a single letter such as x, allows the variable to be identified and its value to be accessed. This value can be changed and retrieved as many times as required.

Types of variables

There are three different types of variables used to store different types of information. These are:

- Integer variables which can only store whole numbers
- Floating point variables, which can store either whole numbers or fractions
- String variables which store characters.

Each type is distinguished by the last character of the variable name. A name by itself, like `Fred`, signifies a floating point variable; `Fred%` is an integer variable, and `Fred$` is a string variable.

Naming variables

The rules for naming variables are as follows:

- they can contain digits, unaccented upper- and lower-case letters, the underscore character (_) and the grave character (`), also known as a backtick
- there must be no spaces within the name but they can be divided into multiple words using the underscore character (_)
- they must not start with a digit
- they must not start with most BASIC keywords.

Naming variables

All the following names are allowed:

```
X
xpos
XPOS
Xpos
x_position
greatest_x_position
position_of_X
XPOS1
```

Note that upper- and lower-case letters are regarded by BASIC as being different, so that XPOS, xpos and Xpos are three separate variables.

The following names are not allowed:

2pos	It does not begin with a letter.
TOTAL_x	It begins with TO, a BASIC keyword.
FOREST	It begins with FOR, a BASIC keyword.
COST	It begins with COS, a BASIC keyword.
x-pos	It contains a minus sign.
X Position	It contains a space.
X.pos	It contains a punctuation mark.

It is very easy to be caught out by the rule which says that the variables must not start with a BASIC keyword. Although some keywords are allowed at the start of a variable name, the best way to avoid this problem is to use lower- or mixed-case names since BASIC keywords only use upper-case. This has the added advantage of making the program easier to read.

The values of the current variables may be displayed at any time by typing the command LVAR at the BASIC prompt and then pressing Return.

6 Numeric expressions

This chapter tells you how to perform arithmetic operations using numeric variables. If you want to know more about the different types of numeric variable which BBC BASIC uses, and how they are represented, see *Appendix A – Numeric implementation*.

Integers and floating point numbers

Integer variables are specified by placing a percent sign (%) at the end of the name. Floating point variables have no percent sign at the end. For instance, a variable called `number%` is an integer variable, whereas a variable called `number` is a floating point variable.

Floating point variables can represent both whole numbers (integers) and decimal fractions, but integer variables can only store whole numbers. For example, the assignments

```
LET number  = 4/3
LET number% = 4/3
```

leave the variables with the following values:

```
number     is 1.33333333
number%    is 1
```

In the case of the integer variable, the decimal fraction part has been lost. The advantages, however, of using integer variables are:

- they are processed more quickly by the computer;
- they occupy less memory;
- they are precise.

Assigning values to variables

The value assigned to a numeric (floating point or integer) variable can be specified as:

- a single number
- the current value of another variable
- an expression
- the result of a function.

For example:

```
LET base   = 3
LET height = 4
LET area   = (base * height)/2
LET hypot  = SQR(base*base + height*height)
```

(base * height)/2 is a mathematical expression consisting of the variables base and height, and arithmetic operations to be performed on them.

SQR is a function which returns the square root of a number, in this case the expression (base*base + height*height).

The above assignments leave the variables with the following values:

```
base    is  3
height  is  4
area    is  6
hypot   is  5
```

Note that giving a new value to base or height does not automatically update area or hypot. Once the expression is evaluated using the values of base and height current at that time, it is forgotten. In other words, area and hypot only know what value they contain, not how it was obtained.

The use of LET is optional. For example,

```
LET x = x+1
```

is equivalent to:

```
x = x+1
```

Using LET, however, makes it easier initially to understand what is happening. On its own x = x+1 looks, to a mathematician, like an unbalanced equation. Using LET makes it clear that the = is not being used in its usual algebraic sense but as shorthand for 'become equal'. LET x = x+1 can be read as 'let x become equal to its old value with one added to it'.

In BBC BASIC, it is usual not to use LET at all; it is principally allowed to provide compatibility with other BASICs which require its presence.

An alternative way of expressing an addition in an assignment is to use:

x += 1

This means 'let x become equal to itself with one added to it'.

Similarly,

x -= 3

means 'let x become equal to itself with three subtracted from it'.

Special integer variables

The 27 integer variables A% to Z% and @% are treated slightly differently from the others. They are called *resident integer variables* because they are not cleared when the program is run, or when NEW is used. This means that they can be used to pass values from one program to another.

A special integer pseudo-variable is TIME. TIME is an elapsed time clock which is incremented every hundredth of a second while the computer is switched on. It can be used to find out how long something takes by putting the following statements around a program:

```
T% = TIME
........
PRINT (TIME - T%)/100 : REM Time in seconds
```

TIME may be assigned a starting value just like any other variable. So, for example, the statement above could be replaced by:

```
TIME = 0
........
PRINT TIME/100
```

Note that you cannot use LET with TIME.

Arithmetic operators

The full list of arithmetic operators and logical operators is given in the following table. Each operator is assigned a priority. When an expression is being evaluated, this priority determines the order in which the operators are executed. Priority 1 operators are acted upon first, and priority 7 last.

Arithmetic operators

Priority	Operator	Meaning
1	–	Unary minus
	+	Unary plus
	NOT	Logical NOT
	FN	Functions
	( )	Brackets
	?	Byte indirection
	!	Word indirection
	$	String indirection
	|	Floating point indirection
2	^	Raise to the power
3	*	Multiplication
	/	Division
	DIV	Integer division
	MOD	Integer remainder
4	+	Addition
	–	Subtraction
5	=	Equal to
	<>	Not equal to
	<	Less than
	>	Greater than
	<=	Less than or equal to
	>=	Greater than or equal to
	<<	Shift left
	>>	Arithmetic shift right
	>>>	Logical shift right
6	AND	Logical and bitwise AND
7	OR	Logical and bitwise OR
	EOR	Logical and bitwise Exclusive OR

For example, 12+3*4^2 is evaluated as 12+(3*(4^2)), producing the result 60.

Operators with the same priority are executed left to right, as they appear in the expression. Thus, 22 MOD 3/7 is evaluated as (22 MOD 3)/7.

Note that the shift operators are entered by typing two (or three) > or < symbols, and should not be confused with the « and » characters in the ISO Latin I alphabet. Note also that although you can say 1+2+3, you cannot write 1<<2<<3. This would have to be bracketed thus: (1<<2)<<3. This is because you may only use one group 5 operator per (unbracketed) expression.

7   Binary and logic

We are most familiar with numbers expressed in terms of powers of ten, or decimal numbers. Sometimes it is more convenient to give numbers in a program in another base. BASIC allows numbers to be given in binary (base 2) and hexadecimal (base 16) as well as base 10.

Binary numbers and bits

You can enter numbers in binary notation, i.e. in base 2, by preceding them with the percent sign %.

Binary numbers consist entirely of the digits 0 and 1. The following table gives the binary equivalents of the decimal values 1 to 10.

Binary	Decimal	Binary	Decimal
%1	1	%110	6
%10	2	%111	7
%11	3	%1000	8
%100	4	%1001	9
%101	5	%1010	10

A one in a particular column represents a power of two:

2^7	2^6	2^5	2^4	2^3	2^2	2^1	2^0
128	64	32	16	8	4	2	1

Thus:

%1000101 = 1*64 + 0*32 + 0*16 + 0*8 + 1*4 + 0*2 + 1*1 = 69

Binary digits are usually referred to as bits.

Hexadecimal numbers

The computer treats any number which is preceded by an & sign as a hexadecimal (hex) number.

Whereas decimal numbers can contain ten separate digits, from 0 to 9, hexadecimal numbers can contain sixteen separate digits, 0 to 9 and A to F. The first 16 hexadecimal numbers and their decimal equivalents are given below:

Shift operators

Hex	Decimal	Hex	Decimal
&0	0	&8	8
&1	1	&9	9
&2	2	&A	10
&3	3	&B	11
&4	4	&C	12
&5	5	&D	13
&6	6	&E	14
&7	7	&F	15

The next hexadecimal number is &10 which is equivalent to 16 in decimal notation. Thus, in hexadecimal notation, one in a column represents a power of sixteen rather than a power of ten. For example, &100 represents 256 which is 16^2.

Shift operators

There are three operators which act upon the 32 bits of an integer, shifting it either left or right by a given number of places.

Shift left

The simplest shift is <<. This shifts the bits of an integer to the left by a given number of places and inserts zeros in the righthand bits. For example:

```
A% = 10
B% = A% << 1
C% = A% << 2
D% = A% << 3
```

This leaves the variables with the following values:

Variable	Value	
A%	10	(%00000000000000000000000000001010)
B%	20	(%00000000000000000000000000010100)
C%	40	(%00000000000000000000000000101000)
D%	80	(%00000000000000000000000001010000)

Shift right (unsigned)

The >>> operator shifts the bits of an integer to the right a given number of times, losing the bits which were in those positions and introducing zeros at the left. For example:

```
A% = %1010
B% = A% >>> 1
C% = A% >>> 2
D% = A% >>> 3
```

This leaves the variables with the following values:

Variable	Value
A%	10 (%00000000000000000000000000001010)
B%	5 (%00000000000000000000000000000101)
C%	2 (%00000000000000000000000000000010)
D%	1 (%00000000000000000000000000000001)

Shift right (signed)

The >> operator is similar to >>>, but instead of introducing zeros at the top at each stage, the left-most bit is set to either one or zero depending on what the current setting is. The left-most bit of an integer is normally used to indicate whether the integer is positive (left-most bit = zero) or negative (left-most bit = one). Consequently, this operator can be used to perform a division by a power of two on a number, retaining its sign. For example:

```
A% = %10100000000000000000000000000000:REM -1610612736
B% = %00100000000000000000000000000000:REM  536870912
C% = A% >>> 2
D% = B% >>> 2
E% = A% >> 2
F% = B% >> 2
```

This leaves the variables with the following binary values:

Variable	Value	
C%	%00101000000000000000000000000000	(671088640)
D%	%00001000000000000000000000000000	(134217728)
E%	%11101000000000000000000000000000	(-402653184)
F%	%00001000000000000000000000000000	(134217728)

Left shift as multiplication

The left shift operator can perform multiplication. The expression `val<<n` is equivalent to `val * 2^n`. So `fred<<3` is the same as `fred*8`. Although using shift can be faster than the equivalent multiply, you should bear in mind that bits may be shifted off the end of the number, so leading to incorrect results which will not be trapped as errors. For example, `&10000<<16` yields 0, whereas the correct 'multiply' result is `&100000000` (which cannot be represented in a 32-bit integer, and would be converted to floating point by BASIC).

Right shift as division

The two right shift operators perform a similar role in division. The `>>` operator gives division of 'signed' numbers by a power of two. This means that both positive and negative numbers may be divided; the result is always rounded towards the integer less than or equal to the exact value. For example, `-3>>1` is the same as `INT(-3/2)=-2`, not `-3 DIV 2`, which is `-1`. The `>>>` operator ignores the sign when shifting negative numbers, so should only be used to divide positive numbers by a power of two.

AND, OR and EOR

The operators AND, OR and EOR produce a result which depends upon the bits of two integer operands:

- In the case of AND, the bits in the two integers are compared and if they are both one, then a one is placed in the corresponding bit of the result.
- In the case of OR, a one is placed in the corresponding bit of the result if either or both of the bits in the integers are one.
- In the case of EOR, a one is placed in the corresponding bit of the result if either (but not both) of the bits in the integers is one.

Inputs		AND	OR	EOR
0	0	0	0	0
0	1	0	1	1
1	0	0	1	1
1	1	1	1	0

For example:

```
A% = %1010
B% = %1100
C% = A% AND B%
D% = A% OR B%
E% = A% EOR B%
```

This leaves the variables with the following values:

Variable	Value	
A%	10	(%1010)
B%	12	(%1100)
C%	8	(%1000)
D%	14	(%1110)
E%	6	(%0110)

The logical operators AND, OR and EOR are symmetrical, like + and *. Thus X AND Y = Y AND X for all possible values of X and Y. This applies to the other two operators as well.

TRUE and FALSE

The truth values TRUE and FALSE have the values −1 and 0 respectively. This means that:

With AND

```
TRUE  AND TRUE      gives    TRUE  (-1 AND -1 =  -1)
TRUE  AND FALSE     gives    FALSE (-1 AND  0 =   0)
FALSE AND FALSE     gives    FALSE ( 0 AND  0 =   0)
```

With OR

```
TRUE  OR TRUE       gives    TRUE  (-1 OR  -1 =  -1)
TRUE  OR FALSE      gives    TRUE  (-1 OR   0 =  -1)
FALSE OR FALSE      gives    FALSE ( 0 OR   0 =   0)
```

With EOR

```
TRUE  EOR TRUE      gives    FALSE (-1 EOR -1 =   0)
TRUE  EOR FALSE     gives    TRUE  (-1 EOR  0 =  -1)
FALSE EOR FALSE     gives    FALSE ( 0 EOR  0 =   0)
```

TRUE and FALSE

8 String expressions

String variables may be used to store strings of characters, constituting words and phrases. This chapter shows you how to assign values to a string variable, and describes several useful operations you can perform on strings in BASIC; such as splitting a string and joining two or more strings together.

Assigning values to string variables

Each string can be up to 255 characters long. The following gives some examples of strings:

```
day$ = "Monday"
Date$ = "29th February"
space$ = " "
Address$ = "10 Downing Street, London"
Age$ = "21"
```

Note that the variable `Age$` is assigned a string containing the two characters 2 and 1, and not the number 21. So, if you type

```
Real_Age$ = 21 * 2
```

the result will not be "42" because BASIC cannot do arithmetic with strings. Instead, the error message:

```
Type mismatch: string needed
```

appears on the screen, indicating that only a string expression can be assigned to a string variable. A type mismatch error can also be caused by an attempt to multiply strings, as in:

```
total$ = "12"*"32"
```

You should note that the 'null' string "" is valid. This is a string containing zero characters. In comparisons, it is less than any other string (except, of course, another null string).

In order to obtain a double quotation character, ", in a string, you use two of them adjacent to each other. For example, to print the text A"here, you would use:

```
PRINT "A""here"
```

39

Joining strings together

Two strings may be joined together, or, more correctly speaking, concatenated. The + operator is used to indicate this:

```
10 Road$ = "Downing Street"
20 City$ = "London"
30 PRINT Road$ + " " + City$
```

Typing RUN produces the following:

```
Downing Street London
```

The += operator can also be used, and as the following program shows, produces the same output as +.

```
10 Address$  = "Downing Street"
20 Address$ += " "
30 Address$ += "London"
40 PRINT Address$
```

Note, however, that the -= operator is meaningless when applied to strings and produces an error message.

Splitting strings

As well as joining two strings together, BASIC can split a string into smaller sequences of characters. Three functions are provided for doing this.

- LEFT$(A$,n) which gives the first (lefthand end) n characters of a string.
- RIGHT$(A$,n) which gives the last (righthand end) n characters of a string.
- MID$(A$,m,n) which gives n characters from the middle, beginning at the mth character.

For example,

```
PRINT LEFT$("HELLO",2),RIGHT$("THERE",2),MID$("GORDON",3,2)
```

gives

HE   RE   RD

and

```
10 title$ = "Moonlight Sonata"
20 left_of_string$ = LEFT$(title$,4)
30 right_of_string$ = RIGHT$(title$,6)
40 middle_of_string$ = MID$(title$,5,9)
50 PRINT left_of_string$
60 PRINT right_of_string$
70 PRINT middle_of_string$
```

produces the following when run:

```
Moon
Sonata
light Son
```

Each of these functions has a convenient shorthand form:

- LEFT$(A$) gives all but the last character of the string
- RIGHT$(A$) gives the last character of the string
- MID$(A$,m) gives all the characters from the *m*th to the last.

For example:

```
10 PRINT LEFT$("Hello")
20 PRINT RIGHT$("Hello")
30 PRINT MID$("Hello",3)
```

produces the following:

```
Hell
o
llo
```

LEFT$, RIGHT$ and MID$ may be used to replace part of a string. In each case the number of new characters equals the number of characters being replaced, and the string stays the same length. The number of characters being changed can be determined by the length of the replacement string. Thus:

```
10 A$ = "Hello there."
20 MID$(A$,7) = "Susan"
30 PRINT A$
40 LEFT$(A$) = "Howdy"
50 PRINT A$
60 RIGHT$(A$) = "!"
70 PRINT A$
```

produces:

```
Hello Susan.
Howdy Susan.
Howdy Susan!
```

Alternatively, you can give the maximum number of characters to be replaced. Then, if the length of the replacement string is less than the given value, all of it is used. Otherwise only the first designated number of characters have an effect. For example,

```
10 A$ = "ABCDEFGHIJ"
20 RIGHT$(A$,3) = "KL"
30 PRINT A$
40 LEFT$(A$,4) = "MNOPQR"
50 PRINT A$
60 MID$(A$,4,3) = "STUVW"
70 PRINT A$
```

produces:

```
ABCDEFGHKL
MNOPEFGHKL
MNOSTUGHKL
```

Other keywords for manipulating strings

There are also BASIC keywords to:

- produce a long string consisting of multiple copies of a shorter string
- find the length of a string
- determine whether one string is contained within the other.

These keywords are:

- STRING$(n,A$), which returns a string consisting of n copies of A$.
- LEN(A$), which gives the length of string A$.
- INSTR(A$,B$), which looks for the string B$ within the string A$ and returns the position of the first place where it is found.

For example,

```
PRINT STRING$(20,"+-")
```

produces the output:

```
+-+-+-+-+-+-+-+-+-+-+-+-+-+-+-+-+-+-+-+-
```

The statement `PRINT LEN("PAUL")` prints the number 4 and

```
A$ = "Great Britain"
PRINT LEN(A$)
```

produces the result 13. Note that the space is treated like any other character.

```
A$ = "Great Britain"
PRINT INSTR(A$,"it")
```

prints 9 because the string `it` is contained in `Great Britain` at the ninth character position. If the substring in the INSTR function is not present in the first string, then 0 is returned. Note also that you can start the search for the substring at any position, not just from the start of the substring. This is done by specifying a third parameter, so that for example,

```
PRINT INSTR("'ello 'ello","'ello",2)
```

will print 7, since the first occurrence of the substring will be skipped.

You can use the relational operators >, =, <= etc, to compare two strings. See the chapter entitled *Control statements* on page 73 for details.

How characters are represented

Every character and symbol which can be reproduced on the screen is represented within the computer by a number in the range 0 to 255. The system used to assign numbers to characters and symbols is known as ISO-8859. This is an extension of the very popular ASCII (American Standard Code for Information Interchange) code, which only applies to characters between 0 and 127. We shall use ASCII as a general term for character codes. It is wise to follow such a standard so that different computers can all understand the same numerical alphabet.

BASIC provides a pair of functions for converting characters to their ASCII number-codes and back again. These are:

- ASC(*a$*), which gives the ASCII code of the first character of a string.
- CHR$(*n*), which gives the one-character string whose ASCII code is *n*.

Converting between strings and numbers

There are three keywords which convert between strings and numbers:

- VAL(*A$*), which converts a string of digits *A$* into a number.
- STR$(*n*), which converts the number *n* into a string.
- EVAL(*A$*), which evaluates the string *A$* as though it were a BASIC expression.

VAL

VAL returns the value of a string, up to the first non-numeric character.

For example:

```
PRINT VAL("10to10")
```

prints the value 10, since all the characters after the t are ignored. The string may, however, begin with a + or −. Thus,

```
number =  VAL("-5")
```

assigns the value −5 to number. If, however, the string does not start with a digit or a plus or minus sign, VAL returns 0.

EVAL

EVAL however, considers the whole string as an expression, allowing operators and variable names to occur within it. Variables must be assigned values beforehand.

```
10 radius = 5
20 area = EVAL("PI*radius^2")
30 PRINT area
```

When this program is run the value printed is 78.5398163, which is the value PI (3.141592653) multiplied by 5 squared.

STR$

STR$ performs the opposite conversion to the above two functions. It takes the number given and returns a string containing the digits in the number.

For example,

```
10 A = 45
20 B = 30.5
30 A$ = STR$(A)
40 B$ = STR$(B)
50 PRINT A + B
60 PRINT A$ + B$
```

produces the following when it is run:

```
75.5
4530.5
```

BBC BASIC can express numbers in base 16 (hexadecimal) as well as base 10 (decimal). This is useful for dealing with certain types of integer. The chapter entitled *Binary and logic* on page 33 explains more about the various ways in which bases can be used. STR$~x gives the hexadecimal string representation of x. Thus

```
10 A% = 45
20 A$ = STR$~(A%)
30 PRINT A$
```

produces:

2D

because 2D is the hexadecimal version of the decimal number 45.

Converting between strings and numbers

9 Arrays

Arrays are groups of variables. An array has a name which applies to all variables in the group. The individual members, known as the elements of the array, are identified by a subscript. This is a whole number (zero or greater) indicating the element's position within the array. For example, A(0) is the first element in the array named A(), and A(1) is the second element, and so on.

The DIM statement

The DIM statement tells BASIC how many elements you wish to use in the array. For example,

```
DIM A(9)
```

allocates space in the computer's memory for ten elements, each called `A()`, but each having a different subscript, zero to nine. The `DIM` statement also assigns the value zero to each of these elements, which may then be individually assigned values, just like any other variables. For example:

```
A(1) = 0.56
A(2) = A(1) + 4
```

The example shown above is of a one-dimensional array: it may be thought of as a line of variables, numbered from 0 to 9 in a sequence. More dimensions may be used.

Two dimensional arrays

Two dimensional arrays in which the individual variables are identified by two subscripts can be thought of as the printing on a computer screen. Each character printed on the screen is at a particular position from the left, and a particular position from the top. (Use the rows and columns as a matrix.)

A two dimensional array may be defined as follows:

```
DIM B(2,2)
```

Two dimensional arrays

This allocates space for nine elements, each called B() in this case, and each identified by two subscripts as shown in the following table:

```
B(0,0)   B(0,1)   B(0,2)

B(1,0)   B(1,1)   B(1,2)

B(2,0)   B(2,1)   B(2,2)
```

Arrays may have as many dimensions as you like, and may hold floating point numbers, integers, or strings. For example,

```
DIM str$(1,3,2)
```

allocates space for 24 string variables (str$(0,0,0) to str$(1,3,2)), each of them containing up to 255 characters.

The subscript need not be specified as a number – a variable or expression can be used instead. For example:

```
10 DIM A(9)
20 X = 6
30 A(X) = 3
40 A(A(X)) = 1
```

This gives A(6) the value 3, and A(3) the value 1.

Any arithmetic expression may be used as a subscript. Since subscripts can only be whole numbers, any expression giving a floating point result has the number truncated to its integer value (the part before the decimal point).

When using arrays, remember that if you DIM the array using a particular number of subscripts, each element of the array must be referenced with the same number of subscripts:

```
10 DIM name$(2,2,2)
20 name$(0) = "FRED"
```

produces an error. Line 20 should be replaced by:

```
20 name$(0,0,0) = "FRED"
```

In addition, the numbers used as subscripts must not be too big or less than zero:

```
10 DIM position(9,4)
20 position(-1,5) = 1
```

If you now type RUN, an error message is displayed because the first subscript must be between zero and nine and the second between zero and four.

When you DIM a string array, the elements are initialised, just as they are for numeric arrays. Each element in the array is set to the null string, "". No space is allocated for the characters of each string element until they are assigned a value.

The operators += and -= are particularly useful with arrays, as they remove the need to evaluate the subscript expressions twice. For example, suppose you had the assignment:

```
a(100*(SINRADangle+1))=a(100*(SINRADangle+1))+increment
```

The expression `100*(SINRADangle+1)` must be calculated twice, which could be quite time-consuming. On the other hand, if you used

```
a(100*(SINRADangle+1)) += increment
```

the complex subscript expression would only be used once, saving time. It is also easier to write and read!

Finding the size of an array

Functions are available to find the number of dimensions of an array, and the size of each dimension. To find the number of dimensions of an array type

```
PRINT DIM(A())
```

To find the number of elements of the nth dimension, type

```
PRINT DIM(A(),n)
```

For example,

```
10 DIM A(4,2,7)
20 n = DIM(A())
30 PRINT n
40 PRINT DIM(A(),n)
```

produces:

```
        3
        7
```

These functions are useful mainly in procedures and functions which take array parameters. See the chapter entitled *Procedures and functions* on page 87 for more details.

Operating on whole arrays

As described above, every element of an array is given the value zero when the array is DIMmed.

It is possible to set every element in an array to any given value using a single assignment as follows:

```
10 DIM A(10), B(10)
20 n% = 2
30 A() = (3*n%)
40 B() = A()
```

Line 10 dimensions two arrays of the same size. Line 30 sets all of the elements of A() to 3*n%, i.e. 6. Then line 40 sets all of the elements of B() from the corresponding elements in A().

> Note: You may be wondering why the righthand side of the assignment in line 30 is in brackets, i.e. why couldn't we have written
>
> ```
> 20 A() = 3*n%
> ```
>
> The answer is that the righthand side of an array assignment must be a single item (number, single variable or expression in brackets) to avoid possible confusion with a more complex array operation, for example
>
> ```
> 20 A() = 3*n%()
> ```
>
> as described below.

Instead of setting all of the elements of an array to one value, you can set them to different values by giving a list of values after the =. For example:

```
10 DIM a(5), b(2,2)
20 a() = 1,2,3,4
30 b() = 6,5,4,3,2,1
```

Any elements omitted from the list are not changed in the array (for example, a(4) and a(5) above wouldn't be assigned). In the case of multi-dimensional arrays, the elements are assigned so that the last subscript changes quickest. For example, in the case of b() above the six values listed would be assigned to b(0,0), b(0,1), b(0,2), b(1,0),... , b(2,1), b(2,2) respectively.

In addition, all the elements in an array can be increased, decreased, multiplied or divided by a given amount:

```
10 DIM A(2,2), B(2,2)
20 A(0,0) = 4
30 A(1,1) = 5
40 A(2,2) = 6

50 n% = 2: m% = 3
60 A() = A() + (n%*n%)
70 A() = A() - m%
80 B() = A() * 6
90 B() = B() / n%
```

When you RUN this program, the elements of the arrays A() and B() are assigned the following values:

Array	Value	Array	Value	Array	Value
A(0,0)	5	A(0,1)	1	A(0,2)	1
A(1,0)	1	A(1,1)	6	A(1,2)	1
A(2,0)	1	A(2,1)	1	A(2,2)	7
B(0,0)	15	B(0,1)	3	B(0,2)	3
B(1,0)	3	B(1,1)	18	B(1,2)	3
B(2,0)	3	B(2,1)	3	B(2,2)	21

Note that in line 60 the brackets around n%*n% are necessary, as with a simple array assignment. The amount being added, subtracted, and so on may be either a constant, a variable, a function result or an expression, provided that it is enclosed in brackets. However, you can use shorthand versions for addition and subtraction which do not require brackets:

```
60 A() += n%*n%
70 A() -= m%
```

It is also possible to add, subtract, multiply or divide two arrays, provided that they are of the same size. In the result, every element is obtained by performing the specified operation on the two elements in the corresponding positions in the operands.

For example, for two arrays which have been DIMmed A(1,1) and B(1,1), the instruction

```
A() = A() + B()
```

is equivalent to the following four instructions:

```
A(0,0) = A(0,0) + B(0,0)
A(0,1) = A(0,1) + B(0,1)
A(1,0) = A(1,0) + B(1,0)
A(1,1) = A(1,1) + B(1,1)
```

BASIC will perform proper matrix multiplication on pairs of two-dimensional arrays using the . operator. The first index of the array is interpreted as the row and the second as the column. For example:

```
10 i=2:j=3:k=4
20 DIM A(i,j),B(j,k),C(i,k)
30 :
40 REM Set up the array contents...
50 :
60 C() = A().B()
```

Note that the second dimension of the first array must be identical to the first dimension of the second array.

Also, the matrix multiplication operation can multiply a vector (a one-dimensional array) by a two dimensional matrix to yield a vector. There are two possible cases:

`row().matrix()`

This gives a row vector as the result. The number of elements is equal to the number of columns in the matrix.

`matrix().column()`

This gives a column vector as the result. The number of elements is equal to the number of rows in the matrix. For example:

```
 10 i = 2: j = 3
 20 DIM row(i), column(j)
 30 DIM matrix(i,j)
 40:
 50 REM lines to set up the arrays
200 column() = matrix().column()
220 PROCprint(column())
260 row() = row().matrix()
270 PROCprint(row())
```

Array operations

Arithmetic operations on arrays are not quite as general as those on simple numbers. Although you can say a=b*b+c, you cannot use the equivalent array expression a()=b()*b()+c(). Instead, you would have to split it into two assignments:

```
a() = b()*b()
a() = a()+c()
```

Also, the only place these array operations may appear is on the righthand side of an assignment to another array. You cannot say

`PRINT a()*2`

for example (or, indeed, `PRINT a()`).

The table below gives a complete list of array operations.

array =	*array*			Copy all elements
array =	-*array*			Copy all elements, negating
array =	*array*	+	*array*	Add corresponding elements
array =	*array*	−	*array*	Subtract corresponding elements
array =	*array*	*	*array*	Multiply corresponding elements
array =	*array*	/	*array*	Divide corresponding elements
array =	*factor*			Set all elements
array =	*factor, expression,*		...	Set several elements
array =	*array*	+	*factor*	Increment (or concatenate) all elements
array =	*factor*	+	*array*	
array +=	*expression*			
array =	*array*	−	*factor*	Decrement all elements
array =	*factor*	−	*array*	
array -=	*expression*			
array =	*array*	*	*factor*	Multiply all elements
array =	*factor*	*	*array*	
array =	*array*	/	*factor*	Divide all elements
array =	*factor*	/	*array*	
array =	*array*	.	*array*	Matrix multiplication

array means any array variable. All of the operations on two arrays require arrays of exactly the same size and type (real and integer arrays are treated as different types for this purpose). Only the assignment and concatenation operations are available on string arrays.

factor means a simple expression, such as 1, LENA$ or "HELLO". If you want to use an expression using binary operators, it must be enclosed in brackets: (a+b).

The arrays used in these operations may all be the same, or all be different, or somewhere in between. For example, you are allowed to use:

```
a() = b() + c()
a() = a() + b()
a() = a() + a()
```

The matrix multiplication operator works on two arrays which must be compatible in size. This means that in the assignment

```
a() = b().c()
```

the following DIMs must have been used:

```
DIM b(i,j) : REM left side  is i rows by j columns
DIM c(j,k) : REM right side is j rows by k columns
DIM a(i,k) : REM result     is i rows by k columns
```

In addition, the following would be permitted:

```
DIM b(i,j) : REM left side is i by j matrix
DIM c(i)   : REM right side is column vector
DIM a(i)   : REM result is column vector
```

or

```
DIM b(k)   : REM left side is row vector
DIM c(j,k) : REM right side is j by k matrix
DIM a(j)   : REM result is row vector
```

There are some functions which act on single arrays:

- SUM *array* gives the sum of all elements of the array or the concatenation of all the strings (up to 255 characters)
- SUMLEN *array* gives the sum of the lengths of all of the strings in an array
- MOD *array* gives the modulus, or square root of the sum of the squares of the elements of a numeric array. For example, if you had the following statements:

```
10 DIM a(100)
20 ...

90 mod=MODa()
```

then to perform the same operation without the MOD operator, you would have to say:

```
10 DIM a(100), b(100)
20 ...

90 b()=a()*a()
100 mod=SQR(SUM(b()))
```

10 Outputting text

You can output text, including special characters defined by yourself, using the PRINT statement.

Print formatting

The PRINT statement provides a number of ways of formatting the printed output.

Using print separators

The items in a PRINT statement can be separated by a variety of different punctuation characters. Each of these characters affects the way in which the text is formatted:

- Items separated by spaces are printed one after the other, with numbers right justified and strings left justified.
- Items separated by semicolons are printed one after the other, with no spaces (numbers are left justified if there is a semicolon before the first number).
- Items separated by commas are tabulated into columns.
- Items separated by apostrophes are printed on separate lines.

The following program demonstrates this:

```
10 PRINT "Hello " "Hello ","Hello"'"What's all this?"
```

Typing RUN produces the following output:

```
Hello Hello      Hello
What's all this?
```

Printing numbers

Numbers are printed right justified in the print field, unless preceded by a semicolon, which causes them to be left justified. Print fields are discussed below. In the example below, the first number is right justified in the default field of ten characters; the second number is left justified because a semicolon comes before it:

```
10 A% = 4
20 PRINT 4;" ";A%
```

Print formatting

Typing RUN produces (spaces are shown as `.`):

`.........4.4`

Numbers are normally printed (displayed) as decimal values unless they are preceded by a ~, in which case they are given in hexadecimal notation (hexadecimal numbers are discussed in the chapter entitled *Binary and logic* on page 33):

```
10 PRINT 10
20 PRINT &10
30 PRINT ~10
40 PRINT ~&10
```

produces:

```
........10
........16
.........A
........10
```

Defining fields

The columns controlled by commas are called fields. By default a field is ten characters wide. Each string which is printed following a comma starts at the lefthand side of the next field. In other words, using commas is a convenient method of left-justifying text. Numbers, on the other hand, are displayed to the right of the next field, so that the units of integers, or the least significant decimal places of floating point numbers, line up.

Thus,

```
10 FOR N% = 1 TO 5
20 A$ = LEFT$("Hello",N%)
30 B% = N%*10^(N%-1)
40 PRINT A$,A$,A$,A$'B%,B%,B%,B%
50 NEXT N%
```

produces the following when RUN:

```
H         H         H         H
          1         1         1         1
He        He        He        He
          20        20        20        20
Hel       Hel       Hel       Hel
          300       300       300       300
Hell      Hell      Hell      Hell
          4000      4000      4000      4000
Hello     Hello     Hello     Hello
          50000     50000     50000     50000
```

Using @% to alter output

Problems may occur when you print out floating point numbers. For example:

PRINT 6,9,7/3,57

produces:

```
         6             92.33333333             57
```

The nine and the decimal equivalent of 7/3 run into each other.

To prevent this, you can alter the default values for the field width or the number of decimal places printed (or both) by using the integer variable @%. Unlike all other integer variables @% can be set using a special format string, as follows:

Setting @% using a format string.

To see the effect of altering the value of @%, type:

@%="F8.4"

then

PRINT 6,9,7/3,57

and the following is produced:

```
  6.0000   9.0000   2.3333  57.0000
```

The value you supply for @% can take one of three forms:

- "G$x.y$" or "Gx,y". The default General (G) format; BASIC uses the number of decimal places it requires up to a maximum of ten.
- "E$x.y$" or "Ex,y". Prints numbers in Exponent (E) format; a number between l and 9.99999999 followed by E and then a power of ten.
- "F$x.y$" or "Fx,y". Prints numbers using Fixed (F) format; a fixed number of decimal places, giving up to a maximum of ten significant figures.

In each case *x* is the field width, *y* is the number of digits and the dot or comma between them is used as the decimal point.

Setting @% using an integer.

To obtain the same format as the previous example, type:

```
@% = &020408
```

The assignment of the variable @% is made up of a number of parts:

- & indicates that a hexadecimal number follows.
- The first digit (0) indicates the decimal point format. It may either be 0 to select a dot or 8 to select a comma.
- The second digit (2) indicates the format of the print field – two tells BASIC to print a fixed number of decimal places.
- The next two digits (04) indicate the number of decimal places required.
- The last two digits (08) give the field width.

The format: the first figure after the & symbol, can take three values:

- 0 is the default General (G) format.
- 1 prints numbers in Exponent (E) format.
- 2 prints numbers in the Fixed (F) format.

For more detailed information on using @%, see the description of PRINT on page 366.

The text cursor

Text cursor coordinates

When text is entered at the keyboard or displayed using the PRINT statement, the position at which it appears on the screen depends on the location of the text cursor. As each character is printed, this cursor moves on to the next character position.

Initially, the text cursor is at the top lefthand corner of the screen, which is position (0,0). The number of possible positions for the cursor depends on the screen mode. For example, in a screen mode which has 80 characters across the screen and 32 rows, the coordinates it can have vary as follows:

Altering the position of the text cursor

You can use TAB with one parameter to control the position of the text cursor. For example:

PRINT TAB(x) "Hello"

It works as follows. If the current value of COUNT (which holds the number of characters printed since the last newline) is greater than the required tab column (i.e. x above), a newline is printed. This moves the cursor to the start of the next line, and resets COUNT to zero. Then x spaces are printed, moving the cursor to the required column.

Note that it is possible to tab to column 60 in a 40 column mode; the cursor will simply move to column 20 of the line below the current one. Using TAB with one parameter to position the cursor on the line will also work, for example, when characters are sent to the printer, as it is just printing spaces to achieve the desired tabulation.

On the other hand, TAB with two arguments works in a completely different way: it uses the operating system to position the cursor at a specified position on the screen – this is relative to the screen 'home' position, which is normally the top left. In this case, if you try to position the cursor on, say, column 60 in a 40 column mode, the command will be ignored. Furthermore, this kind of tabbing does not affect any characters being sent to the printer.

Defining your own characters

The VDU statement

In addition to TAB, there are other methods of altering the position of the cursor. If, for example, you type

```
10 PRINT "A";
20 VDU 8
30 PRINT "B"
```

`PRINT "A";` prints an A at the current cursor position and moves the cursor one place to the right. `VDU 8` moves the cursor back one position so that it is underneath the A. Hence, `PRINT "B"` prints a B at the same position as the A, and so rubs it out.

VDU 8	moves the cursor back one space.
VDU 9	moves the cursor forward one space.
VDU 10	moves the cursor down one line.
VDU 11	moves the cursor up one line.
VDU 12	clears the screen and puts the cursor at the top left.
VDU 13	moves the cursor to the beginning of the line.
VDU 30	moves the cursor to the 'home' position.

For details of these and other effects available with VDU see the chapter entitled VDU *control* on page 177.

Defining your own characters

Each character is made up of a pattern of dots on an eight by eight grid. All normal letters, numbers and so on are pre-defined in this way. It is possible, however, to define your own characters with ASCII values in the range 32 to 255.

To do this, use the VDU 23 command, followed by the code of the character you wish to define and then eight integers, each representing one row of the character, from top to bottom. The bit pattern of each integer defines the sequence of dots and spaces: one gives a dot and zero gives a space.

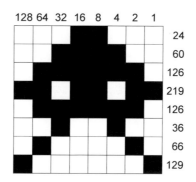

To set up character 128 to be the shape shown above, use the following:

VDU 23,128,24,60,126,219,126,36,66,129

Then, to display this character, type

PRINT CHR$(128)

Note that characters 129-133 and 136-139 can be redefined by the Wimp and so should be avoided in window managed programs.

Defining your own characters

11   Inputting data

This chapter describes several methods by which you can input data into your BASIC program:

- from the keyboard
- from predefined data within your program
- by programming keys on the keyboard
- from a mouse.

Inputting data from the keyboard

There are three commands you can use to input data from the keyboard:

- The INPUT command allows a program to request information.
- The GET command waits for the user to press a single key.
- The INKEY command waits a specified length of time for the user to press a single key.

Note that you are advised **not** to use these three commands in BASIC programs written under the window manager environment (see the section entitled *Window managed programs* on page 7).

INPUT

The INPUT statement allows a program to request information from the user.

The following program gives an example:

```
10 PRINT "Give me a number and I'll double it";
20 INPUT X
30 PRINT "Twice ";X " is ";X*2
```

When you run this program, the INPUT command on line 20 displays a question mark on the screen and waits for you to enter data. The number you type is assigned to the variable X. If you do not type anything, or type letters or symbols instead, X is assigned the value 0.

INPUT may also be used with string and integer variables:

```
10 PRINT "What is your name ";
20 INPUT A$
30 PRINT "Hello ";A$
```

Line 10 in each of the above two programs is used to print a message on the screen indicating the type of response required. The INPUT statement allows text prompts to be included, so the program above could be written more neatly as:

```
10 INPUT "What is your name ",A$
20 PRINT "Hello ";A$
```

The comma in line 10 tells the computer to print a question mark when it wants input from the keyboard. If you leave out the comma, the question mark is not printed. A semi-colon may be used, with exactly the same effect as the comma.

When the program is being executed, the INPUT statement requires you to press Return if you wish to send what you have typed to the computer. Until you press Return, you can delete all or part of what you have typed by pressing Backspace or Ctrl-U to erase the whole line.

When you are inputting a string, the computer ignores any leading spaces and anything after a comma, unless you put the whole string inside quotation marks.

To input a whole line of text, including commas and leading spaces, INPUT LINE (or LINE INPUT) may be used:

```
10 INPUT A$
20 INPUT LINE B$
30 PRINT A$
40 PRINT B$
```

RUN the above program and, in response to each of the question marks, type

```
Hello, how are you?
```

This produces the following output:

```
Hello
```

```
Hello, how are you?
```

Several inputs may be requested at one time:

```
10 INPUT A,B,C$
```

You may enter the data individually, pressing Return after each item. In this case you are prompted with a question mark until you enter the number required. Alternatively, you can give all the inputs on one line, separated by commas.

GET and GET$

Single-character input may be used to read a single key press:

```
10 PRINT "Press a key"
20 A$ = GET$
30 PRINT "The key you pressed was ";A$
```

In this example the program waits at line 20 until you press a key. As soon as you do so, the character that key represents is placed in A$. You do not have to press Return and so do not get the chance to change your mind.

GET is similar to GET$ but returns the ASCII code of the key pressed, instead of the character.

INKEY and INKEY$

INKEY$ is similar to GET$, except that it does not wait indefinitely for a key to be pressed. You give it a time limit and it waits for that length of time only (unless a key is pressed first). For example:

```
10 PRINT "You have 2 seconds to press a key"
20 A$ = INKEY$(200)
```

The number following the INKEY$ is the number of hundredths of a second it waits. If a key is pressed in time, A$ holds the character which was typed. Otherwise, A$ is the null string.

INKEY can be used in a similar manner to INKEY$: it waits for a given time for a key to be pressed, and then returns the ASCII code for the key pressed, or −1 if no key is pressed within this time.

Including data as part of a program

Predefined data may be included within a program and saved as part of it. When the program is run, individual items of data are read and assigned to variables as follows:

```
10 FOR I% = 1 TO 4
20 READ age%, dog$
30 PRINT "Name: ";dog$ " Age: ";age%
40 NEXT I%
50 DATA 9,"Laddie",3,"Watson"
60 DATA 1
70 DATA "Mungo",3,"Honey"
```

Including data as part of a program

You may use as many DATA statements as you like, but you must make sure that the type of each item of data matches the type of the variable into which it is being read. Each DATA statement can be followed by one or more items of data separated by commas.

You can usually leave out the quotation marks around strings, but they are needed if you want to include leading or trailing spaces, commas or quotation marks in the string.

For example,

```
10 DATA Hello, my name is
20 DATA Marvin
30 READ A$,B$
40 PRINT A$;B$
```

produces:

```
Hellomy name is
```

To obtain the sentence Hello, my name is Marvin, change the program as follows:

```
10 DATA "Hello, my name is"
20 DATA " Marvin"
30 READ A$,B$
40 PRINT A$;B$
```

A DATA statement must appear as the first statement on a line, otherwise it will not be found. If BASIC encounters a DATA statement while executing a program, it ignores it and goes on to the next line.

When it attempts to READ the first item of data, it scans through the lines of the program from the start until it finds the first DATA statement and uses the first item of data on this line. The next READ uses the second item and so on until the DATA statement has no more items left, at which point the next DATA statement is searched for and used.

If there is insufficient data, the computer produces an error message, such as:

```
Out of data at line 20
```

This indicates that it has tried to READ an item of data, but that all items have already been read.

You might have a lot of different sections of DATA, and want to start reading from a certain point. You can do this using the RESTORE statement. It is followed by a line number. BASIC will start subsequent searches for DATA from that line instead of from the start of the program. For example, the program below

Inputting data

```
10 RESTORE 60
20 READ A$
30 PRINT A$
40 END
50 DATA First line of data
60 DATA Second line of data
```

will print out

```
Second line of data
```

because the RESTORE causes BASIC to start the search for DATA statements at line 60.

Because line numbers can't be used in procedure libraries, a special form of RESTORE is provided so that you can still include data in them. If you say RESTORE +*offset*, BASIC will start searching for DATA statements at *offset*+1 lines from where the RESTORE statement is located. For example, if you had the following lines:

```
1000 RESTORE +0
1010 DATA ...
1020 DATA ...
```

the next READ would read data from line 1010. If line 1000 was RESTORE +1, then data would be read next from line 1020, and so on.

A further useful feature is the ability to remember where data is currently being read from (LOCAL DATA), read data from another part of the program, then restore the original place (RESTORE DATA). This is mainly useful in functions and procedures, so is explained in the section dealing with them.

A note about line numbers. In general, if you use line numbers anywhere in a program (and there should be very few situations where you have to), they should be simple numbers in the range 0 to 65279, not expressions like start%+10*n%. Otherwise, if the program is renumbered, it will stop working since BASIC does not know how to change the expression in the right way.

Programming the keyboard

Waiting for input

A program can wait for a key to be pressed, either indefinitely using GET and GET$, or for a defined length of time using INKEY and INKEY$. Normally, every time you press a key, it is placed in the keyboard buffer which is a temporary block of memory used to store key presses until BASIC is ready to read them. Up to 31 key presses may be typed ahead like this.

Programming the keyboard

The GET and GET$ instructions look in the keyboard buffer for a key. Hence they take note of keys which were pressed before the input instructions were executed. If, for instance, you want to ensure that you only read keys pressed *after* a prompt has been displayed, you can empty or flush the buffer before using these instructions. Then you can be sure that the key obtained is in response to the prompt and not just an accidental press of the keyboard a few moments before. To do this, use the operating system command:

```
*FX 15,1
```

Using the Tab & cursor keys to get ASCII code

The cursor editing keys can be made to generate ASCII codes when they are pressed, rather than performing their normal cursor editing functions, by typing

```
*FX 4,1
```

The codes they return are:

Key	Code
End (Copy)	135
←	136
→	137
↓	138
↑	139

You can restore cursor copying by giving the command

```
*FX 4
```

The Tab key can be made to return any ASCII value you choose by typing

```
*FX 219,n
```

where *n* is the ASCII code you want it to return.

The following program uses these features to move a block around the screen until End is pressed, and then to leave it at its current location. Don't worry if you don't understand all of the statements (e.g. RECTANGLE and REPEAT); they are all described later on in the manual.

Note that this method of redefining keys to generate ASCII codes is not compatible with BASIC programs written under the window manager environment (described in the section entitled *Window managed programs* on page 7).

Inputting data

```
10 MODE MODE
20 *FX 4,1
30 x = 600 : y = 492
40 oldx = x : oldy = y
50 RECTANGLE FILL x,y,80,40
60 REPEAT
70   *FX 15,1
80   key = GET
90   CASE key OF
100    WHEN 135 : END
110    WHEN 136 : x -= 20
120    WHEN 137 : x += 20
130    WHEN 138 : y -= 20
140    WHEN 139 : y += 20
150  ENDCASE
160  RECTANGLE FILL oldx,oldy,80,40 TO x,y
170  oldx = x : oldy = y
180 UNTIL FALSE
```

Scanning the keyboard

When you give INKEY a positive parameter, it waits for a given length of time for a particular key to be pressed; but it has an additional function. If you give INKEY a negative parameter it tests to see if a particular key or range of keys is pressed at that instant.

This feature is particularly useful for real-time applications where the computer is constantly reacting to the current input it is being given, rather than stopping and waiting for you to decide what to do next. For example:

```
210 IF INKEY(-66) THEN PRINT "You were pressing A"
```

Another advantage is that it lets you check for keys like Shift and Ctrl being pressed, which you cannot do with the other input functions.

The list of negative values associated with each of the keys is given in *Appendix D – INKEY values*.

Using the mouse in programs

The mouse provides a convenient method of supplying information to a program. This information is in three parts:

- a position on the screen
- details of which of the buttons are currently being pressed

Using the mouse in programs

- the time of the last mouse 'event'.

To input this information, type

`MOUSE x,y,buttons,when`

The values returned in x and y give the position of the mouse. The variable buttons gives details of the mouse buttons currently pressed. Finally, when gives the value of a centi-second timer. This timer starts at 0 when the machine is switched on. So, when gives the last time a mouse button was pressed or released, or the current time if no presses or releases are 'pending'. You can omit the last comma and variable if you are not interested in the time.

The buttons variable has a value whose meaning is as follows:

Buttons	Details
0	No buttons pressed
1	Adjust (righthand) only pressed
2	Menu (middle) only pressed
3	Adjust and Menu pressed
4	Select (lefthand) only pressed
5	Select and Adjust pressed
6	Select and Menu pressed
7	All three buttons pressed

Linking the mouse to a pointer

The following program is a very simple sketchpad program which draws lines as you move the mouse around and hold down its buttons:

```
10 MODE MODE
20 MOVE 0,0
30 REPEAT
40   MOUSE x,y,button
50   GCOL button + 1
40   DRAW x,y
50 UNTIL FALSE
```

In order to be able to see the position of the mouse on the screen, it can be linked to a pointer. The easiest way to show the mouse pointer is to use the BASIC statement MOUSE ON. This gives the pointer an arrow shape and displays it on the screen. To turn the pointer off, use MOUSE OFF.

Now, whenever you move the mouse, the pointer moves with it on the screen indicating its current position. This enables the sketchpad program shown above to be altered so that you can move to the position you want and then draw a line to this new position by pressing any button:

```
10 MODE MODE
20 MOUSE ON
30 MOVE 0,0
40 REPEAT
50   REPEAT
60     MOUSE x,y,button%
70   UNTIL button% <> 0
80   DRAW x,y
90 UNTIL FALSE
```

For more details about the MOUSE statement see the chapter entitled *Keywords* on page 215.

Programming function keys

The keys across the top of the keyboard labelled F1 to F12 are function keys. These can be programmed so that they generate any string you like when they are pressed. For example, type

`*KEY1 "*CAT"`

Now when you press F1 the string *CAT is printed on the screen as though you had typed it.

Try changing the definition to:

`*KEY1 "*CAT|M"`

The | sign means that the character following it is to be interpreted as a control character. In this case it is a Ctrl-M which is being included in the string. This performs the same function as pressing Return. A full list of the control characters is given in *Chapter 25 - VDU control*.

Now when you press F1, the string *CAT is printed and Return is 'pressed' automatically so the current directory is catalogued immediately.

Storing a series of commands

A whole series of commands can be stored in one key. The following defines a key to clear the screen and list the current program in paged mode.

`*KEY2 "CLS|M|N LIST|M"`

Storing a small BASIC program

You can even define a key so that it contains a small BASIC program:

`*KEY 3 "10 MODE MODE|M 20 FOR I% = 1 TO 100|M 30 CIRCLE RND(1279), RND(1024), 50 + RND (300)|M 40 N.|M RUN|M"`

The quotation marks around the string are not strictly necessary. However, it is important to remember that everything on the line after the *KEY command is treated as part of the string. So if *KEY is used in a program, it must be the last statement on the line.

Using other keys as additional function keys

The key labelled PRINT or Print Scrn acts as function key 0. In addition, the cursor editing keys and End (Copy) can be made to behave as function keys 11 to 15 by giving the command:

`*FX 4,2`

Following this command, the keys, instead of having their normal cursor editing effects, return the function key strings assigned to them:

Key	*KEY number
End (Copy)	11
←	12
→	13
↓	14
↑	15

To return them to their normal state, type `*FX 4`

Symbols in function key strings

The following special characters are allowed in function key strings:

			means	
	!ch	means the following character code + 128
	?	means Delete (i.e. CHR$(127))
	"	means " (useful for making " the first character)
<n>	means CHR$n
	<	means <

12 Control statements

Normally, lines in a BASIC program are executed in sequence, one after the other. However, the language includes two types of structure which alter this sequence:

- Conditional structures allow statements to be executed only if certain conditions are met.
- Loop structures allow statements to be executed repeatedly, either for a fixed number of times, or until a certain condition is met.

In all cases, the code is easier to read if it is clear which statements are in the loop and which are conditional on certain factors. This clarity can be achieved by use of the LISTO command before listing the programs, to indent the conditional and loop structures in the listing. All programs included in this chapter are listed as if the command:

LISTO 3

had been typed beforehand; this gives a space after the line number and indents structures.

IF... THEN... ELSE

The IF (single line) statement may be used to enable the computer to make a choice about whether or not to execute a statement or group of statements. It has the form

IF condition [THEN] statements [ELSE statements]

A condition is an expression that gives a number. It is said to be TRUE if the number if not zero, or FALSE if the number is zero. Usually the relational operators described below are used in conditional expressions.

The statements after the THEN keyword (which is optional, as indicated by the square brackets) are only executed if the condition is TRUE. If it is FALSE, the statements are skipped. However, if there is an ELSE, then the statements following that are executed if the condition is FALSE.

Operators

For example:

```
10 PRINT "What is 2 * 4"
20 INPUT ans%
30 IF ans% = 8 THEN PRINT "Well done" ELSE PRINT "Wrong"
```

Line 30 contains a conditional expression. In the example shown the expression is TRUE (i.e. has a non-zero value) when `ans%` is equal to 8, and is FALSE (i.e. has a zero value) otherwise. Note that in an IF statement, either the THEN part or the ELSE part (if present) is executed, never both.

Any non-zero number is treated as TRUE in an IF statement, however, the comparison operators described in the following section return a particular value meaning TRUE: −1. They return 0 for FALSE, of course. In addition, there are two functions called FALSE and TRUE which return 0 and −1 respectively.

Operators

Two kinds of operators may be used in expressions:

- relational operators
- logical operators (on TRUE and FALSE values).

Relational operators

Relational operators can be used to evaluate numbers or strings:

Numbers

In the following, A and B can be integers or floating point numbers.

Operator	Meaning
A = B	TRUE when A is equal to B
A < B	TRUE when A is less than B
A > B	TRUE when A is greater than B
A <= B	TRUE when A is less than or equal to B
A >= B	TRUE when A is greater than or equal to B
A <> B	TRUE when A is not equal to B

Strings

Operator	Meaning
A$ = B$	TRUE when A$ and B$ are the same
A$ <> B$	TRUE when A$ and B$ are different
A$ < B$	String comparisons; see below:
A$ > B$	
A$ <= B$	
A$ >= B$	

When strings are compared, corresponding characters of each string are examined until either they are different, or the end of a string is reached. If the strings are the same length, and the corresponding characters are the same, the strings are said to be equal; otherwise, the shorter string is 'less than' the longer one.

In the case where the two corresponding characters differ, the relationship between the strings is the same as that between the ASCII codes of the mismatched characters. For example, `"HI" < "Hi"` yields TRUE, because the ASCII code of upper case I is less than that of lower case i. Similarly, `"SIX" > "FIFTEEN"` is TRUE because `"SIX"` starts with S, and the ASCII value of S is larger than that of F.

Logical operators (on TRUE and FALSE values)

Operator	Meaning
NOT A	TRUE when A is FALSE
A AND B	TRUE if both A and B are TRUE
A OR B	TRUE if either A or B or both are TRUE
A EOR B	TRUE if either A or B but not both are TRUE

IF... THEN... ELSE... ENDIF

A block structured IF... THEN... [ELSE ...] ENDIF statement is available. It executes a series of statements, which may be split over several lines, conditionally on the result of the IF expression.

IF... THEN... ELSE... ENDIF

```
 10 n% = RND(10)
 20 m% = RND(10)
 30 PRINT "What is ";n% " * "m%;
 40 INPUT ans%
 50 IF ans% = n%*m% THEN
 60    PRINT "Well done"
 70 ELSE
 80    PRINT "Wrong"
 90    PRINT n%;" * ";m% " = ";n%*m%
100 ENDIF
```

The ENDIF on line 90 terminates the statement. It indicates that execution of the following statements is not dependent on the outcome of the conditional expression on line 50, so these statements are executed as normal. Without the ENDIF the computer has no way of knowing whether or not the statements on line 100 belongs to the ELSE part.

There are certain rules which must be obeyed when using IF... THEN... |ELSE...| ENDIF constructions:

- The first line must take the form:

  IF *condition* THEN

  with THEN being the last item on the line.

- The ELSE part need not be present, but if it is, the ELSE must be the first thing on a line (excluding spaces).

- The ENDIF statement must be the first thing on a line (excluding spaces).

- IF... THEN ... |ELSE ...| ENDIF statements may be nested: one may occur inside another. For example:

```
 10 DIM A%(10)
 20 count% = 0
 30 PRINT "Give me an integer between 0 and 9 ";
 40 INPUT number%
 50 IF number% >= 0 AND number% <= 9 THEN
 60    IF A%(number%) = 0 THEN
 70       PRINT "Thank you"
 80       A%(number%) = 1 : count% = count% + 1
 90    ELSE
100       PRINT "You've already had that number"
110    ENDIF
120 ELSE
130    PRINT number% " is not between 0 and 9 !"
140 ENDIF
150 IF count% < 10 GOTO 30
```

FOR... NEXT

The FOR and NEXT statements are used to specify the number of times a block of a program is executed. These statements are placed so that they surround the block to be repeated:

```
10 FOR N% = 1 TO 6
20    PRINT N%
30 NEXT N%
```

Type RUN and the following is produced:

```
       1
       2
       3
       4
       5
       6
```

The variable N% is called the control variable. It is used to control the number of times the block of code is executed. The control variable can be started at any number you choose, and you may alter the step size; the amount by which it changes each time round the loop.

```
10 FOR N% = -5 TO 5 STEP 2
20    PRINT N%
30 NEXT N%
```

This program produces:

```
      -5
      -3
      -1
       1
       3
       5
```

The step size can be negative so that the control variable is decreased each time. It does not have to be an integer value. You can also use a decimal step size, although this is not generally advisable. The reason is that numbers such as 0.1 are not exactly representable in the internal format used by the computer. This means that when the step is added to the looping variable several times, small errors may accumulate. You can see this by typing the following program:

```
10 FOR i=0 TO 100 STEP 0.1
20    PRINT i
30 NEXT i
```

FOR... NEXT

The looping variable i doesn't reach exactly 100.

FOR ... NEXT loops may be nested. For example,

```
10 FOR N = 3.0 TO -1.0 STEP -2.0
20    FOR M = 2.5 TO 2.9 STEP 0.2
30       PRINT N,M
40    NEXT M
50 NEXT N
```

produces:

```
         3         2.5
         3         2.7
         3         2.9
         1         2.5
         1         2.7
         1         2.9
        -1         2.5
        -1         2.7
        -1         2.9
```

You do not need to specify the control variable to which NEXT refers. The following program produces the same results as the one above:

```
10 FOR N = 3.0 TO -1.0 STEP -2.0
20    FOR M = 2.5 TO 2.9 STEP 0.2
30       PRINT N,M
40    NEXT
50 NEXT
```

The program will now run slightly faster because the computer assumes that NEXT applies to the most recent FOR.

If you put variable names after NEXT you should not mix them up as shown below:

```
10 FOR N = 3.0 TO -1.0 STEP -2.0
20    FOR M = 2.5 TO 2.9 STEP 0.2
30       PRINT N,M
40 NEXT N
50    NEXT M
```

The output produced by this example is:

```
       3.0       2.5
       1.0       2.5
      -1.0       2.5
Not in a FOR loop at line 50
```

Loops must be nested totally within each other: they must not cross. In the above example, the N and M loops are incorrectly nested. BASIC tries to run the program, but when line 50 is reached, it gives an error message indicating that it cannot match the FOR statements with the NEXT statements.

Note: The reason the error wasn't given sooner, i.e. as soon as the mismatched NEXT was met, was that it is actually legal, though not advisable, to close more than one loop with a single NEXT. When BASIC meets a NEXT *var* statement, it terminates all open FOR loops until it meets one which started FOR *var*. Thus the NEXT N in the example above closed the FOR M loop before performing the NEXT N.

A FOR loop is ended when the control variable is:

- greater than the terminating value (value in the FOR statement) when a positive step size is used.
- less than the terminating value (value in the FOR statement) when a negative step size is used.

The loop is performed in the following sequence:

1. Assign the initial value to the control variable.
2. Execute the block of code.
3. Add the step to the control variable.
4. Test against terminating value, and if it is to be performed again, go back to step 2.

The initial and terminating values and the step size are calculated only once, at the start of the loop.

One of the consequences of the way in which the loop is performed is that the block of code is always executed at least once. Thus,

```
10 FOR N = 6 TO 0
20    PRINT N
30 NEXT
```

produces:

         6

FOR ... NEXT loops are very versatile, since the initial and terminating values and the step size can be assigned any arithmetic expression containing variables or functions. For example:

REPEAT... UNTIL

```
10 REM Draw a sine curve
20 MODE MODE: MOVE 0,512
30 PRINT "Please give me a step size (eg 0.1) "
40 INPUT step
50 FOR angle = -2*PI TO 2*PI STEP step
60    DRAW 100*angle, 100*SIN(angle)+512
70 NEXT
80 END
```

REPEAT... UNTIL

The REPEAT ... UNTIL loop repeats a block of code until a given condition is fulfilled. For example:

```
10 REM Input a number in a given range
20 REPEAT
30    PRINT "Please give me a number between 0 and 9 "
40    INPUT N
50 UNTIL N >= 0 AND N <= 9
60 PRINT "Thank You"
```

If the result of the conditional expression following the UNTIL is TRUE, then the loop is ended and the statement following the UNTIL is executed. If, however, the result of the expression is FALSE, the block of code after the REPEAT is executed again and the conditional expression is re-evaluated.

REPEAT ... UNTIL loops may be nested in the same way as FOR ... NEXT loops. They are also similar to FOR loops in that the body of the loop is always executed once, since no test is performed until the end of the loop is reached.

```
10 REM Repeat questions until answered right first time
20 REPEAT
30    tries% = 0
40    REPEAT
50       PRINT "What is 20 * 23 + 14 * 11 ";
60       INPUT ans%
70       tries% += 1
80    UNTIL ans% = 20 * 23 + 14 * 11
90    REPEAT
100      PRINT "What is 12 + 23 * 14 + 6 / 3 ";
110      INPUT ans%
120      tries% += 1
130   UNTIL ans% = 12 + 23 * 14 + 6 / 3
140 UNTIL tries% = 2;
```

WHILE... ENDWHILE

The WHILE ... ENDWHILE loop repeats a block of code while a given condition holds true. For example:

```
10 X = 0
20 WHILE X < 100
30    PRINT X
40    X += RND(5)
50 ENDWHILE
```

The WHILE ... ENDWHILE loop has a conditional expression at the start of it. If this expression returns TRUE, the block of statements following the WHILE, down to the matching ENDWHILE statement, is executed. This is repeated until the expression returns FALSE, in which case execution jumps to the statement following the matching ENDWHILE. We say 'matching' ENDWHILE because WHILE loops may be nested. This means that when BASIC is looking for an ENDWHILE to terminate a loop, it might skip nested WHILE ... ENDWHILE loops.

Here is an example of nested WHILE loops:

```
10 A%=256
20 WHILE A%<>0
30    B%=1
40    WHILE B%<8
50       PRINT A%,B%
60       B%=B%*2
70    ENDWHILE
80    A%=A% DIV 2
90 ENDWHILE
```

WHILE ... ENDWHILE is similar to REPEAT ... UNTIL except that the conditional expression is evaluated at the beginning of the loop (so the body of the loop may never be executed if the condition is initially FALSE) and the loop repeats if the result is TRUE. The following program demonstrates the fact that REPEAT ... UNTIL loops are always executed at least once, whereas the WHILE ... ENDWHILE loops need not be executed at all.

```
10 REPEAT
20    PRINT "Repeat"
30 UNTIL TRUE
40
50 WHILE FALSE
60    PRINT "While"
70 ENDWHILE
80
90 PRINT "All done"
```

This program produces the following output:

```
Repeat
All done
```

CASE... OF... WHEN... OTHERWISE... ENDCASE

The IF ... THEN ... ELSE ... ENDIF construct is useful if you wish to make a choice between two alternatives. The CASE statement can be used when there are many alternatives to be acted upon in different ways.

The following program is a keyboard-controlled sketch pad. The statements after the WHENs alter the values of X% and Y%, and then DRAW a line.

```
10 REM Draw a line depending on the L,R,U,D keys
20 MODE MODE
30 MOVE 640,512
40 X% = 640: Y% = 512
50 REPEAT
60    CASE GET$ OF
70       WHEN "L","l": X% -= 40: DRAW X%,Y% :REM go left
80       WHEN "R","r": X% += 40: DRAW X%,Y% :REM go right
90       WHEN "D","d": Y% -= 40: DRAW X%,Y% :REM go down
100      WHEN "U","u": Y% += 40: DRAW X%,Y% :REM go up
110   ENDCASE
120 UNTIL FALSE : REM go on forever ...
```

This program reads in the character of the next key pressed and checks it against each of the strings following the WHEN statements. If it matches one of these values, the statements following it are executed. Execution continues until another WHEN or the ENDCASE is reached. When this happens, control passes to the statement after the ENDCASE.

If you press a key which is not recognised by any of the four WHEN statements, the program goes round again and waits for another key to be pressed. You can include another line to warn you that you pressed the wrong key. For example:

Control statements

```
105    OTHERWISE VDU 7 : REM Make a short noise
```

The OTHERWISE statement is used if none of the WHENs finds a matching key. The VDU 7 makes a short bell sound to warn you that you have pressed the wrong key.

The following rules apply to CASE statements:

- CASE must be followed by an expression, and then OF. This statement must be at the end of the line.

- Each WHEN must start at the beginning of a line. It may be followed by one or more values, separated by commas.

- The statements dependent on a WHEN may follow it on the same line after a colon :, or be spread over several lines following it.

- The OTHERWISE part is optional. If present it must be at the beginning of a line. The statements following OTHERWISE may be spread over several lines.

- An ENDCASE statement must be present. Like WHEN and OTHERWISE, it must be the first non-space item on a line.

Whenever the result of the expression matches one of the values listed after a WHEN, all the statements following this WHEN down to the next WHEN, OTHERWISE or ENDCASE are executed. BASIC then skips to the statement following the ENDCASE. This means that if the result matches a value in more than one WHEN, only the statements following the first one are executed: the others are ignored. Since OTHERWISE matches any value, having WHEN statements following an OTHERWISE is pointless since they can never be reached.

The following gives another example of using the CASE statement:

```
10 REM Guess a number
20 X% = RND(100)
30 Still_guessing% = TRUE
40 tries% = 0
50 WHILE Still_guessing%
60   INPUT "What is your guess ",guess%
70   CASE guess% OF
80     WHEN X%
90       PRINT "Well done, you've guessed it after ";tries% " attempts"
100      Still_guessing% = FALSE
110    WHEN X%-1,X%+1
120      PRINT "Very close"
130      tries% += 1
140    OTHERWISE
150      IF guess%<X% THEN PRINT "Too low" ELSE PRINT "Too high"
160      tries% += 1
170    ENDCASE
180 ENDWHILE
```

Like all the other BASIC structures, CASE statements may be nested.

GOTO

The GOTO instruction may be used to specify a line number from which the computer is to continue executing the program. For example:

```
10 PRINT "Hello"
20 GOTO 10
```

Whenever the computer executes line 20 it is sent back to line 10 once again. Left on its own, this program never ends. To stop it, press Esc.

GOTO instructions send the control of the program either forwards or backwards. The specified line number may be given as an expression. For example:

```
 10 start% = 100
 20 GOTO (start%+10)
 30 PRINT "This line should not be executed"
100 REM start of the action
110 PRINT "Hello"
120 END
```

Using a variable, however, as the destination for a GOTO is not recommended because while RENUMBER changes the line numbers, it does not alter GOTO destinations that are given as anything other than a simple number. If you must use an expression, it is best to put in inside brackets, since BASIC may get confused if the expression starts with a number.

If you wish to make your programs easy to read, especially for other people, use as few GOTOs as possible. They make a program very difficult to follow. It is far better to use one of the loop constructs like REPEAT ... UNTIL which have been described above.

GOSUB... RETURN

GOSUB stands for 'go to subroutine' and is another variation of GOTO. Instead of continuing indefinitely from the line number which is jumped to, the lines are executed until a RETURN statement is reached. Control then passes back to the instruction which comes after the GOSUB. For example,

```
 10 GOSUB 100
 20 PRINT "This is printed after the first GOSUB returns"
 30 GOSUB 100
 40 PRINT "This is printed after the second GOSUB returns"
 50 END
100 PRINT "This is printed in the GOSUB"
110 RETURN
```

produces:

```
This is printed in the GOSUB
This is printed after the first GOSUB returns
This is printed in the GOSUB
This is printed after the second GOSUB returns
```

Like GOTO, GOSUB should be used sparingly, if at all. It is provided in this version of BASIC for compatibility with weaker dialects of the language. Better methods of providing blocks of code, which once executed then return control back to the point from which they were called are described in the chapter entitled *Procedures and functions* on page 87.

ON... GOTO/GOSUB

The ON ... GOTO statement is used to choose one of a number of different lines depending on the value of a given expression. For example:

```
10 PRINT "Input a number between 1 and 4"
20 INPUT N%
30 ON N% GOTO 60, 100, 80, 120
60 PRINT "Your number is 1"
70 GOTO 999
80 PRINT "Your number is 3"
90 GOTO 999
100 PRINT "Your number is 2"
110 GOTO 999
120 PRINT "Your number is 4"
999 END
```

The computer checks the value of `N%` which is input, then jumps to the `N%`th line number in the list. If `N%` is 3, the computer starts executing at line 80 and so on. If `N%` is less than 1 or greater than 4, the error message

```
ON range at line 30
```

is displayed.

ELSE can be used to catch all other values. It is followed by a statement which is executed if the value of the expression after ON has no corresponding line number. For example, line 30 above could be replaced by:

```
30 ON N% GOTO 60, 100, 80, 120 ELSE PRINT "Number out of range"
40 GOTO 999
```

Now, when the program is run, if `N%` is not between 1 and 4 the message `Number out of range` is displayed and the program ends normally.

ON... GOTO/GOSUB

ON ... GOSUB acts in exactly the same way:

```
10 PRINT "Input a number between 1 and 4"
20 INPUT N%
30 ON N% GOSUB 60, 100, 80, 120
40 END
60 PRINT "Your number is 1"
70 RETURN
80 PRINT "Your number is 3"
90 RETURN
100 PRINT "Your number is 2"
110 RETURN
120 PRINT "Your number is 4"
130 RETURN
```

There is also an ON ... PROC statement which is described in the chapter entitled *Procedures and functions* on page 87. Note, however, that when writing new programs, it is better to use the more versatile CASE structures rather than the ON ... GOTO/GOSUB/PROC constructs. Again, this old-fashioned construct is provided mainly for backwards compatibility with less powerful versions of BASIC.

13 Procedures and functions

Procedures (PROCs) and functions (FNs) provide a way of structuring a program by grouping statements together and referring to them by a single name. The statements can be executed from elsewhere in the program simply by specifying the procedure or function name. A function returns a value, but a procedure does not.

The two structures are very similar, but they are used in slightly different circumstances. PROCs are used wherever a statement can be executed. FNs are used in expressions, wherever a built-in function might be used. Whereas procedures end with an ENDPROC statement, functions return using =expression. The expression is returned as the result of the function call. Functions can return integers, floating point numbers or strings.

Defining and calling procedures

Procedure names begin with the keyword PROC, followed by a name. The following shows how a procedure may be defined and called:

```
 10 CLS
 20 PRINT TAB(0,10)"Countdown commencing ";
 30 FOR N% = 30 TO 1 STEP -1
 40   PRINT TAB(22,10) "  " TAB(22,10);N%;
 50   PROCwait_1_second
 60 NEXT
 70 PRINT TAB(0,10) "BLAST OFF";STRING$(14," ")
 80 END
 90
100 DEF PROCwait_1_second
110 T% = TIME
120 REPEAT
130 UNTIL TIME - T% >= 100
140 ENDPROC
```

Parameters and local variables

The important points about procedures are:

- The procedure definition must start with DEF PROC (or, more simply, DEFPROC) followed by the procedure name. There must be no spaces between PROC and the name.
- The procedure definition must end with the keyword ENDPROC.
- Procedures are called by the keyword PROC followed by the procedure name, again with no spaces.
- Procedure names obey the same rules as variable names, except that they are allowed to start with a digit and may include the character @. Procedure names can also include or start with reserved words, e.g. PROCTO.
- The main body of the program must be separated from the procedure definitions by an END statement. That is, you should only enter the body of a procedure by a PROC statement, not by 'falling' into it. DEF statements are treated as REMs if they are encountered in the usual execution of a program.

Procedures enable you to split up a large amount of code into smaller distinct sections which are easy to manage. The main body of a program can then consist almost entirely of procedure calls, so that it can remain short and easy to follow (since it should be obvious from the procedure names what each call is doing).

Parameters and local variables

Consider the following program:

```
10 REM Draw boxes centred on the screen
20 CLS
30 FOR N% = 1 TO 10
40   PRINT "What size do you want the next box to be ";
50   INPUT size
60   IF size<1024 PROCbox(size) ELSE PRINT "Too large"
70 NEXT N%
80 END
100 DEF PROCbox(edge)
110 RECTANGLE 640-edge/2, 512-edge/2, edge, edge
120 ENDPROC
```

The procedure PROCbox draws a box around the centre of the screen. The size of this box is determined by the value of the variable edge. This variable has the current value of `size` assigned to it each time the procedure is called from line 60. The values being passed to the procedure are known as actual parameters. The variable edge used within the procedure is known as a formal parameter.

A procedure can be defined with more than one parameter. However, it must always be called with the correct number of parameters. These parameters may be:

- integers
- floating point numbers
- strings
- arrays.

If a string variable is used as a formal parameter, it must have either a string expression or a string variable passed to it. Floating point and integer parameters may be passed to one another and interchanged freely, but remember that the fractional part of a floating point variable is lost if it is assigned to an integer variable. Array formal and actual parameters must be of exactly the same type. That is, if the formal parameter is an integer, then only integer arrays may be passed as actual parameters.

Local variables

The formal parameters of a procedure are local to that procedure. This means that assigning a value to any variable within the procedure does not affect any variable elsewhere in the program which has the same name.

In the following program, the procedure PROCsquare has a parameter S% which is automatically local. It also contains a variable, J%, which is declared as being LOCAL.

```
 10 FOR I% = 1 TO 10
 20    PROCsquare(I%)
 30    PROCcube(I%)
 40 NEXT
 50 END
 60
100 DEF PROCsquare(S%)
110 LOCAL J%
120 J% = S% ^ 2
130 PRINT S% ", squared equals "J%;
140 ENDPROC
150
200 DEF PROCcube(I%)
210 I% = I% ^ 3
220 PRINT " and cubed equals ";I%
230 ENDPROC
```

Parameters and local variables

In the case of PROCcube, the actual parameter passed and the formal parameter referred to within it are both called I%. This means that there are two versions of the variable, one inside the procedure and another outside it.

Adding the line

```
35 PRINT I%
```

to the program above prints out the numbers 1 to 10, showing that the assignment to I% within PROCcube does not affect the value of I% in the main body of the program.

Declaring local variables

It is good practice to declare all variables used in a procedure as local, since this removes the risk that the procedure will alter variables used elsewhere in the program.

When you declare a local array, the LOCAL statement must be followed by a DIM statement to dimension the local array. For example, consider the following function which, when passed two vectors of the same size, returns their scalar product:

```
100 DEF FNscalar_product(A(),B())
110 REM ** Both arrays must have a dimension of 1 **
120 IF DIM(A()) <> 1 OR DIM(B()) <> 1 THEN
130 PRINT "Vectors required"
140 =0
150 ENDIF
160 REM ** Both arrays must be the same size **
170 IF DIM(A(),1) <> DIM(B(),1) THEN
180 PRINT "Vectors must be of same size"
190 =0
200 ENDIF
210 REM ** Create a temporary array of the same size **
220 LOCAL C()
230 DIM C(DIM(A(),1))
240 REM ** Multiply the corresponding elements and place in C() **
250 C() = A()*B()
260 REM ** Finally sum all the elements of C() **
270 =SUM(C())
```

This example uses a function instead of a procedure. Note that SUM is a built-in function.

Notice that although function definitions may be multi-line, the syntax is such that single line functions as found in older dialects of BASIC may be defined in a compatible manner. Thus you can say either:

```
1000 DEF FNdisc(a,b,c)
1010 REM find the discriminant of a, b and c
1020 =b*b-4*a*c
```

or, using the old-fashioned form:

```
1000 DEF FND(a,b,c)=b*b-4*a*c
```

(Another limitation of the non-BBC BASIC syntax was that often only single-letter function names were allowed.)

Value-result parameter passing

The simple parameter passing scheme described above is known as 'value' parameter passing because the value of the actual parameter is copied into the formal parameter, which is then used within the procedure. The result of any modification to the formal parameter is not communicated back to the actual parameter. Thus the formal parameter is entirely local.

BASIC provides a second method of parameter passing known as 'value-result'. This is just like the simple value mechanism in that the actual parameter's value is copied into the formal parameter for use inside the procedure. The difference is, however, that when the procedure returns, the final value of the formal parameter is copied back into the actual parameter. Thus, a result can be passed back. (This means that the actual parameter can only be a variable, not an expression.)

A statement specifying that you wish to pass a result back for a particular parameter should be preceded by the keyword RETURN. For example:

```
100 DEF PROCorderedswap(RETURN A,RETURN B)
110 IF A > B SWAP A,B
120 ENDPROC
```

SWAP is a built-in statement to swap the values of two variables or arrays.

Specifying RETURN before an array formal parameter does not make any difference to the way the parameter is passed.

Arrays passed by reference

Arrays are always passed by reference. That is, the array formal parameter acts as an 'alias' for the actual parameter within the procedure or function, and if you change the elements of the formal parameter, the actual parameter will also be altered. If you want to simulate value passing of array parameters, you should use a local array of the same dimensions as the actual parameter, for example:

```
1000 DEF PROCfred(a())
1010 LOCAL b()
1020 DIM b(DIM(a(),1), DIM(a(),2))  :REM assume a() is 2D
1030 b()=a() : REM now b() can be altered at will
1040 ...
```

LOCAL DATA and LOCAL errors

Because procedures and functions often set up their own error handlers and local data, it is possible to make these local so that nothing outside the procedure or function is affected. In fact, both these may be made 'local' outside of a procedure. For example, you can make an error handler local to a WHILE loop. However, the constructs are mentioned here for completeness. More information can be found about local error handlers in the chapter entitled *Error handling and debugging* on page 169.

To make the current DATA pointer local, and then restore it, a sequence of the following form is used:

```
1000 LOCAL DATA
1010 RESTORE +0
1020 DATA ...
1030 ...
1080 RESTORE DATA
...
```

LOCAL DATA stores the current data pointer (i.e. the place where the next READ will get its data from) away. It can then be changed by a RESTORE to enable some local data to be read, and finally restored to its original value using RESTORE DATA. Thus a procedure or function which uses its own local data can read it without affecting the data pointer being used by the calling program.

As mentioned above, LOCAL DATA and RESTORE DATA can be used anywhere that localised data is required, not just in functions and procedures. They can also be nested. However, if LOCAL DATA is used within a function or procedure definition, it must come after any LOCAL variables. BASIC will perform an automatic RESTORE DATA on return from a PROC or FN, so that statement isn't strictly required at the end of PROCs and FNs.

ON... PROC

ON ... PROC is similar to ON ... GOTO which is described in the chapter entitled *Control statements* on page 73. It evaluates the expression given after the ON keyword. If the value N% is given, it then calls the procedure designated by N% on the list. For example:

Procedures and functions

```
 10 REPEAT
 20   INPUT "Enter a number ",num
 30   PRINT "Type 1 to double it"
 40   PRINT "Type 2 to square it"
 50   INPUT action
 60   ON action PROCdouble(num), PROCsquare(num)
 70 UNTIL FALSE
100 DEF PROCdouble(num)
110 PRINT "Your number doubled is ";num*2
120 ENDPROC
200 DEF PROCsquare(num)
210 PRINT "Your number squared is ";num*num
220 ENDPROC
```

Note, however, that in most circumstances, the CASE statement provides a more powerful and structured way of performing these actions.

Recursive procedures

A procedure may contain calls to other procedures and may even contain a call to itself. A procedure which does call itself from within its own definition is called a recursive procedure:

```
 10 PRINT "Please input a string :"
 20 INPUT A$
 30 PROCremove_spaces(A$)
 40 END
100 DEF PROCremove_spaces(A$)
110 LOCAL pos_space%
120 PRINT A$
130 pos_space%=INSTR(A$," "):REM =0 if no spaces
140 IF pos_space% THEN
150   A$=LEFT$(A$,pos_space%-1)+RIGHT$(A$,pos_space%+1)
160   PROCremove_spaces(A$)
170 ENDIF
180 ENDPROC
```

In the example above, PROCremove_spaces is passed a string as a parameter. If the string contains no spaces, the procedure ends. If a space is found within the string, the space is removed and the procedure is called again with the new string as an argument to remove any further spaces. For example, typing the string The quick brown fox causes the following to be displayed:

Functions

```
The quick brown fox
Thequick brown fox
Thequickbrown fox
Thequickbrownfox
```

Recursive procedures often provide a very clear solution to a problem. There are two reasons, however, which suggest that they may not be the best way to solve a problem:

- Some operations are more naturally expressed as a loop, that is, using FOR ... NEXT, REPEAT ... UNTIL, or WHILE ... ENDWHILE.
- Recursive procedures often use more of the computer's memory than the corresponding loop.

As an example, the following two programs both print Good morning! backwards. The first one uses a WHILE ... ENDWHILE loop. The second uses a recursive technique to achieve the same result.

First example:

```
 10 PROCreverseprint("Good morning !")
100 DEF PROCreverseprint(A$)
110 FOR i% = LEN A% TO 1 STEP -1
120    PRINT MID$(A$,i%,1)
130 NEXT
140 ENDPROC
```

Second example:

```
 10 PROCreverseprint("Good morning !")
100 DEF PROCreverseprint(A$)
110 IF LEN(A$) > 0 THEN
120    PRINT RIGHT$(A$);
130    PROCreverseprint(LEFT$(A$))
140 ENDIF
160 ENDPROC
```

Functions

Functions are similar in many ways to procedures, but differ in that they return a result. BASIC provides many functions of its own, like the trigonometric functions SIN, COS, TAN and RND. If you give RND a parameter with an integer value greater than 1, it returns a random value between 1 and the number given inclusive. For example,

```
X = RND(10)
```

produces random numbers between 1 and 10.

You may define functions of your own using the keyword DEF followed by FN and the name of your function. The function definition ends when a statement beginning with an = sign is encountered. This assigns the expression on the right of the sign to the function result. This result may be assigned to a variable in the normal way.

Functions obey the same rules as procedures with regard to naming conventions, the use of parameters and local variables.

We have already seen an example function definition in FNscalar_product above. The following is another example of how a function may be defined and used:

```
 10 FOR N% = 1 TO 10
 20   PRINT "A sphere of radius ";N%;" has a volume "; FNvolume(N%)
 30 NEXT N%
 40 END
100 DEF FNvolume(radius%)
110 = 4/3*PI*radius%^3
```

Function and procedure libraries

Libraries provide a convenient way of adding frequently-used procedures and functions to a BASIC program.

The libraries are kept in memory (unless they are OVERLAYed), and if a reference is made to a procedure or function which is not defined in your program, a search of each library in turn is made until a definition is found. If the routine is found in a library, it is executed exactly as though it were part of the program.

The advantages of using libraries are:

- They standardise certain routines between programs.
- They reduce the time required to write and test a program. (The library routines only need to be written and tested once, not each time a new program is developed.)
- They make programs shorter and more modular.

Loading a library into memory

There are three methods of loading a library into memory, INSTALL, LIBRARY and OVERLAY.

INSTALL and LIBRARY are followed by a string giving a filename. This file should contain a set of BASIC procedure and function definitions, perhaps with local DATA statements to be used by those procedures and functions.

Function and procedure libraries

INSTALL loads the library at the top of BASIC's memory. It then lowers the upper memory limit that BASIC programs can use. INSTALLed libraries are therefore 'permanent' in that they occupy memory (and may be called) until BASIC is re-started (e.g. by another *BASIC command). You can not selectively remove INSTALLed libraries. INSTALL must be used before the BASIC program is first run rather than from within a program – it is a command, and cannot be used as a program statement.

LIBRARY reserves a sufficient area of memory for the library just above the main BASIC program and loads the library. Any library loaded in this way remains only until the variables are cleared. This occurs, for example, when the CLEAR or NEW commands are given, when the program is edited in some way, or when a program is run. Thus LIBRARY-type libraries are much more transient than INSTALLed ones (as temporary as normal variables, in fact), so you would generally use LIBRARY from within a program.

For example:

```
 10 CLS
 20 REM Print out a story
 30 REM Load output library
 40 LIBRARY "Printout"
 50 REM Read and print the heading
 60 READ A$
 70 PROCcentre(A$)
 80 REM Print out each sentence in turn
 90 REPEAT
100   READ sentence$
110   REM if sentence$ = "0" then have reached the end
120   IF sentence$ = "0" END
130   REM otherwise print it out
140   PROCprettyprint(sentence$)
150 UNTIL FALSE
200 DATA A story
210 DATA This,program,is,using,two,procedures:
220 DATA 'centre',and,'prettyprint',from,a,library
230 DATA called,'Printout'.
240 DATA The,library,is,loaded,each,time,
245 DATA the,program,is,run.
250 DATA The,procedure,'centre',places,a,string,in,the
260 DATA centre,of,the,screen.
270 DATA The,procedure,'prettyprint',prints,out,
280 DATA a,word,at,the,current,text,cursor,
290 DATA position,unless,it,would,be,split,over,
300 DATA a,line,in,which,case,it,starts,the,word,
305 DATA on,the,next,line,down.
310 DATA 0
```

The library `Printout` could be as follows:

```
 10 REM >Printout - Text output library
 20 REM ******************************
 30 DEF PROCPrintouthelp
 40 REM Print out details of the library routines
 50 PRINT "PROCcentre(a$)"
 60 PRINT "Place a string in the centre"
 70 PRINT "of a 40 character line"
 80 PRINT "PROCprettyprint(a$)"
 90 PRINT "Print out a word at the current"
100 PRINT "text cursor position, starting"
110 PRINT "a new 40 character line if required"
120 PRINT "to avoid splitting it over two lines"
130 ENDPROC

140 REM ******************************
200 REM Place a string in the centre
210 REM of a 40 character line
220 DEF PROCcentre(a$)
230 LOCAL start%
240 start% = (40 - LEN(a$))/2
250 PRINT TAB(start%);a$
260 ENDPROC

270 REM ******************************
300 REM Print out a word at the current
310 REM text cursor position, starting
320 REM a new 40 character line if required
330 REM to avoid splitting it over two lines
340 DEF PROCprettyprint(a$)
350 LOCAL end%
360 end% = POS + LEN(a$)
370 IF end% < 40 PRINT a$;" "; : ENDPROC
380 PRINT 'a$;" ";
390 ENDPROC
400 REM ******************************
```

In the above example the library `Printout` contains three procedures:

PROCPrintouthelp	prints out details of the library structure
PROCcentre	prints a string in the middle of a 40 character line
PROCprettyprint	prints a word at the current position or, if necessary, on the next line to avoid splitting it

To make PROCprettyprint and PROCcentre more general-purpose a further refinement would be for them to take an additional parameter specifying the number of characters there are on the line, instead of a fixed length of 40.

Overlaying

OVERLAY enables you to give a list of filenames which contain libraries. When BASIC can't find a PROC or FN within the program or within any of the current libraries, it will start to look in the OVERLAY files. You give OVERLAY a string array as a parameter. For example:

```
10 DIM lib$(5)
20 lib$()="lib1","lib2","lib3","lib4"
30 OVERLAY lib$()
40 ...
```

When the OVERLAY statement is executed, BASIC reserves enough space for the largest of the files given in the string array. Then, when it can't find a PROC or FN definition anywhere else, it will go through the list, loading the libraries in order until the definition is found or the end of the array is met.

Once a definition has been found, that library stays in memory (and so the other definitions in it may be used) until the next time a definition can't be found anywhere. The search process starts again, so the current overlay library will be overwritten with the first one in the list. Once BASIC has found a definition, it will remember which file it was in (or more precisely, which element of the array held the filename), so that file will be loaded immediately the next time the definition is required and it is not in memory.

Because of the way one area of memory is used to hold each of the overlay files (and only one at any one time), you are not allowed to call a procedure whose definition is in an overlay library if one of the overlay definitions is currently active. Another way of putting this is that you can't nest overlay calls.

If you know that a given overlay file will never be needed again in the program, you can speed up the search through the overlay list by setting the no-longer-required elements of the array to the null string. You can also add new names to the end of the array, as long as none of the new library files is bigger than the largest one specified in the original OVERLAY statement.

You can execute OVERLAY more than once in a program. Each time it is called, the memory set aside for the previous set of files will be lost, and a new block based on the size of the new ones will be allocated.

Building your own libraries

There are certain rules which should be obeyed when writing library procedures and functions:

- Line number references are not allowed.

    Libraries must not use GOTO, GOSUB, etc. Any reference to a line number is to be taken as referring to the current program, not to the line numbers with which the library is constructed. You can use RESTORE+ to access DATA statements in a library.

- Only local variables referring to the current procedure or function should be used.

    It is advisable that library routines only use local variables, so that they are totally independent of any program which may call them.

- Each library should have a heading.

    It is recommended that a library's first line contains the full name of the library and details of a procedure which prints out information on each of the routines in the library. For example:

```
10000 REM>hyperlib - gives hyperbolic functions.
      Call PROChyperHelp for details
```

This last rule is useful because BASIC contains a command, LVAR, which lists the first line of all libraries which are currently loaded. As a result, it is important that the first line of each library contains all the essential information about itself.

The name of the library is also suffixed to the error message when an error occurs in library code. When libraries are not being used from the command line, and LVAR is not available, it might be more appropriate for the heading to just be the library name.

Function and procedure libraries

14 Data and command files

This chapter describes how you can create data files to read information from files, and how you can create command files to build up a sequence of commands to BASIC.

Data files

Programs can create and read information from files, called data files. For example, if you write a program that creates a list of names and telephone numbers, you may wish to save the names and telephone numbers as a data file.

Creating a data file

The data file is specified in a program by one of the OPEN*xx* keywords. For example you can create a data file using the keyword OPENOUT.

For example, typing

```
A = OPENOUT "books"
```

creates a data file named books and opens it so that it is ready to receive data. The value stored in the variable A is called a *channel number* and allows the computer to distinguish this data file from other open data files. All future communication with the file books is made via the file channel number in A rather than via the name of the file.

Writing information to a data file

Writing information to a data file is done using PRINT#. For example:

```
 10 A = OPENOUT "books"
 20 FOR I = 1 TO 5
 30   READ book$
 40   PRINT#A, book$
 50 NEXTI
 60 CLOSE#A
 70 END
 80 DATA "Black Beauty"
 90 DATA "Lord of the Rings"
100 DATA "The Wind in the Willows"
110 DATA "The House at Pooh Corner"
120 DATA "The BBC BASIC Reference Manual"
```

Closing a data file

Use CLOSE# to close a data file. This ensures that any data belonging to the file which is still in a memory buffer is stored on the disc. The buffer can then be re-used for another file. After a CLOSE#, the file handle is no longer valid.

Reading data from a file

You can read data from a file using OPENIN and INPUT#. OPENIN opens an existing data file so that information may be read from it. INPUT# then reads the individual items of data. For example:

```
10 channel = OPENIN "books"
20 REPEAT
30   INPUT#channel, title$
40 UNTIL EOF#channel
50 CLOSE#channel
60 END
```

EOF# is a function which returns TRUE when the end of a file is reached.

Writing or reading single bytes

Other useful keywords for reading or writing data are:

- BPUT# which writes a single byte to a file
- BGET# which reads a single byte from a file.

The following writes all the upper-case letters to a file using BPUT# as part of the program:

```
10 channel = OPENOUT "characters"
20 FOR N% = ASC("A") TO ASC("Z")
30   BPUT#channel,N%
40 NEXT N%
50 CLOSE#channel
```

BGET# is used as part of a program that allows each character to be read into a string as follows:

```
10 channel = OPENIN "characters"
20 string$ = ""
30 REPEAT
40   string$ += CHR$(BGET#channel)
50 UNTIL EOF#channel
60 CLOSE#channel
```

Writing or reading ASCII strings

The BPUT# statement and GET$# function can also be used to write text to a file, and read text from a file. These write and read the text in a form compatible with other programs, such as text editors like Edit, unlike PRINT# and INPUT# which write and read strings in BASIC string format.

When you PRINT# an expression to a file, it is written as an encoded sequence of bytes. For example, an integer is stored on the file as the byte &40 followed by the binary representation of the number. A string is written as &00 followed by the length of the string, followed by the string itself in reverse order.

To write information as pure text, you can use:

BPUT#*channel*,*string$*[;]

The characters of the string, which may be any string expression, are written to the file. If there is no semi-colon at the end of the statement, then a newline character (ASCII 10) is written after the last character of the string. If the semi-colon is present, no newline is appended to the string.

To read an ASCII string from a file, you can use:

*str$*=GET$#*channel*

This function reads characters from the file until a newline (ASCII 10) or carriage return (ASCII 13) character is read. This terminates the string, but is not returned as part of it. Thus any newlines will look like new strings when you read the file. The end of file also terminates the string.

Command files

A command file is a file whose contents are a sequence of commands to be executed as if they had been typed at the keyboard. You can use a variety of methods to create a command file. Using Edit is probably the easiest, especially if that application is already loaded and can be activated from the desktop. See the RISC OS *User Guide* for details on using Edit.

Another way of creating a command file is to use the *BUILD command. If you type

```
*BUILD keyfile
```

everything subsequently typed from the keyboard is sent directly to the file called `keyfile`. If there is a file named `keyfile` already, it is deleted when the *BUILD command is given.

Press Return at the end of each line. When you finish entering the commands, press Esc to end keyboard input to keyfile.

Executing a command file

There are two main ways of executing a command file. If the file contains a sequence of commands to a language, such as BASIC, then you should *EXEC it. For example, suppose you create a file called `install` which contains the following lines:

```
INSTALL "basiclib.shell"
INSTALL "basiclib.hyperlib"
INSTALL "basiclib.debugger"
INSTALL "basiclib.FPasm"
```

The lines in the file are designed to save the programmer from having to type in a list of INSTALL commands whenever BASIC is started. To execute these commands, enter BASIC then type the command

```
*EXEC install
```

This causes the contents of `install` to be taken as input, exactly as if it had been typed in (but much quicker!). You can make the command even shorter by setting the file type of `install` to COMMAND using the command

```
*SETTYPE install COMMAND
```

This converts the file into a runnable file. Once you have done this, you can *EXEC the file just by giving its name as a command, for example:

```
*install
```

The other way in which a command file can be executed is to *OBEY it.

Note: If you do this, each line in the file is executed as a * command, i.e. it is passed to the operating system command line interpreter only – not to BASIC. In this case you do not see the lines that are being executed on the screen, and *OBEY allows parameter substitution.

See the section *Command scripts* in appendix *The command line* in the RISC OS *User Guide* for more details on *OBEY.

Command files

15   Screen modes

The display produced on a standard monitor can be in one of many different modes. Each mode gives a different combination of values to the following four attributes:

- the number of characters you can display on the screen
- the graphics resolution
- the number of colours available on the screen at any one time
- the amount of memory allocated to the screen display.

The graphics resolution is specified by the number of pixels (rectangular dots) which can be displayed horizontally and vertically. The greater the number of pixels which the screen can be divided into, the smaller each pixel is. Since all lines have to be at least one pixel thick, smaller pixels enable the lines to appear less chunky.

Different modes use different amounts of memory to hold the picture; the amount of memory is determined by the resolution and by the number of colours.

Note: BASIC screen mode and graphics commands control the computer when BASIC is being run from the command line. When it is being run from a Task Window, these functions are controlled by the Window Manager, so these BASIC commands should not be used.

Changing screen modes

If you are using RISC OS 3.50 or later then to change mode, use MODE followed by a *mode string*. This is a list of space or comma separated attributes, which must contain an X parameter giving the horizontal resolution, a Y parameter giving the vertical resolution and a C parameter giving the required number of colours. For example,

MODE "X640 Y480 C256"

changes the display to a mode that is 640 pixels wide and 480 pixels high with 256 colours. Note that only certain combinations of resolutions and colours are available, depending on the capabilities of your computer's video hardware and the monitor you are using. If you specify a mode that is not supported you will get a Screen mode not available error.

When you type a MODE command from the command line, the desktop is cleared automatically.

The following resolutions are typically available on most RISC OS computers:

- 640 × 480
- 800 × 600
- 1024 × 768

For a full list of the attributes that may be specified in a mode string see *Appendix* E *– Specifying screen modes*

A second way to select a mode is to use MODE followed by three integer parameters. The first two give the horizontal and vertical resolution you want and the third is the requested number of bits per pixel, which specifies how many colours are available. For example,

```
MODE 640,480,8
```

changes the display to a mode that is 640 pixels wide and 480 pixels high with 256 colours. The bits per pixel parameter can take the following values:

Bits per pixel	Number of colours
1	2
2	4
4	16
6	256 (VIDC-1 style palette, see below)
8	256 (full palette)
16	32,768
32	16,777,216

A third method is to use MODE followed by five integer parameters. The first two are the resolution, as in the previous example, and the next three specify the ModeFlags, NColour and Log2BPP mode variables. For example,

```
MODE 640,480,&80,255,3
```

selects the same mode as the previous example (640 pixels wide and 480 pixels high with a fully controllable palette of 256 colours). For a detailed explanation see *Appendix* E *– Specifying screen modes*.

Numbered screen modes

For compatibility with versions of RISC OS older than RISC OS 3.50, numbered screen modes are supported. Full details of the numbered screen modes are given in the Appendix on old-type screen modes in the RISC OS *User Guide*.

To change to a numbered mode, use MODE followed by the mode number you want. For example,

```
MODE 12
```

changes the display to mode 12. This provides 640 × 256 pixel resolution graphics in 16 colours (if your monitor supports this resolution).

Banked modes

By adding 128 to the mode number you can select a mode that uses the so-called 'shadow' memory. If you imagine that there are two separate areas of memory which may be used to hold the screen information, then selecting a normal mode will cause one area to be used, and selecting a shadow mode (in the range 128 to 255) will cause the alternative bank to be used.

You can force all subsequent mode changes to use the shadow bank with the command:

```
*SHADOW
```

After this, you can imagine 128 to be added to any mode number in the range 0 to 127. To disable the automatic use of the shadow memory, issue the command:

```
*SHADOW 1
```

Using the shadow bank

In order to use the shadow bank, the ScreenSize configuration must reserve at least twice as much screen memory as the amount required for the non-shadow mode. For example, if you want to use both mode 0 and mode 128, 40K of screen memory must be available, as mode 0 takes 20K.

In fact, for a given mode, there may be several banks available. You can work out how many by dividing the amount of configured screen memory by the requirement of the current mode.

The normal, non-shadow bank is numbered bank 1, and the shadow bank, used by mode 128, is bank 2. There are two more, banks 3 and 4. Using operating system calls, you can choose which of the four banks is displayed, and which is used by the VDU drivers when displaying text and graphics.

Text size

The number of characters displayed on the screen is affected by the number which are allowed per row (i.e. the width of each character) and the number of rows which can be displayed on the screen (i.e. the spacing between the rows).

Changing text size

You can change the size of text characters in the modes which support graphics. However, you can only do this when the display is in what is called VDU 5 mode. This mode is explained in the section entitled *Printing text at the graphics cursor* on page 125.

To set the size of characters in VDU 5 mode, type:

VDU 23,17,7,6,sx;sy;0;

where sx is the horizontal size of characters and sy is the vertical size. Characters are normally eight pixels square so to get double height you would use:

VDU 23,17,7,6,8;16;0;

Single- and double-height character plotting is much faster than other sizes, but you can choose any numbers for sx and sy between 1 and 32767.

Colour modes

The number of colours available on the screen at any given time depends on the number of bits per pixel in the mode. The value stored in memory for each pixel is called a colour number and varies between zero and the number of available colours, minus one.

In modes with more than 256 colours the colour number of each pixel directly defines the physical colour that is displayed, but in modes with 256 or fewer colours it is instead a logical colour number which identifies an entry in a table called the palette that defines the physical colour.

When you first enter a mode that uses a palette, the computer selects the default colours which it uses for that particular mode. These are assigned to the logical colour numbers (see *Appendix F – Default palettes* on page 481).

The computer chooses one colour to display text and graphics and another for the background. These two colours are chosen so that under default conditions the text and graphics are in white and the background is black. For example, in four-colour modes the computer chooses to draw text and graphics in colour 3 (white) on a background which is colour 0 (black).

VIDC1-style 256-colour modes

RISC OS still provides compatibility with the VIDC1 hardware found in the Acorn Archimedes series of computers. In VIDC1-style 256-colour modes, there are 64 different colours, and each colour may have four different brightnesses, resulting in a total of 256. The colours themselves are referred to as numbers 0-63. The brightness levels are called 'tints' and are in the range 0-255. However, because there are only four different tints, the numbers normally used are 0, 64, 128 and 192.

The VIDC1-style 256-colour modes are described in more detail on page 113.

Changing colours

You may choose to display your text, graphics, or background in a different colour from the defaults. To do this, use the following commands:

Modes with less than 256 colours

- COLOUR n selects colour n for text
- GCOL n selects colour n for graphics.

Each command can affect both the foreground and background colours, depending on the value it is given:

- If n is less than 128, the foreground colour is set to colour n.
- If n is 128 or greater, the background colour is set to colour $n-128$.

If the colour number is greater than the number of colours available in a particular mode then it is reduced to lie within the range available. For example, in a four-colour mode COLOUR 5 and COLOUR 9 are both equivalent to COLOUR 1.

Try the following example in a four-colour mode:

```
10 MODE "X640 Y480 C4"  : REM four-colour mode
20 COLOUR 129           : REM red background
30 COLOUR 2             : REM yellow foreground
40 PRINT "Hello There"
```

If your computer does not support a resolution of 640 × 480, change the first line to select a valid mode. If you are using RISC OS 3.10 change it to use MODE 1 instead.

Modes with 256 colours or more

Text, graphics and background colours are specified by the amount of red, green, and blue (as one of 256 levels) which go to make up the colour.

- COLOUR OF r,g,b selects a text colour with the given amounts of red, green and blue. COLOUR ON r,g,b selects the text background colour. These two forms can be combined to set both the foreground and background colours
- Similarly, GCOL OF r,g,b selects the graphics colour and GCOL ON r,g,b selects the graphics background colour.

Each of r, g and b must be values between 0 and 255. A value of zero specifies that none of that colour should be used and a value of 255 that the maximum intensity of that colour should be used. Thus setting all of them to zero gives black and setting all to 255 gives white. The actual colour selected will be the closest one available in the current mode.

The following example gives the same result as the previous one:

```
10 MODE "X640 Y480 C256" : REM 256-colour mode
20 REM yellow foreground, red background
30 COLOUR OF 255,0,0 ON 255,255,0
40 PRINT "Hello There"
```

If your computer does not support a resolution of 640 × 480, change the first line to select a valid mode. If you are using RISC OS 3.10 change it to use MODE 15 instead.

Changing the colour palette

In addition to being able to select the colour in which numbers, text and so on are displayed, in modes with 256 or fewer colours you can also change the physical colour associated with each colour number.

Changing the shade of the colour

You can define the amount of red, green, and blue (as one of 256 levels) which go to make up the colour displayed for each of the logical colour numbers. Thus, any of the available colour numbers can be made to appear as a shade selected from the full range, or 'palette', of 256*256*256 = 16,777,216 colours.

You can assign any of the shades available to a logical colour using the command:

COLOUR n,r,g,b

This assigns r parts red, g parts green and b parts blue to logical colour n. Each of r, g and b must be values between 0 and 255. A value of zero specifies that none of that colour should be used and a value of 255 that the maximum intensity of that colour should be used. Thus setting all of them to zero gives black and setting all to 255 gives white.

Returning to the default colour settings

To return to the default settings for each of the colours type

VDU 20

Note: you should not use VDU 20 if you are writing a BASIC program under the Wimp (described in the section entitled W*indow managed programs* on page 7).

Experimenting with colour

The following program allows you to mix and display various colours:

```
10 REPEAT
40    MODE "X640 Y480 C16"
50:
60 REM Input values from the user
70:
80     INPUT"Amount of red    (0 - 255) "red%
90     INPUT"Amount of green  (0 - 255) "green%
100    INPUT"Amount of blue   (0 - 255) "blue%
110:
120    COLOUR 1,red%,green%,blue%
130    GCOL 1
140    RECTANGLE FILL 540,380,200,200
150:
160    Now=TIME
170    REPEAT UNTIL TIME > Now + 500
180:
190 UNTIL FALSE : REM Repeat forever
```

This program asks you for three values, one for each of the amounts of red, green and blue you require. It then plots a rectangle in that colour. After it has displayed it for five seconds it clears the screen and starts again. To stop the program at any stage press Esc.

VIDC1-style 256-colour modes

Full control is not available over the colour palette setting in VIDC1-style 256-colour modes.

As noted above, in these modes, a choice of 64 colours is available directly from the simple COLOUR and GCOL commands.

For example:

```
10 MODE "X640 Y480 C64"
20 FOR Col% = 0 TO 63
30    COLOUR Col%
40    PRINT ":";Col%;
50 NEXT
```

As in the other modes the colour of the background can be changed by adding 128 to the parameter of the COLOUR command. Try modifying line 30 of the above program and running it again.

About colour numbers in VIDC1-style 256 colour modes

To understand the manner in which the colour number dictates the actual shade of colour which you see you need to consider the binary pattern which makes up the colour number. Only the right-most six bits are relevant. For an explanation of % and binary numbers, see the chapter entitled *Binary and logic* on page 33.

In common with the other modes colour zero (%000000) is black.

Colour	binary pattern	shade of colour
1	(%000001)	dark red
2	(%000010)	mid-red
3	(%000011)	bright red
4	(%000100)	dark green
8	(%001000)	mid-green
12	(%001100)	bright green
16	(%010000)	dark blue
32	(%100000)	mid-blue
48	(%110000)	bright blue
63	(%111111)	white

Of the six bits which are used for the colour, the right-most two control the amount of red, the middle two the amount of green and the left-most two the amount of blue.

For example, COLOUR 35 is composed as follows: 35 = %100011, and so contains two parts of blue, no green and three parts of red, and appears as a purple shade. The remaining two bits of the eight bits of colour information are supplied via a special TINT keyword, already mentioned above.

The TINT keyword

The effect of TINT on the shade of the colour is to change the small amount of white tint used in conjunction with the base colour. This gives four subtle variations to each colour.

The range of the TINT value is 0 to 255; but there are only four distinct tint levels within this range, and so all the number values within the following ranges have the same effect:

0-63	No extra brightness
64-127	Some extra brightness
128-191	More extra brightness
192-255	Maximum extra brightness

For example:

```
COLOUR 35 TINT 128
```

or

```
GCOL 17 TINT 0
```

Displaying 256 shades

Here is a program which shows all possible tints and colours:

```
10 MODE "X640 Y480 C64"
20 FOR col%=0 TO 63
30   FOR tint%=0 TO 192 STEP 64
40     GCOL col% TINT tint%
50     RECTANGLE FILL tint%*4,col%*15,256,15
60   NEXT tint%
70 NEXT col%
```

Using the screen under the Wimp

When writing programs which run under the window environment, you should not use the standard commands such as COLOUR and MODE as these will interfere with the running of other active programs. Instead you should use the facilities provided by the Wimp (see the section entitled *Window managed programs* on page 7 for more details).

16 Simple graphics

Text and graphics plotting is performed by the operating system. Many graphics operations require strings of control characters to be sent to the VDU drivers. However, BASIC provides keywords to perform some of the more common operations, such as plotting points, lines and circles and changing colours. This chapter describes those keywords.

The graphics screen

Whichever graphics mode your program is in, the actual range of coordinates that can be addressed is −32768 to +32767 in each direction. The coordinate range of the graphics screen that you actually use, and which is dependent upon the mode you select, is really a window on this area.

The coordinates used for graphics are specified in OS *units* where there are approximately 180 units per inch on most screens. In many graphics modes a pixel is two units wide and two units high, so a 640 by 480 pixel mode would be 1280 units wide by 960 units high.

A program can find out the resolution of the screen and the conversion factor between pixels and OS units by using the VDU keyword to read the following VDU variables:

Name	No.	Meaning
XEigFactor	4	This indicates the number of bits by which an X coordinate must be shifted right to convert to screen pixels. Thus if this value is n, then one screen pixel corresponds to 2^n OS units in the X direction.
YEigFactor	5	This indicates the number of bits by which a Y coordinate must be shifted right to convert to screen pixels. Thus if this value is n, then one screen pixel corresponds to 2^n OS units in the Y direction.
XWindLimit	11	Number of x pixels on screen−1.
YWindLimit	12	Number of y pixels on screen−1.

This means that you can find out the size of the screen in OS units by using the following statements:

The point command

```
ScreenW% = (VDU 11 + 1) << VDU 4
ScreenH% = (VDU 12 + 1) << VDU 5
```

The origin (0,0) is located initially at the bottom left corner of the screen. So, for example, you could draw a line between (−1300,−900) and (850,1500) and what would appear on the screen in a 640 by 480 mode is the portion of the line which crosses the region (0,0) to (1279,959):

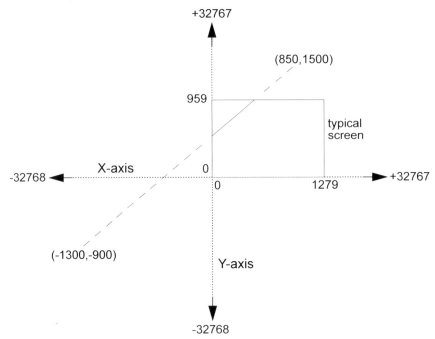

Note: Many of the graphics examples in this and the following chapters start with the command MODE MODE. This performs a mode change to the mode you are currently in, resetting the state of the VDU drivers and clearing the screen, but leaving the resolution and number of colours unchanged.

The point command

The simplest type of object you can plot on the screen is a single pixel, or point. To plot a point, you use the statement POINT followed by the x and y coordinates of the pixel you want plotted. For example:

```
POINT 640,480
```

will plot a pixel in the middle of the screen (or near to it, depending on the resolution of the current mode) in the current graphics foreground colour.

Simple graphics

The program below plots random points within a radius of 200 units from the centre of the screen:

```
10 MODE MODE
20 ScreenW%=(VDU 11 + 1) << VDU 4
30 ScreenH%=(VDU 12 + 1) << VDU 5
40 CentreX%=ScreenW%/2
50 CentreY%=ScreenH%/2
60 REPEAT
70   rad%=RND(199)
80   angle=RADRND(360)
90   GCOL RND(255),RND(255),RND(255)
100  POINT CentreX%+rad%*COSangle, CentreY%+rad%*SINangle
110 UNTIL FALSE
```

POINT may also be used as a function to discover the colour of a pixel. It has the form:

```
col = POINT(x%,y%)
```

In modes with less than 256 colours POINT returns the logical colour number. In 256-colour modes it returns a number between 0 and 63. To find the tint of the pixel, you use the TINT keyword as a function in a similar way:

```
tint = TINT(x%,y%)
```

If you are using a 256-colour mode with a full palette it is possible to convert the values returned by POINT and TINT into the logical colour number used by the palette, but the mapping is not straightforward. It can be found as follows:

```
pal = (col AND 33)<<2 OR (col AND 14)<<3 OR (col AND 16)>>1 OR tint>>6
```

In modes with more than 256 colours POINT returns the colour number of the pixel, the format of which depends on the number of bits per pixel (which can be determined by reading VDU 9, Log2BPP), and the colour format (which can be determined from bits 12-15 of VDU 0, ModeFlags).

For example, in a 32-bit per pixel mode with a TBGR format (Log2BPP=5, ModeFlags=0) the lowest 8 bits of the returned number is the amount of red, the next 8 bits are the amount of green and the next 8 bits are the amount of blue.

The line command

BASIC provides a very simple way of drawing lines on the screen. All you need to do is to work out the positions of the two ends of the line. You can then draw a line with a single instruction such as:

```
LINE 120,120, 840,920 : REM line (120,120) to (840,920)
```

You could draw the line the other way and produce the same result:

```
LINE 840,920, 120,120
```

The following program uses LINE four times to draw a box on the screen:

```
10 MODE MODE
20 left%    = 100
30 right%   = 400
40 bottom%  = 200
50 top%     = 800
60:
70 LINE left%,bottom%, right%,bottom%
80 LINE left%,top%,    right%,top%
90 LINE left%,bottom%, left%,top%
100 LINE right%,bottom%, right%,top%
```

Rectangle and rectangle fill

The RECTANGLE statements provide an easier way of drawing boxes on the screen. The first two parameters of RECTANGLE are the x and y coordinates of the bottom left corner. The second two parameters are the width and height of the rectangle. For example:

```
RECTANGLE 440,412, 400,200
```

If the width and height are equal, as in a square, the fourth parameter may be omitted:

```
RECTANGLE 400,312,400
```

RECTANGLE FILL is used in exactly the same way as RECTANGLE, but instead of drawing the outline of a rectangle, it produces a solid rectangle. The following program plots solid squares of gradually decreasing size in different colours:

```
10 MODE MODE
20 ScreenW%=(VDU 11 + 1) << VDU 4
30 ScreenH%=(VDU 12 + 1) << VDU 5
40 CentreX%=ScreenW%/2:CentreY%=ScreenH%/2
50 FOR I% = 63 TO 1 STEP -1
60   GCOL RND(255),RND(255),RND(255)
70   RECTANGLE FILL CentreX%-I%*8,CentreY%-I%*8,I%*16
80 NEXT I%
```

Circle and circle fill

To draw the outline of a circle or to plot a solid circle, you need to provide the centre of the circle and the radius. For example:

```
CIRCLE 640,512, 100 : REM centre (640,512) radius 100
CIRCLE FILL 640,512, 50
```

This produces the outline of a circle centred at (640,512), which is the centre of the screen, and of radius 100. Inside this is a solid circle, again centred at (640,512), which has a radius of 50.

Try the following program:

```
10 MODE MODE
20 REPEAT
30   GCOL RND(255),RND(255),RND(255)
40   MOUSE x,y,z
50   CIRCLE FILL x,y, RND(400)+50
60 UNTIL FALSE
```

This program produces circles in random colours, centred on the current mouse position and with a radius of between 51 and 450. To stop it press Esc.

Ellipse and ellipse fill

To draw the outline of an ellipse or to plot a solid ellipse you need to provide its centre point and the size of its major and minor axes. In addition, you may also give the angle by which it is rotated from the horizontal.

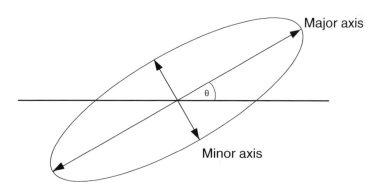

For example:

```
ELLIPSE 640,512, 200,100, PI/4
```

This produces the outline of an ellipse centred at (640,512). The length of it is 200, the width is 100 and it is rotated by pi/4 radians (45 degrees) from the horizontal. If you omit the angle, an axis-aligned ellipse is produced:

```
ELLIPSE 400,500, 320,80
```

Try the following program, which plots eight ellipses of two different sizes with the same centre point to form multi-petalled flowers:

```
 10 MODE MODE
 20 ScreenW%=(VDU 11 + 1) << VDU 4
 30 ScreenH%=(VDU 12 + 1) << VDU 5
 40 CentreX%=ScreenW%/2:CentreY%=ScreenH%/2
 50 GCOL 255,0,0
 60 FOR angle = 0 TO 3*PI/4 STEP PI/4
 70   ELLIPSE FILL CentreX%,CentreY%,200,60,angle
 80 NEXT angle
 90 GCOL 255,255,0
100 FOR angle = PI/8 TO 3*PI/4+PI/8 STEP PI/4
110   ELLIPSE FILL CentreX%,CentreY%,100,30,angle
120 NEXT angle
```

Graphics colours

In previous examples, GCOL has taken three parameters selecting the amount of red, green and blue respectively. This form of GCOL works in any mode and will select the closest colour available to the requested colour. In modes with fewer than 256 colours, GCOL can also be used with a single parameter to select the current logical colour for the graphics foreground or background. For example,

```
GCOL 3
GCOL 129
```

selects the graphics foreground colour to be logical colour three and the background colour to be one.

GCOL may also take two parameters: GCOL *m*, *c*. In this case the second (*c*) selects the foreground and background graphics colours, and the first (*m*) selects the manner in which *c* is applied to the screen as follows:

m	**Meaning**
0	Store the colour *c* on the screen
1	OR the colour on the screen with *c*
2	AND the colour on the screen with *c*
3	EOR the colour on the screen with *c*
4	Invert (NOT) the colour on the screen (disregards *c*)
5	Leave the colour on the screen unchanged (disregards *c*)
6	AND the colour on the screen with NOT *c*
7	OR the colour on the screen with NOT *c*.

Two of the options ignore the second parameter and either leave the colour on the screen unchanged or invert it. Inverting a colour means that all the bits in the colour number are altered: zeros are set to ones and vice versa. For example:

```
10 REM Pick a mode with 16 colours 0(%0000) - 15 (%1111)
20 MODE "X640 Y480 C16" : REM Use MODE 12 on RISC OS 3.10
30 GCOL 128+5
40 CLG
50 GCOL 4,0 : REM plot in NOT (screen colour)
60 LINE 0,0, 100,100
```

The colour on the screen is colour 5 (%0101). The colour used to draw the line is, therefore, NOT (%0101) or colour 10 (%1010).

The OR, AND and EOR operators act on the bits of the colour already on the screen and on the colour given as the second GCOL parameter as described in the chapter *Bases*. Thus:

```
 10 REM Pick a mode with 16 colours 0(%0000) - 15 (%1111)
 20 MODE "X640 Y480 C16" : REM Use MODE 12 on RISC OS 3.10
 30 GCOL 128+5 : REM clear screen to magenta
 40 CLG
 50 GCOL 0,6 : LINE 0,0,     100,100
 60 GCOL 1,6 : LINE 100,100, 200,200
 70 GCOL 2,6 : LINE 200,200, 300,300
 80 GCOL 3,6 : LINE 300,300, 400,400
 90 GCOL 6,6 : LINE 400,400, 500,500
100 GCOL 7,6 : LINE 500,500, 600,600
```

The colour already on the screen when the lines are drawn is colour 5 (%0101). The foreground colour is selected as colour 6 (%0110) in all cases. The method of applying it to the screen, however, alters the actual colour displayed as follows:

- The first line appears in colour 6
- The second line appears in colour 7 (%0101 OR %0110 = %0111)
- The third line appears in colour 4 (%0101 AND %0110 = %0100)

- The fourth line appears in colour 3 (%0101 EOR %0110 = %0011)
- The fifth line appears in colour 1 (%0101 AND NOT %0110 = %0101 AND &1001 = %0001)
- The sixth line appears in colour 13 (%0101 OR NOT %0110 = &0101 OR %1001 = %1101)

The graphics cursor

In the examples shown so far, we have always explicitly mentioned where objects are to be plotted, for example by giving both end points of a line in the LINE statement. This isn't always necessary, because of the graphics cursor. The graphics cursor is an invisible point on the screen which affects where lines and other items are drawn from.

For example:

```
10 CLG
20 MOVE 100,100
30 DRAW 200,200
```

This moves the graphics cursor to (100,100), then draws a line to (200,200) and leaves the graphics cursor at this position. Now, if a further line is added to the program as follows:

```
40 DRAW 300,100
```

This adds a line from (200,200) to (300,100). BASIC's LINE command is actually shorthand for a MOVE followed by a DRAW.

Many of the graphics entities described in the next chapter rely on the current position of the graphics cursor, and some of them also use its previous positions.

Relative coordinates and BY

All coordinates used so far are termed *absolute* because they tell the computer where to plot the object with respect to the graphics origin (0,0). However, it is also possible to use *relative* coordinates. When these are used, the coordinates given are added to the current graphics cursor position to find the new point. To use relative coordinates in POINT, MOVE and DRAW statements, you follow the keyword by the word BY.

Here is a program that starts in the middle of the screen and 'walks' randomly around:

```
 10 MODE MODE
 20 ScreenW%=(VDU 11 + 1) << VDU 4
 30 ScreenH%=(VDU 12 + 1) << VDU 5
 40 CentreX%=ScreenW%/2:CentreY%=ScreenH%/2
 50 MOVE CentreX%,CentreY%
 60 REPEAT
 70   dx%=8*(RND(3)-2)
 80   IF dx%=0 THEN dy%=8*(RND(3)-2) ELSE dy%=0
 90   DRAW BY dx%,dy%
100 UNTIL FALSE
```

Printing text at the graphics cursor

Printing text at the text cursor positions gives only limited control over the places at which characters may be located. In addition it does not allow characters to overlap. Attempting to print one character on top of an existing one deletes the existing one. You may find that you would like to be able to place text in different positions, for example to label the axes of a graph or to type two characters on top of each other, in order to add an accent, e.g. ^, to a letter. To do either of these type

VDU 5

You are now in VDU 5 mode. Whilst you are in this mode of operation, any characters you print are placed at the graphics cursor position. The text cursor is ignored. You can use the MOVE statement to locate the text precisely.

Since this method of printing makes use of graphics facilities, it is not possible in text-only modes. If the command VDU 5 is given in any of these screen modes it has no effect.

Each character is actually placed so that its top left corner is at the graphics cursor. After the character has been printed, the graphics cursor moves to the right by the width of one character. Although the graphics cursor also automatically moves down by the height of a character (32 units in modes 0 to 17) when the righthand side of the screen is reached, the screen does not scroll when a character is placed in the bottom righthand corner. Instead the cursor returns to the top left.

To return to the normal mode of operation type

VDU 4

Printing text at the graphics cursor

17   Complex graphics

The commands such as MOVE, DRAW, CIRCLE, etc are special cases of the more general PLOT command. This command can give a far wider range of options over what kind of shape you produce and how you produce it. Of course, the added functionality it provides makes it more complicated to use.

PLOT takes the following format:

PLOT k,x,y

where k is the mode of plotting, and x and y are the coordinates of a point to be used to position the shape. PLOT takes one pair of coordinates. To produce shapes which need more than one pair to define them, such as rectangles, it uses the previous position or positions of the graphics cursor to provide the missing information. This means that you must pay careful attention to the position of the graphics cursor after a shape has been drawn. Otherwise future plots may produce unexpected results.

Each type of plot has a block of eight numbers associated with it. These are listed below in both decimal and hexadecimal notation. (See the chapter entitled *Binary and logic* on page 33).

Decimal	Hexadecimal	Description
0-7	(&00 - &07)	Solid line including both end points
8-15	(&08 - &0F)	Solid line excluding final points
16-23	(&10 - &17)	Dotted line including both end points
24-31	(&18 - &1F)	Dotted line excluding final points
32-39	(&20 - &27)	Solid line excluding initial point
40-47	(&28 - &2F)	Solid line excluding both end points
48-55	(&30 - &37)	Dotted line excluding initial point
56-63	(&38 - &3F)	Dotted line excluding both end points
64-71	(&40 - &47)	Point plot
72-79	(&48 - &4F)	Horizontal line fill (left & right) to non-background
80-87	(&50 - &57)	Triangle fill
88-95	(&58 - &5F)	Horizontal line fill (right only) to background
96-103	(&60 - &67)	Rectangle fill
104-111	(&68 - &6F)	Horizontal line fill (left & right) to foreground
112-119	(&70 - &77)	Parallelogram fill
120-127	(&78 - &7F)	Horizontal line fill (right only) to non-foreground

128-135	(&80 - &87)	Flood to non-background
136-143	(&88 - &8F)	Flood to foreground
144-151	(&90 - &97)	Circle outline
152-159	(&98 - &9F)	Circle fill
160-167	(&A0 - &A7)	Circular arc
168-175	(&A8 - &AF)	Segment
176-183	(&B0 - &B7)	Sector
184-191	(&B8 - &BF)	Block copy/move
192-199	(&C0 - &C7)	Ellipse outline
200-207	(&C8 - &CF)	Ellipse fill
208-215	(&D0 - &D7)	Graphics characters
216-223	(&D8 - &DF)	Reserved for Acorn expansion
224-231	(&E0 - &E7)	Reserved for Acorn expansion
232-239	(&E8 - &EF)	Sprite plot
240-247	(&F0 - &F7)	Reserved for user programs
248-255	(&F8 - &FF)	Reserved for user programs

Within each block of eight, the offset from the base number has the following meaning:

offset   meaning

0   move cursor relative (to last graphics point visited)
1   plot relative using current foreground colour
2   plot relative using logical inverse colour
3   plot relative using current background colour
4   move cursor absolute (i.e. move to actual coordinate given)
5   plot absolute using current foreground colour
6   plot absolute using logical inverse colour
7   plot absolute using current background colour

PLOT is a good example of where using hexadecimal notation helps to make things clearer. Each block of eight starts at either $&x0$ or $&x8$, where x represents any hexadecimal digit, so a plot absolute in the current foreground colour, for example, has a plot code of $&x5$ or $&xD$. Thus, it is obvious which mode of plotting is being used. Similarly, it is obvious which shape is being plotted, and so, for example, if the plot is between &90 and &9F, then it is a circle. This is a far easier range to recognise than 144 to 159.

Each of the types of plot is described in further detail below.

Plotting simple lines

A line is plotted between the coordinates given by the PLOT and the previous position of the graphics cursor. The following examples draw a line from (200,200) to (800,800):

```
10 MODE MODE
20 PLOT &04,200,200
30 PLOT &05,800,800
```

These two PLOT statements are equivalent to MOVE 200,200 and DRAW 800,800 respectively.

The same line can be drawn by a different PLOT code:

```
10 MODE MODE
20 PLOT &04,200,200
30 PLOT &01,600,600
```

This demonstrates the use of relative plotting. The coordinate (600,600) which has been given in line 30 is relative to the position of the graphics cursor. The absolute value is obtained by adding this offset to the previous position i.e. (600,600) + (200,200) which gives a position of (800,800). This is equivalent to DRAW BY 600,600.

Dot-dash lines

Straight lines do not have to be drawn as a solid line. Instead you can set up a pattern of dots and dashes and use that to determine which pixels along the line will be plotted.

A dot-dash pattern is set up using:

VDU 23,6,$n1$,$n2$,$n3$,$n4$,$n5$,$n6$,$n7$,$n8$

where $n1$ to $n8$ define a bit pattern. Each bit which is set to one represents a point plotted and each bit set to zero represents no point. The pattern starts at bit 7 of $n1$, then for each pixel plotted moves one bit to the right in $n1$. After bit 0 of $n1$ has been used, bit 7 of $n2$ is used, and so on.

The pattern can be made to repeat (i.e. go back to bit 7 of $n1$) after a given number of pixels. The maximum pattern repeat is 64. However, you can set up any repeat between one and 64 using:

*FX 163,242,n

If you set n to zero, this sets up the default pattern which has a repeat length of eight bits and is alternately on and off, i.e. $n1$ is %10101010 (&AA).

There are four different methods which may be used to plot the line:

PLOT range	Effect
&10-&17	Both end points included, the pattern being restarted when each new line is drawn.
&18-&1F	Final point omitted, the pattern being restarted when each new line is drawn.
&30-&37	Initial point omitted, the pattern being continued when each new line is drawn.
&38-&3F	Both end points omitted, the pattern being continued when each new line is drawn.

Triangles

To draw a triangle plot, you need the coordinates given with the triangle PLOT code and two previous points which mark the other corners. For example:

```
10 MODE MODE
20 MOVE 200,200
30 MOVE 600,200
40 PLOT &55,400,400
```

This plots a triangle with corners (200,200), (600,600) and (400,400).

Adding a further line:

```
50 PLOT &55,800,400
```

plots a further triangle using corners (600,200), (400,400) and (800,400).

Rectangles

An axes-aligned (filled) rectangle plot can be plotted between the coordinates given by the PLOT and the previous position of the graphics cursor. For example:

```
MOVE 200,200
PLOT &61,600,600
```

This is equivalent to RECTANGLE FILL 200,200, 600,600. You can also specify absolute coordinates in the PLOT version, for example:

```
MOVE 200,200
PLOT &65,800,800
```

Parallelograms

A parallelogram plot is constructed as a rectangle which has been sheered sideways. For example:

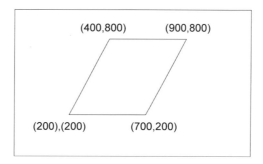

These require three points to define them. Thus to plot the parallelogram shown above the following could be used:

```
MOVE 200,200
MOVE 700,200
PLOT &75,900,800
```

Although any three corners of the parallelogram may be used to define it, the order in which these are given affects which way round the parallelogram appears. Consider the three points given below:

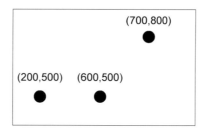

These could produce any of three parallelograms, depending on the order in which they were used. The rule to determine what the final parallelogram will look like is as follows: the three points specify adjacent vertices, with the fourth vertex being calculated from these. From this, it can be seen that the unspecified corner is the one which appears diagonally opposite the second point given.

Plotting simple lines

Suppose, for example, you used the following sequence of statements with the three points shown above:

```
MOVE 200,500
MOVE 600,500
PLOT &75,700,800
```

The final point is calculated by the computer to have the coordinates (300,800), diagonally opposite the point (600,500).

The other two possible parallelograms that would be obtained using these three sequences are:

```
MOVE 600,500 : MOVE 700,800 : PLOT &75,200,500
MOVE 700,800 : MOVE 200,500 : PLOT &75,600,500
```

When specifying the corners, you can give them in 'clockwise' or 'anti-clockwise' order; the same shape is drawn regardless.

Circles

To plot a circle, define the centre by moving to it, and then use PLOT with the relevant plot code and the coordinates of a point on its circumference. For example, to plot a solid circle centred at (640,512) with a radius of 100, type

```
MOVE 640,512       :REM centre
PLOT &9D,740,512   :REM Xcentre+radius,Ycentre
```

Alternatively you could use relative plotting:

```
MOVE 640,512       :REM centre
PLOT &99,100,0     :REM radius,0
```

In both these examples the circles are solid and could have been produced using the CIRCLE FILL command. The equivalent of the CIRCLE command for producing outlines of circles would be PLOT &95 and PLOT &91.

Complex graphics

Ellipses

Ellipses are more complicated to define than circles:

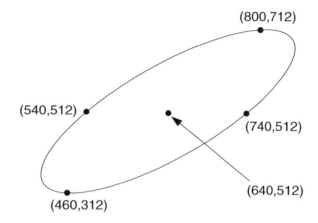

To plot the above ellipse, the following information is required:
- the centre point
- an outermost point (either to the right or left) at the same height as the centre
- the highest or lowest point of the ellipse.

For example, to draw the ellipse above, you could use:

```
MOVE 640,512        :REM the centre
MOVE 740,512        :REM the righthand point
PLOT &C5,800,712    :REM the top point
```

or alternatively:

```
MOVE 640,512        :REM the centre
MOVE 540,512        :REM the lefthand point
PLOT &C5,480,312    :REM the bottom point
```

Note that only the x coordinate of the second point is relevant, although for clarity it is good practice to give the same y coordinate as for the centre point.

The following example creates a pattern using a number of differently shaped ellipses:

```
10 MODE MODE
20 FOR step% = 0 TO 400 STEP 25
30   MOVE 640,512
40   MOVE 215+step%,512
50   PLOT &C5,640,512+step%
60 NEXT step%
```

Solid ellipses are drawn in the same way using the plot codes &C8 to &CF.

The ELLIPSE keyword provides an easier way of specifying rotated ellipses.

Arcs

We saw above how circle outlines are defined and drawn. In a similar way, just a portion of the circle outline may be drawn to produce an arc. In this case, three points are required: the centre of the circle and two points to indicate the starting and finishing points of the arc. Ideally, these would be given as follows:

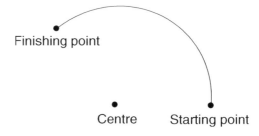

In the example above, however, both the starting and finishing points are on the arc itself. This is a design which requires a large amount of calculation. It is easier for the starting point to be taken as being on the arc and used to calculate the radius, the finishing point being used just to indicate the angle the arc subtends. For example:

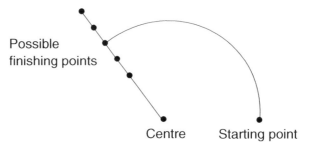

This is the method used by the VDU drivers. To draw an arc, you need to specify the centre of the circle it is based upon and the starting point of the arc, and then to plot to a third point to specify the angle.

The example below draws an arc based on a circle whose centre is at (640,512). It draws the portion of the arc from 0 to 270. Since arcs are drawn anticlockwise this means that its starting position is the point (440,512) (270) and its finishing position (640,512+n) (0):

```
MOVE 640,512
MOVE 440,512
PLOT &A5,640,1000
```

The resulting arc would look like that drawn below:

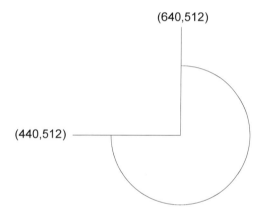

Sectors

A sector is a filled shape enclosed by two straight radii and the arc of a circle.

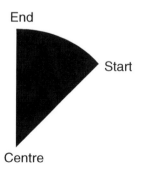

Segments

Sectors are defined in a similar manner to arcs. For example:

```
MOVE 640,512       :REM centre point
MOVE 440,512       :REM starting point on the circumference
PLOT &B5,640,1000  :REM point indicating angle of sector
```

Again the sector is taken as going anti-clockwise from the starting point to the finishing point.

Segments

A segment is an area of a circle between the circumference and a chord as shown below:

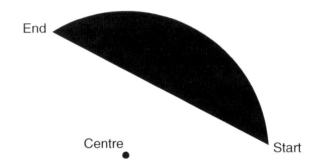

Segments are defined in exactly the same way as arcs and sectors.

Flood-fills

This section is concerned with how to fill the inside of any closed region, however awkward the shape. The method used is flood-filling; with this you can start off at any point within the boundaries of the shape. The whole shape is then filled at once.

Note that flood-filling is not compatible with BASIC programs written under the window manager environment (described in the section entitled *Window managed programs* on page 7).

Flood to non-background

This can be used on shapes which are in the current background colour and bordered by non-background colours. The shape is filled with the current foreground colour.

To use this flood-fill method, type, for example:

`FILL 640,512`

This starts filling from the point (640,512). If this point is in a non-background colour then it returns immediately. Otherwise it fills in all directions until it reaches either a non-background colour or the edge of the screen.

Flood-fills may be performed using either pure colours or colour patterns. Note that if you wish to colour in a shape it must be totally enclosed by a solid border. If there is a gap anywhere then the colour 'leaks' out into other regions.

Flood until foreground

Whereas the previous flood-fill filled a shape currently in the background colour, this one fills a shape currently in any colour except the present foreground one, with the present foreground colour. This is performed by a `PLOT` command with plot codes &88 to &8F.

For example:

`PLOT &8D,640,512`

Flood-filling will only succeed when the region being filled does not already contain any pixels in the colour being used. For example, if you are attempting a flood to non-background when the background colour is black, you should not try to flood in black or in a pattern which contains black pixels.

Copying and moving

Using RECTANGLE... TO and RECTANGLE FILL... TO, you can pick up a rectangular area of the screen and either make a copy of it elsewhere on the screen or move it to another position, replacing it with a block of the background colour.

For example:

`RECTANGLE FILL 400,600,60,80 TO 700,580`

This marks out the source rectangle as having one corner at co-ordinates (400,600), a width of 60 and a height of 80. It then moves this rectangular area so that the bottom left of it is at the co-ordinates (700,580). The old area is replaced by background.

The new position can overlap with the rectangular area, as in the example above, and the expected result is still obtained.

Copying and moving

The rectangle move and copy commands may also be expressed in terms of PLOT codes. The relevant range of codes is &B8 to &BF: first move to two points which denote the bottom left and top right of the rectangle to be copied or moved; then plot, using one of the range of codes described above, to the bottom left corner of the destination rectangle. The meanings of the plot codes are as follows:

&B8   Move relative (no copy/move operation)
&B9   Relative rectangle move
&BA   Relative rectangle copy
&BB   Relative rectangle copy
&BC   Move absolute (no copy/move operation)
&BD   Absolute rectangle move
&BE   Absolute rectangle copy
&BF   Absolute rectangle copy

The rectangle move operations erase the source rectangle, whereas the copy operations leave it intact. So, the RECTANGLE FILL ... TO example above could also be expressed as:

```
MOVE 400,600
MOVE BY 60,80
PLOT &BD,700,580
```

18 Graphic patterns

Any of the colours which are available in a given mode may be 'interwoven' to give a tremendous range of colour patterns. When using modes with a limited number of colours, for example any of the four-colour modes, this feature may be used to extend the colours available, since combining similar colours produces further shades which look like pure colours. Alternatively, contrasting colours may be used to give checks, wavy lines, and so on.

Default patterns

Default patterns are set up for you as follows, depending on the number of bits per pixel in the current mode:

Bits per pixel	Pattern	Pattern
1	1	Dark grey
	2	Grey
	3	Light grey
	4	Hatching
2	1	Red-orange
	2	Orange
	3	Yellow-orange
	4	Cream
4	1	Orange
	2	Pink
	3	Yellow-green
	4	Cream
8	1	White-grey stripes
	2	Black-grey stripes
	3	Green-black stripes
	4	Pink-white stripes

To use these patterns you issue a GCOL with a plot action which depends on the pattern desired. In general, to use pattern n, the GCOL command should be

GCOL n*16+*action*, *col*

where `action` is the plotting action you want to use with the pattern (for example 0 for store, 1 for OR etc, as described earlier), and `col` is 0 if you want to set the foreground colour as a pattern or 128 for a background pattern. The parameter *n* is in the range 1 to 4 for the normal patterns, or 5 for a large pattern which is formed by placing patterns 1 to 4 next to each other.

Plotting using pattern fills

All the shapes which have been described above can be plotted using these colour patterns. A pattern may be selected using GCOL. The first parameter to GCOL affects the plotting action as was seen earlier in the chapter entitled *Screen modes*. Patterns can be used in future plots by using values in the following ranges:

    16-31   Pattern 1
    32-47   Pattern 2
    48-63   Pattern 3
    64-79   Pattern 4

Try the following:

```
10 MODE "X640 Y480 C16":REM Use MODE 9 on RISC OS 3.10
20 GCOL 16,0
30 MOVE 100,100
40 MOVE 800,800
50 PLOT &55,700,200
```

or

```
10 MODE "X640 Y480 C4":REM Use MODE 1 on RISC OS 3.10
20 GCOL 32,0
30 CIRCLE FILL 640,512,100
```

It is possible to plot lines using these colour patterns in a similar manner, but the effects may be rather strange. Consider, for example, a line drawn at 45 degrees. If the pattern being used were alternate black and white pixels, then this line would be drawn either in all white or all black, the latter not being visible on a black background.

Defining your own patterns

You may define your own colour patterns using VDU commands as follows:

VDU 23,2,*n1,n2,n3,n4,n5,n6,n7,n8* defines GCOL 16,0 i.e. pattern 1

VDU 23,3,*n1,n2,n3,n4,n5,n6,n7,n8* defines GCOL 32,0 i.e. pattern 2

VDU 23,4,*n1,n2,n3,n4,n5,n6,n7,n8* defines GCOL 48,0 i.e. pattern 3

Graphic patterns

VDU 23,5,*n1,n2,n3,n4,n5,n6,n7,n8* defines GCOL 64,0 i.e. pattern 4

The pattern produced by a set of parameters depends upon which pattern mode is being used. There are two modes available, one where the parameters are interpreted in the same manner as on the BBC Master series and another simpler method native to RISC OS. The default is the BBC Master series mode. To change to native mode type

VDU 23,17,4,1|

To revert back again to the Master mode type

VDU 23,17,4|

Note: the | character sends nine zero bytes, so it is equivalent to adding ,0,0,0,0,0,0,0,0,0 to the VDU command.

The pattern fill works with blocks of pixels. The size of these blocks depends on the number of bits per pixel in the mode:

Bits per pixel	Horizontal pixels	Vertical pixels
1	8	8
2	4	8
4	2	8
8	1	8
16	1	4
32	1	2

In all cases, each pixel may be assigned a colour independently of the others. The way the value of the parameters is interpreted depends on the mode being used.

Native mode patterns

In native mode the bits of the parameter are used in a straightforward manner to give the colour of the pixels.

One bit per pixel modes

Each parameter of the VDU command corresponds to a row in the pixel block. The first parameter contains the value of the top row, the second the value of the second row, and so on.

Each bit of the parameter is assigned to a pixel, the least significant bit applying to the pixel on the left, i.e. the pixels appear on the screen in the opposite order to which the bits are written down on paper. For example, to set a row of the pattern as follows:

141

Native mode patterns

black	white	white	white	black	black	black	white
%0	%1	%1	%1	%0	%0	%0	%1

the value required is 142 (%10001110).

Two bits per pixel modes

As before each parameter of the VDU command corresponds to a row in the pixel block. Each pair of bits of the parameter is assigned to a pixel, the least significant pair applying to the pixel on the left. For example, to set a row of the pattern as follows:

yellow	red	white	yellow
%10	%01	%11	%10

the value required is 182 (%10110110).

Four bits per pixel modes

Each set of four bits of each parameter is assigned to a pixel, the least significant set applying to the pixel on the left. For example, to set a row of the pattern as follows:

green	white
%0010	%0111

the value required is 114 (%01110010).

Eight bits per pixel modes

The value of the parameter defines the colour assigned to the pixel directly. Patterns in these cases are more complex since they involve interleaving the bits from the colour to obtain the parameter value.

16 bits per pixel modes

Each row of the pattern is defined by two consecutive parameters. The first parameter of each pair is the least significant 8 bits of the colour number and the second parameter of the pair is the most significant 8 bits.

32 bits per pixel modes

Each of the two rows of the pattern is defined by four consecutive parameters where the least significant byte of the colour number comes first. For example, a pattern consisting of alternate read and yellow lines can be set as follows:

red	green	blue	alpha	red	green	blue	alpha
255,	0,	0,	0,	255,	255,	0,	0

BBC Master mode patterns

In BBC Master series mode, the bits of the parameter are used in the following manner to give the colour of the pixels:

Two-colour modes

This is the easiest case to understand. Each pixel in the block corresponds to one bit of the parameter, the least significant bit applying to the pixel on the right, so pixels on the screen appear in the same order as the bits are written down on paper. For example, to set a row of the pattern as follows:

black	white	white	white	black	black	black	white
%0	%1	%1	%1	%0	%0	%0	%1

the value required is 113 (%01110001).

Defining a pattern in a two-colour mode is similar to setting up a user-defined character.

Four-colour modes

In four-colour modes each colour is defined using two bits as follows:

	yellow (%10)		red (%01)		white (%11)		yellow (%10)	
bit	7	6	5	4	3	2	1	0
	1				0				10 (yellow)
		0				1			01 (red)
			1				1		11 (white)
				1				0	10 (yellow)
	1	0	1	1	0	1	1	0	

The value required is 182 (%10110110).

16-colour modes

In 16-colour modes the situation is different again. There are just two pixels in a row, four bits of the parameter being used to hold the value of each colour. However, it is not the case that the left-most four bits correspond to the first colour and the right-most four bits to the other. Instead, the bits of each are interleaved, as shown:

Giant patterns

		green (%0010)			white (%0111)				
bit	7	6	5	4	3	2	1	0	
	0		0		1		0		0010 (green)
		0		1		1		1	0111 (white)
	0	0	0	1	1	1	0	1	

and the value required is 29 (%00011101).

To get the colours the other way around different numbers are required:

		white (%0111)			green (%0010)				
bit	7	6	5	4	3	2	1	0	
	0		1		1		1		0111 (white)
		0		0		1		0	0010 (green)
	0	0	1	0	1	1	1	0	

and the value required is 46 (%00101110).

Thus a cross-hatch pattern of alternate white and green pixels can be defined:

VDU 23,2,29,46,29,46,29,46,29,46

Giant patterns

Giant patterns can be set up which take all four of the separate patterns and place them side by side, giving an overall pixel size as shown below:

Bits per pixel	Horizontal pixels	Vertical pixels
1	32	8
2	16	8
4	8	8
8	4	8
16	4	4
32	4	2

To produce a giant pattern in this way, the first parameter given to GCOL should be in the range 80 to 95.

Simple patterns

Often the most effective way of using the pattern fills is for simple cross-hatch patterns. If you want to use this sort of colour pattern in a mode with less than 256 colours, a simpler way of defining it is available. In this method, just a small block of eight pixels is defined which is used to form the normal-sized block.

The eight pixel colours in the following diagram are set up using

VDU 23,12,*n1*,*n2*,*n3*,*n4*,*n5*,*n6*,*n7*,*n8* defines pattern 1

VDU 23,13,*n1*,*n2*,*n3*,*n4*,*n5*,*n6*,*n7*,*n8* defines pattern 2

VDU 23,14,*n1*,*n2*,*n3*,*n4*,*n5*,*n6*,*n7*,*n8* defines pattern 3

VDU 23,15,*n1*,*n2*,*n3*,*n4*,*n5*,*n6*,*n7*,*n8* defines pattern 4

where *n1* to *n8* correspond to the actual colours to be used as follows:

n1	n2
n3	n4
n5	n6
n7	n8

In 256 colour modes VDU 23,12-15 will define a 1×8 pattern, but the difference from using VDU 23,2-5 is that the values given to the parameters are interpreted in the same way as the values specified for COLOUR and TINT commands, so if the default palette is in use this will work as follows:

Bit	Meaning
0	Red bit 2
1	Red bit 3 (high)
2	Green bit 2
3	Green bit 3 (high)
4	Blue bit 2
5	Blue bit 3 (high)
6	Tint bit 0 (red + green + blue bit 0)
7	Tint bit 1 (red + green + blue bit 1)

Simple patterns

19 Viewports

The operating system allows the programmer to set up special rectangular areas of the screen, called viewports, in order to restrict where text or graphics can appear on the screen.

Text viewports provide automatic scrolling of text written into the viewport area, and so are also referred to as 'scrolling viewports'.

Graphics viewports restrict the area affected by graphics operations, so that, for example, lines are clipped to lie within the viewport area. Graphics viewports are therefore also referred to as 'clipping viewports'.

Note: the text and graphics viewports described here are supported directly by the VDU drivers, and are quite distinct from the bordered, moveable windows used by the window manager software, which uses graphics viewports as a stepping stone to greater functionality (for more details see the section entitled *Window managed programs* on page 7).

Text viewports

Normally, text may appear anywhere on the screen. However, you can define a text viewport, which allows the text to appear only inside the viewport. To set up a text viewport, use the VDU 28 command as follows:

VDU 28, *left*, *bottom*, *right*, *top*

where *left*, *bottom* is the bottom lefthand and *right*, *top* the top righthand position inside the viewport given in text coordinates:

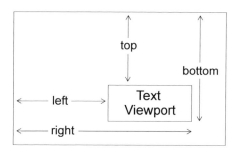

Text viewports

Nothing outside the text viewport is affected by text statements, such as CLS to clear the text screen, or screen scrolling. Note that TAB(*X, Y*) positions the text cursor relative to the position of the top left of the current text viewport. The following program demonstrates how text viewports behave:

```
10 MODE MODE
20 REM Set up a text viewport 6 characters square
30 VDU 28,5,10,10,5
40 REM Change the background colour to red
50 COLOUR ON 255,0,0
60 REM Clear the text screen to show where it is
70 CLS
80 REM Demonstrate scrolling
90 FOR N% = 1 TO 20
100    PRINT N%
110 NEXT N%
120 REM Show position of character (2,3)
130 PRINT TAB(2,3);"*"
140 END
```

To revert back to having the whole screen as the text viewport type

VDU 26

The precise actions of the VDU 26 command are as follows:

- Restore text viewport to the whole screen
- Restore graphics viewport to the whole screen
- Home the text cursor
- Restore graphic origin to bottom left of screen
- Home graphics cursor to (0,0).

Graphics viewports

Just as text may have a text viewport defined, so a graphics viewport may be set up using

VDU 24,*left;bottom;right;top;*

where (*left,bottom*) and (*right,top*) are the coordinates of the lower lefthand and upper righthand pixels inside the viewport. Be sure to use semi-colons as indicated, not commas.

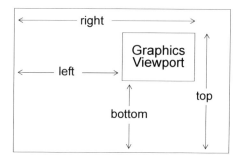

Nothing outside the graphics viewport is affected by graphics commands, such as CLG to clear the graphics screen. When a graphics viewport is set up, the graphics origin (0,0) is unaltered.

The following program demonstrates how graphics viewports behave:

```
 10 MODE "X640 Y480 C16":REM Use MODE 12 on RISC OS 3.10
 20 REM Set up a graphics viewport,a quarter of the screen size
 30 VDU 24,320;240;960;720;
 40 REM Change the background colour to colour 1 (red)
 50 GCOL 129
 60 REM Clear the graphics viewport
 70 CLG
 80 REM Show position of 0,0
 90 CIRCLE 0,0,600
100 END
```

To revert back to having the whole screen as the graphics viewport type

VDU 26

Graphics viewports

20 Sprites

A sprite is just a graphic shape made up of an array of pixels. You can create and manipulate sprites using Paint. This is a general-purpose painting program whose output happens to be stored in a sprite. It is fully described in the RISC OS *User Guide*.

Having created one or more sprites in a Sprite file (using Paint), you can then:

- load this file;
- manipulate and plot one or more sprites from it.

For a full description of how to load, manipulate and plot sprites see the *Sprites* chapter of the RISC OS *Programmer's Reference Manual*.

Loading a user sprite

In the program fragment below the function FNload_sprites takes the name of a sprite file as a parameter and loads sprites from this file into a user sprite area:

```
 60 DEF FNload_sprites(sprite_file$)
 70   LOCAL length%, area_ptr%
 80   REM Find size of sprite file
 90   SYS "OS_File",13,sprite_file$ TO ,,,,length%
100   REM Reserve memory for user sprite area
110   REM Size of area should be size of file + 4 bytes for length
120   DIM area_ptr% length%+4-1
130   REM Initialise area with size...
140   area_ptr%!0 = length%+4
150   REM ...and with offset to first sprite
160   area_ptr%!4 = 16
170   REM Finish initialising with this sprite op
180   SYS "OS_SpriteOp",9+256,area_ptr%
190   REM Load sprites
200   SYS "OS_SpriteOp",10+256,area_ptr%,sprite_file$
210   REM Return pointer to user sprite area
220 = area_ptr%
```

The function FNload_sprites (defined above) calls OS_SpriteOp to initialise a sprite user area and load the specified sprite file into it. OS_SpriteOp is the SWI which controls the sprite system (SWI stands for **S**oft**W**are **I**nterrupt, and is one of the ARM's built-in instructions). In BASIC, SWIs are called using the SYS statement, and the first parameter this SWI takes is a number between 1 and 62 specifying the particular action to be taken. Adding 256 to this number indicates that it is a user sprite. These actions include:

OS_SpriteOp   9 + 256   initialise a sprite area
OS_SpriteOp 10 + 256   load sprites from a sprite file into a sprite area
OS_SpriteOp 34 + 256   plot a sprite at the coordinates supplied

Plotting a user sprite

The following program calls the function FNload_sprites to load a sprite file and return a pointer to the control block of the user sprite area. It then calls OS_SpriteOp 34+256 (i.e. 290) to plot a sprite from this sprite file on the screen at coordinates (200,300), using a plot action of 0:

```
10 REM Load sprite file from RISC OS !Boot application
20 sprite_area% = FNload_sprites("Boot:Themes.!Sprites")
30 REM plot sprite to screen at (200,300)
40 SYS "OS_SpriteOp",34+256,sprite_area%,"!boot",200,300,0
50 END
```

The parameters that OS_SpriteOp 290 takes are:

pointer to control block of sprite area
sprite name
x coordinate
y coordinate
plot action:

Value	Action
0	Overwrite colour on screen
1	OR with colour on screen
2	AND with colour on screen
3	exclusive OR with colour on screen
4	Invert colour on screen
5	Leave colour on screen unchanged
6	AND with colour on screen with NOT of sprite pixel colour
7	OR with colour on screen with NOT of sprite pixel colour
&08	If set, then use the mask, otherwise don't
&10	Use palette when plotting 1/2/4/8bpp sprite to 16/32bpp if set
&20	Indicates a *wide translation table* is being used when set
&40	If set, use dithering when plotting 16/32bpp sprite to a reduced depth

21 Teletext mode

The teletext mode, mode 7, is unique in the way it displays text and graphics. Commands such as COLOUR, GCOL, MOVE and DRAW do not work in this mode (or in the Wimp). Instead colourful displays are produced using teletext control codes.

Mode 7 is compatible with the teletext pages that were broadcast in many countries before the introduction of digital television. You can produce your own teletext displays using the limited but effective graphics which are available.

In mode 7 the screen is 40 characters wide and 25 characters high, but with RISC OS 5.24 and later it is possible to select a Teletext mode of a different size by using the T, TX and TY attributes in a mode string. See *Appendix E – Specifying screen modes* for further details.

Coloured text

Type in the following program and run it:

```
10 MODE 7
20 PRINT"THIS";CHR$(129);"demonstrates";CHR$(130);"the";CHR$(131);"use"
30 PRINT CHR$(132);"of";CHR$(133);"control"; CHR$(134); "codes"
```

The characters 129, etc, which are printed using CHR$(129) are the control codes. Although the control codes are invisible they still take up a character position, so the words are separated by a space.

Each control code affects the way in which the remaining characters on that particular line are displayed. For example, printing CHR$(129) makes the computer display the text in red. The full list of colours and their associated control codes is:

Code	Text colour
129	Red
130	Green
131	Yellow
132	Blue
133	Magenta
134	Cyan
135	White (default)

Every line starts off with the text in white. So, if you want several rows of text to appear in red, for example, you must start each of these rows with CHR$(129).

Making text flash

Text can be made to flash. For example:

```
10 MODE 7
20 PRINT CHR$(136)"Flash";CHR$(137)"Steady";CHR$(136); "Flash"
```

Flashing coloured text can be produced by using two control codes:

```
10 MODE 7
20 PRINT "Steady white";CHR$(129);CHR$(136)"Flashing red"
```

Since each control code occupies a character position, the words `white` and `Flashing` are separated by two spaces on the screen.

Double-height text

Double-height text can be produced as follows:

```
10 MODE 7
20 PRINT CHR$(141)"Double height"
30 PRINT CHR$(141)"Double height"
```

To obtain double-height text, the same text must be printed on two successive lines beginning with CHR$(141). If the text is only printed once, only the top half of the letters is displayed.

To revert to single-height graphics on the same line, the control code is 140. For example:

```
10 MODE 7
20 PRINT CHR$(141)"Double Height";CHR$(140); "Single Height"
30 PRINT CHR$(141)"Double Height";CHR$(140); "Single Height"
```

Changing the background colour

Changing the background colour requires two codes:

```
10 MODE 7
20 PRINT CHR$(131);CHR$(157)"Hello"
```

The first code is for yellow text. The second tells the computer to use the previous control code as the background colour. The net effect of the two codes is to give yellow text on a yellow background as you can see when you run the program above. Hence to print text visibly on a coloured background, three control codes are required, two to change the background colour, and a third to change the colour of the text.

For example:

```
10 MODE 7
20 PRINT CHR$(131);CHR$(157);CHR$(132)"Blue on yellow"
```

Concealing and revealing text

Text can be concealed and revealed as follows:

```
10 MODE 7
20 PRINT "Press a key to see";CHR$(152);"hidden";CHR$(135);"text"
30 A=GET
40 VDU 23,18,2,1|:REM Reveal
50 A=GET
60 VDU 23,18,2,0|:REM Conceal
```

Text following CHR$(152) is concealed until the next colour control code. The VDU 23,18,2 command selects whether this text is hidden (replaced by spaces) or displayed.

Teletext graphics

Certain characters, such as the lower-case letters, may either be printed normally as text or made to appear as graphics shapes by preceding them with one of the graphics control codes. These are:

Code	Graphics colour
145	Red
146	Green
147	Yellow
148	Blue
149	Magenta
150	Cyan
151	White
156	Set background to black
157	Set background colour to the current foreground colour

Each line of the teletext display starts with the following attributes: white, alpha (i.e. non-graphics) characters on a black background.

Teletext graphics

Each graphics shape is based on a two by three grid:

A B

It is possible to calculate the code for any particular graphics shape, since each of the six cells contributes a particular value to the code as follows:

1	2
4	8
16	64

The base value for the codes is 160, so that they lie in the ranges 160 to 191 and 224 to 255. For example,

has a code of 160 + 1 + 8 + 16 = 185 and so may be produced on the screen in red. To do this, type

```
PRINT CHR$(145);CHR$(185)
```

Outlining blocks of colour

Normally, the blocks of colours are continuous. For example,

```
PRINT CHR$(145);CHR$(255)
```

produces a solid block of red. Nevertheless, the graphics can be separated, with a thin black line around all the segments. To see the effect of this, try typing

```
PRINT CHR$(145);CHR$(154);CHR$(255)
```

Placing blocks of colour next to each other

So far we have seen that each of the teletext control characters appears on the screen as a space. This means that it is not normally possible to have graphics blocks of different colours touching each other. They have to be separated by at least one space to allow for the graphics colour control codes.

However, if you wish to use different colours next to each other, you can do so by using some of the more advanced teletext controls. For example, try typing

PRINT CHR$(145)CHR$(152)CHR$(255)CHR$(158)CHR$(146)CHR$(147)CHR$(159)

Code 152   conceals the display of all graphics characters until a colour change occurs. Hence the solid red graphics block is not displayed.

Code 158   holds the graphics. This means that it remembers the previous graphics character, in this case the solid block, and displays all future graphics shapes and control codes as the remembered character.

Code 146   first colour change. As a result, it reverses the concealing effect of code 152 so that future characters are displayed, and also selects green graphics.

Code 147   control code displayed as a solid graphics block in the current colour which is green. It selects yellow graphics.

Code 159   control code displayed as a solid graphic block in the current colour which is yellow. It releases the graphics, i.e. it reverses the effect of any previous 158 codes.

Teletext graphics

22 Sound

The computer contains a sound synthesizer which enables you to emulate up to eight different instruments playing at once, giving either mono or stereo sound production for each instrument.

Activating the sound system

The sound system can be activated or de-activated using the statements SOUND ON and SOUND OFF.

Selecting sound channels

You can select how many different sound channels you want to use. The default value is 1, but you can alter this by typing

```
VOICES n
```

The maximum number allowed is eight. Any number between one and eight can be specified, but the number which the computer can handle has to be a power of two, and so the number you give is rounded up by the computer to either one, two, four or eight.

Allocating a wave-form to each channel

After you have specified the number of channels you require, you will need to allocate a wave-form to each one. This is done with the VOICE statement, the syntax of which is:

```
VOICE channel,voicename
```

Since the bell uses channel 1, you can get an idea of how the command works by entering

```
VOICE 1,"Percussion-Snare"
```

and then sounding the bell by typing Ctrl-G.

As you will notice, the sound of the bell has changed, since the sound channel has been allocated a new voice – in this case a percussion snare sound.

A full list of the resident voices can be obtained, along with their channel allocations, using the *VOICES command. With "Percussion-Snare" allocated to channel 1, the list appears as follows:

```
            Voice Name
                1 WaveSynth-Beep
                2 StringLib-Soft
                3 StringLib-Pluck
                4 StringLib-Steel
                5 StringLib-Hard
                6 Percussion-Soft
                7 Percussion-Medium
     1          8 Percussion-Snare
                9 Percussion-Noise
     ^^^^^^^^ Channel Allocation Map
```

Note that *VOICES indicates only the mapping of voices to channels – it does not specify how many channels have been selected with BASIC's VOICES command.

Setting the stereo position

For each active channel, the stereo position of the sound can be altered using:

STEREO *chan*, *pos*

pos can take any value between −127 (indicating the sound is fully to the left) and +127 (indicating the sound is fully to the right). The default value for each channel is zero which gives central (mono) production.

Although the range of the *pos* argument in the STEREO keyword is −127 to 127, there are actually only seven discrete stereo positions. These are:

−127 to −80	Full left
−79 to −48	2/3 left
−47 to −16	1/3 left
−15 to +15	Central
+16 to +47	1/3 right
+48 to +79	2/3 right
+80 to +127	Full right

Sound

Creating a note

BASIC provides a SOUND statement to create a note on any of the channels. This requires four parameters which can be summarised as follows:

SOUND channel, amplitude, pitch, duration [, after]

Channel

There are eight different channels, numbered 1 to 8. Each of these is identical, except for the voice assigned to it.

Setting the volume

The second parameter amplitude determines how loud a note is to be played. You set the amplitude to an integer between 0 and −15. −15 is the loudest, −7 is half-volume and zero produces silence.

Alternatively, a logarithmic scale can be used, by giving a value between 256 (&100) and 383 (&17F). A change of 16 represents a doubling or halving of the volume.

Pitch

The pitch can be controlled in steps of a quarter of a semitone by giving a value between 0 and 255. The lowest note (0) is the A# one octave and two semitones below middle C. The highest note is the D four octaves and a tone above middle C. A value of 53 produces middle C itself. The following table is a quick reference guide to help you find the pitch you require:

Note	Octave number					
	1	2	3	4	5	6
A		41	89	137	185	233
A#	0	45	93	141	189	237
B	1	49	97	145	193	241
C	5	53	101	149	197	245
C#	9	57	105	153	201	249
D	13	61	109	157	205	253
D#	17	65	113	161	209	
E	21	69	117	165	213	
F	25	73	121	169	217	
F#	29	77	125	173	221	
G	33	81	129	177	225	
G#	37	85	133	181	229	

Alternatively, a finer control is available by giving a value between 256 (&0100) and 32767 (&7FFF). Each number consists of 15 bits. The left-most three bits control the octave number. The bottom 12 bits control the fractional part of the octave. This means that each octave is split up into 4096 different pitch levels. Middle C has the value 16384 (&4000).

Using hexadecimal notation is a particularly useful way of seeing what pitch a given value defines. Each value in hexadecimal notation comprises four digits. The left-most one gives the octave number and the right-most the fractional part of the octave. The following table illustrates this:

Note	\multicolumn{9}{c}{Octave number}								
	1	2	3	4	5	6	7	8	9
A		&0C00	&1C00	&2C00	&3C00	&4C00	&5C00	&6C00	&7C00
A#		&0D55	&1D55	&2D55	&3D55	&4D55	&5D55	&6D55	&7D55
B		&0EAA	&1EAA	&2EAA	&3EAA	&4EAA	&5EAA	&6EAA	&7EAA
C		&1000	&2000	&3000	&4000	&5000	&6000	&7000	
C#	&0155	&1155	&2155	&3155	&4155	&5155	&6155	&7155	
D	&02AA	&12AA	&22AA	&32AA	&42AA	&52AA	&62AA	&72AA	
D#	&0400	&1400	&2400	&3400	&4400	&5400	&6400	&7400	
E	&0555	&1555	&2555	&3555	&4555	&5555	&6555	&7555	
F	&06AA	&16AA	&26AA	&36AA	&46AA	&56AA	&66AA	&76AA	
F#	&0800	&1800	&2800	&3800	&4800	&5800	&6800	&7800	
G	&0955	&1955	&2955	&39AA	&49AA	&59AA	&69AA	&79AA	
G#	&0AAA	&1AAA	&2AAA	&3AAA	&4AAA	&5AAA	&6AAA	&7AAA	

Duration of sound

The fourth SOUND parameter determines the duration of a sound. A value of 0 to 254 specifies the duration in twentieths of a second. For example, a value of 20 causes the note to sound for one second. A value of 255 causes the note to sound continuously, stopping only when you press Esc. Values between 256 and 32767 also give the duration in 20ths of a second.

Synchronising the channels

The channels can be synchronised by using the beat counter. The counter increases from zero to a set limit, then starts again at zero. Typically, you would use the time it takes for the counter to complete one cycle to represent a 'bar' in the music, and use the *after* parameter in the SOUND statement to determine where in the bar the note is sounded.

Sound

You can set the value that this counter will count up to by typing

```
BEATS n
```

The counter then counts from 0 to $n-1$ and when it reaches n it resets itself to zero.

To find the current beat counter limit, type

```
PRINT BEATS
```

Increasing the number of beats increases the time taken before two notes are repeated. It has no effect on the time interval between the two notes themselves.

Finding the value of the current beat

In addition, the current beat counter value is found by typing

```
PRINT BEAT
```

Finding the current tempo

The rate at which the beat counter counts depends on the tempo which can be set as follows:

```
TEMPO n
```

n is a hexadecimal fractional number, in which the three least-significant digits are the fractional part. A value of &1000 corresponds to a tempo of one tempo beat per centi-second; doubling the value (&2000) causes the tempo to double (2 tempo beats per centi-second), halving the value (&800) halves the tempo (to half a beat per centi-second).

Suppose you are working in 4/4 time, and want to have a resolution of 8 computer beats per musical beat (i.e. there are 32 computer beats to the bar). Furthermore, suppose you want the musical tempo to be 125 beats per minute. This is 125*8/60 computer beats per second, or 125*8/60/100 computer beats per centi second. If you calculate this, you obtain 0.6666667 computer beats per centi-second. Multiply this by the scaling factor of &1000 (4096), and you get a TEMPO value of 683. Therefore you would use the following two commands:

```
TEMPO 683
BEATS 32
```

To find the current tempo, type

```
PRINT TEMPO
```

Increasing the tempo decreases both the time taken before two notes are repeated and the time interval between the two notes.

Executing a sound on a beat

Sounds can be scheduled to execute a given number of beats from the last beat counter reset by giving the fifth parameter *after* to the SOUND statement.

The optional *after* parameter in the SOUND statement specifies the number of beats which should elapse before the sound is made. The beats are counted from the last time the beat counter was set to zero (i.e. the start of the bar). If the beat counter is not enabled (because no BEATS statement has been issued), the beats are counted from the time the statement was executed.

For example, the listing below repeatedly waits for the start of the bar, then schedules the sounds to be made after 50 beats and 150 beats respectively. If a bar is 200 beats long, this corresponds to the second and fourth beat of a 4/4 time:

```
10 BEATS 200
15 VOICES 2
20 VOICE 1,"WaveSynth-Beep"
30 VOICE 2,"WaveSynth-Beep"
40 REPEAT
50   REPEAT UNTIL BEAT=0
60   SOUND 1, -15, 100, 5, 50
70   SOUND 2, -15, 200, 5, 150
80   REPEAT UNTIL BEAT<>0
90 UNTIL FALSE
```

Having scheduled the sounds, the program waits in another REPEAT loop until the current beat is not zero. This prevents the sounds from being scheduled more than once in a bar.

Note: Where other things are happening in a program, such as screen updating, it is not safe to test for BEAT=0, in case the program misses the short period where that was true. It is better to test, for example, for BEAT<10 and treat beat 10 as the 'start' of the bar.

Synchronising sounds

If you give −1 as the *after* parameter, the sound, instead of being scheduled for a given number of beats, is synchronised with the last sound that was scheduled. For example,

```
SOUND 1,-10,200,20,100
SOUND 2,-10,232,20,-1
```

will cause two sounds, an octave apart, to be made 100 beats from the present moment, assuming that at least two channels are active and have voices assigned.

Note: If you alter the sound system, you should restore it before returning to the desktop, or running any other programs.

23   Accessing memory locations

Individual memory locations can be accessed from BASIC by using four indirection operators:

Symbol	Purpose	Number of bytes
?	Byte indirection operators	1
!	Integer indirection operator	4
|	Floating point indirection operator	5 (BASIC V)
		8 (BASIC VI)
$	String indirection operator	1 to 256

These operators can either be used to read the value(s) in one or more memory locations or to alter the value(s) there. You must be very careful that you only read from or write to memory locations which you have set aside specially. Using these operators on other areas of the memory can have undesirable effects.

Reserving a block of memory

You can reserve a block of memory using a special form of the DIM command. For example:

```
DIM pointer% 99
```

This reserves a block of (uninitialised) memory and sets the variable `pointer%` to the address of the first byte of the block. The bytes are at addresses `pointer%+0` to `pointer%+99`, a total of 100 bytes. Note that the address assigned to `pointer%` will always be a multiple of four. This means that consecutive DIMs will not necessarily allocate contiguous blocks of memory.

Note also that this differs from the usual use of DIM to dimension an array in that the size is not contained in brackets, and the variable cannot be a string.

Inside a procedure or function you can temporarily reserve a block of memory that will be released when the procedure or function exits by adding LOCAL to the DIM command, for example:

```
DIM pointer% LOCAL 99
```

In this case the memory will be reserved on BASIC's stack.

The '?' indirection operator

You can set the contents of the first byte of this block of memory to 63 by typing

```
?pointer% = 63
```

To check that this value has been inserted correctly, type

```
PRINT ?pointer%
```

The ? indirection operator affects only a single byte. Only the least significant byte of the number is stored. Thus, if you give it a value of n, where n > 256, only n AND &FF will be stored.

For example,

```
?pointer% = 356
PRINT ?pointer%
```

produces the result:

```
     100
```

because 356 AND &FF gives 100.

If you wish to set or examine the contents of the location which is five bytes after pointer%, you can do this by typing

```
?(pointer% + 5) = 25
```

Alternatively, a shorter form is available as follows:

```
pointer%?5 = 25
```

The following program prints out the contents of all the memory locations in the reserved block:

```
10 DIM block_of_memory% 100
20 FOR N% = 0 TO 100
30   PRINT "Contents of ";N%;" are ";block_of_memory%?N%
40 NEXT N%
```

The '!' indirection operator

BASIC integer variables are stored in four consecutive bytes of memory. The ! operator can be used to access these four bytes. For example, type

```
DIM pointer% 100
!pointer% = 356
PRINT !pointer%
```

The least significant byte of the integer is stored in the first memory location, and the most significant byte in the fourth location. This can be seen in the following example:

```
10 DIM pointer% 100
20 !pointer% = &12345678
30 PRINT ~pointer%?0
40 PRINT ~pointer%?1
50 PRINT ~pointer%?2
60 PRINT ~pointer%?3
```

This prints:

```
78
56
34
12
```

The '|' indirection operator

Floating point numbers, which are stored in five bytes (in BASIC V) or eight bytes (in BASIC VI), can be accessed using the unary operator |. For example:

```
10 DIM pointer% 100
20 |pointer% = 3.678
30 PRINT |pointer%
```

There is no dyadic form of |. You cannot say, for example, a|5=1.23.

Appendix A – Numeric implementation explains how floating point numbers are stored in BBC BASIC.

The '$' indirection operator

Strings can be placed directly in memory, each character's ASCII code being stored in one byte of memory. For example:

```
DIM pointer% 100
$pointer% = "STRING"
PRINT $pointer%
```

The $ indirection operator places a carriage return (ASCII 13) after the last character of the string. Thus, the example above uses seven bytes: six for the characters of the word STRING, plus one for the terminating carriage return. To see this, run the following program:

The '$' indirection operator

```
 10 DIM space% 10
 20 REM set all bytes to zero
 30 FOR N% = 0 TO 10
 40   space%?N% = 0
 50 NEXT N%
 60 REM Store the string
 70 $space% = "STRING"
 80 REM Print out the bytes
 90 FOR N% = 0 TO 10
100   PRINT space%?N% "  ";CHR$(space%?N%)
110 NEXT N%
```

As with |, there is no dyadic form of $. For example, although you may use $(string+1), the form string$1 is not allowed.

24 Error handling and debugging

By default, when the BASIC interpreter finds an error it halts execution of the program and prints an error message on the screen. Most errors are generated by incorrect programming, such as using a variable which has not had a value assigned to it. You have to correct this kind of error to make the program work. However, even if the syntax of the program is correct, errors can occur whilst it is being executed, because it cannot cope with the data it is given.

For example:

```
10 REPEAT
20   INPUT "Number",N
30   L = LOG(N)
40   PRINT "LOG of ";N" is ";L
50 UNTIL FALSE
```

This program takes a number from the keyboard and prints the logarithm of that number. If you type in a negative number, however, the program gives the message:

```
Logarithm range at line 30
```

The same thing happens if you type 0, or a character such as W, or a word such as TWELVE.

Trapping an error

You may decide that you would like to trap such an error and print a message to tell the user what he or she has done wrong instead of having the program end abruptly. You can do this using the ON ERROR statement.

169

Trapping an error

For example:

```
  5 ON ERROR PROCerror
 10 REPEAT
 20   INPUT "Number",N
 30   L = LOG(N)
 40   PRINT "LOG of ";N" is ";L
 50 UNTIL FALSE
 60 END

100 DEFPROCerror
110 IF ERR=22 THEN
120   PRINT "The number must be greater than 0"
130 ELSE REPORT
140   PRINT " at line ";ERL
150   END
160 ENDIF
170 ENDPROC
```

The ON ERROR statement can be followed by a series of statements given on the same line. In many cases, it is more convenient to follow it with a call to an error handling procedure, as in the example above, which can then be as complex as you like.

When an error occurs, BASIC passes control to the first statement on the ON ERROR line, as if it jumped there using a GOTO. It will 'forget' about any loops or procedures that were active when the error occurred, as if the program had been re-started. Of course, the values of all the variables and so on will still be intact.

Each error has an error number associated with it. When a particular error occurs, its number is placed in a variable called ERR (these numbers are guaranteed to remain the same). A full list of error numbers is given in *Appendix C – Error messages*.

In the example above, the error handling procedure tests for error 22 which is the Logarithm range error. If it was this error which occurred, it is dealt with appropriately. If a different error occurred, the program executes the REPORT instruction which prints out the error message and then prints the number of the line where the error occurred which is given in the function ERL. Then it executes the END to end the execution of the program. Trapping all errors is not necessarily a good idea since you then would not be able to press Esc, which is treated as an error, to stop the program.

If a program contains more than one ON ERROR statement, the most recently executed one is used when an error occurs.

Turning off the error handler

Error handling can be turned off, and BASIC's default handler restored, at any stage in the program using the instruction ON ERROR OFF.

Errors in libraries

If an error occurs in a library, the error message displayed by REPORT is suffixed with the name of the library, for example `Mistake in "MyLib"`. The name that will be printed is everything that follows REM or REM> on the first line of the library.

Generating errors

In addition to the error messages that the interpreter itself generates when it discovers a mistake in the program, you can cause your own errors. This can be useful when, for example, you find a mistake in the user's input data and want to notify the user through your standard error handler. To generate an error, use the statement:

ERROR *errnum*, *errstring*

The *errnum* expression is a number which will be passed to the error handler via the ERR function, as usual. The *errstring* is accessible to the error handler through the REPORT statement and REPORT$ function. ERL will be set to the line number at which the ERROR statement was executed.

If you use 0 as the error number, the error will be a 'fatal' one. As with built-in errors with that number, it cannot be trapped by using ON ERROR.

An example of the use of ERROR is:

```
1000 ch=OPENIN(f$)
1010 IF ch=0 THEN ERROR 214,"File '"+f$+"' not found"
```

External errors

If an error occurs in a program, you may wish to leave BASIC altogether and pass the error back to the program that called BASIC in the first place. You can do this using the ERROR EXT statement. Its syntax is very similar to ERROR, described above. If you say:

```
ERROR EXT 0,"Can't find template file"
```

then BASIC will quit and the error message and number will be passed back to the error handler of the program that called BASIC (e.g. the RISC OS Supervisor prompt or error box).

BASIC's default error handler uses this form of the ERROR statement if the program being executed was called from a command of the form

`*BASIC -quit `*filename*

(A BASIC program filename typed as a * command will behave like this.)

When BASIC is called like this, it loads and executes the program stored in *filename*, and then QUITs automatically when the program terminates. In addition, the function QUIT will return TRUE instead of FALSE, as it usually does. This is used in BASIC's default error handler, which reads as follows:

```
TRACE OFF
IF QUIT THEN
   ERROR EXT ERR,REPORT$
ELSE
   RESTORE
   IF ERL THEN
     REM Equivalent to PRINT REPORT$+" at line "+STR$(ERL)
     CALL !ERRXLATE:PRINT $STRACC
   ELSE
     REPORT:PRINT
   ENDIF
   END
ENDIF
```

The `CALL !ERRXLATE` statement calls a function that stores a translated version of `REPORT$+" at line "+STR$(ERL)` at `$STRACC`.

Local error handling

When an error occurs, the ON ERROR command can be used to deal with it. BASIC, however, forgets all about what it was doing at the time the error happened. For example, if it was in the middle of a FOR ... NEXT loop or executing a procedure, it is not possible to jump back to the place the error occurred and carry on as though nothing had happened.

Trapping an error; procedures & functions

The ON ERROR LOCAL command can be used to get around this problem. This command traps errors which occur inside an individual procedure or function and then continues executing within the procedure or function rather than jumping back to the top level. For example:

Error handling and debugging

```
 10 PROCcalculate(100)
 20 END
100 DEFPROCcalculate(A)
110 LOCAL I
120 LOCAL ERROR
130 FOR I = -15 TO 15
140 ON ERROR LOCAL PRINT"Infinite Result":NEXT I:ENDPROC
150 PRINT A / I
160 NEXT I
180 ENDPROC
```

Local error handlers can be used in any loops, not just inside procedures and functions.

Restoring the previous error handler

Normally, when one ON ERROR or ON ERROR LOCAL statement is used, all previous ON ERROR statements are forgotten about. It is possible, however, to use one error handler and then restore the previous one. To do this, use the instruction LOCAL ERROR to store the old error handler, and RESTORE ERROR to activate it again.

For example:

```
  1 ON ERROR PRINT "Error ";REPORT$;:END
 10 PROCcalculate(100)
 15 this line will give an error !!!
 20 END
100 DEFPROCcalculate(A)
110 LOCAL I
120 LOCAL ERROR
130 FOR I = -15 TO 15
140 ON ERROR LOCAL PRINT"Infinite Result":NEXT I:ENDPROC
150 PRINT A / I
160 NEXT I
170 RESTORE ERROR
180 ENDPROC
```

This shows that the local error handler is in force during the procedure, but that the original one set up by the first line of the program is restored when the PROC has finished.

Strictly speaking, the RESTORE ERROR is not required here because it is done automatically when the ENDPROC is reached. RESTORE ERROR is also executed automatically at the end of a user-defined function. However, if you set up a local error handler in a loop at the top level, then you would need to use it explicitly.

173

Debugging

For example:

```
100 LOCAL ERROR
110 WHILE ...
120   ON ERROR LOCAL ...
130   ...
140 ENDWHILE
150 RESTORE ERROR
160 ...
```

Debugging

A program may contain errors which cause it to behave differently from the way you intended. In these circumstances, you may wish to watch more closely how the program is being executed.

Stopping execution of the program

One option you have available is to place a STOP statement at a particular point in the program. When this line is reached, execution of the program stops and you can then investigate the values assigned to any of its variables using the PRINT statement or LVAR command.

Tracing the path through the program

Another option is to use the TRACE facility. The standard trace prints the BASIC line numbers in the order these lines are executed, thus showing the path being taken through the program. This can be invoked by typing

```
TRACE ON
```

To trace only those lines with a line number below 1000, for example, type

```
TRACE 1000
```

Alternatively you may trace procedures and functions only as follows:

```
TRACE PROC
```

You can also trace both at once if you wish by typing

```
TRACE 1000 : TRACE PROC
```

To trace when procedures and functions exit use:

```
TRACE ENDPROC
```

Tracing can be performed in single-step mode where the computer stops after each line or procedure call and waits for a key to be pressed before continuing. Single-step tracing can be invoked by typing

Error handling and debugging

```
TRACE STEP ON
```

to stop after every line traced, or

```
TRACE STEP n
```

to trace all lines below *n* and stop after each one, or

```
TRACE STEP PROC
```

to stop after every procedure call.

Instead of having TRACE output displayed on the screen, you can send it to a file. To do this, type

```
TRACE TO filename
```

This means that you have a permanent record of the path taken through your program.

Any TRACE option affects all programs which are subsequently run until tracing is turned off by

```
TRACE OFF
```

or until an error occurs.

Because TRACE is a statement, you can also use it from within a program. Thus if you know that a program is going wrong within a particular procedure, you could insert a TRACE ON statement at the start of the procedure, and a TRACE OFF just before the ENDPROC. That way, trace information will only be produced while the procedure is executing.

Error service call

When an error occurs, BASIC will issue the service call Service_Error to allow external debuggers to see this happening. In addition to the standard registers for this service call, information about BASIC's state is passed in registers R2 to R5:

R0	pointer to error block
R1	&06 (reason code)
R2	pointer to BASIC's workspace (ARGP)
R3	BASIC's LINE pointer (points to the current statement)
R4	pointer to BASIC's full, descending stack
R5	environment information pointer

The error number in the error block will be the BASIC error number with &81FB00 added to it. Registers R2 to R5 contain information about BASIC's environment corresponding to the information passed in registers R8, R12, R13 and R14 by the CALL statement. Further information can be found in the section describing CALL on page 234. If a service call handler wishes to call any of the internal BASIC routines then it must first switch to user mode and transfer the state information to the correct registers.

25 VDU control

The Visual Display Unit (VDU) driver is a part of the operating system which provides a set of routines used to display all text and graphical output. Any bytes sent to the VDU driver are treated either as characters to be displayed or as VDU commands: instructions which tell the driver to perform a specific function. Their interpretation depends on their ASCII values as follows:

ASCII value	Interpretation
0-31	VDU commands
32-126	Characters to be displayed
127	Delete
128-159	Characters to be displayed / teletext control codes
160-255	International characters to be displayed

The nearest equivalent to the statement VDU X is PRINT CHR$(X); with the exception that VDU ignores the value of WIDTH and does not affect COUNT.

In addition, the VDU commands can be given from the keyboard by holding down Ctrl and one further key as shown in the table below. For example, to give the command VDU 0, you would press Ctrl-@. Some VDU commands require extra data to be sent. The number of bytes extra is also given in the table.

VDU Code	Ctrl plus	Extra bytes	Meaning
0	2 or @	0	Do nothing
1	A	1	Send next character to printer only
2	B	0	Enable printer
3	C	0	Disable printer
4	D	0	Write text at text cursor
5	E	0	Write text at graphics cursor
6	F	0	Enable VDU driver
7	G	0	Generate bell sound
8	H	0	Move cursor back one character
9	I	0	Move cursor on one space
10	J	0	Move cursor down one line
11	K	0	Move cursor up one line
12	L	0	Clear text viewport
13	M	0	Move cursor to start of current line
14	N	0	Turn on page mode
15	O	0	Turn off page mode

16	P	0	Clear graphics viewport
17	Q	1	Define text colour
18	R	2	Define graphics colour
19	S	5	Define logical colour
20	T	0	Restore default logical colours
21	U	0	Disable VDU drivers
22	V	1	Select screen mode
23	W	9	Multi-purpose command
24	X	8	Define graphics viewport
25	Y	5	PLOT
26	Z	0	Restore default viewports
27	[	0	Does nothing
28	\	4	Define text viewport
29	]	4	Define graphics origin
30	6 or ^	0	Home text cursor
31	– or _	2	Move text cursor

In the VDU commands described below, note the following three points:

- Expressions followed by a semi-colon are sent as two bytes (low byte first) to the operating system VDU drivers.

- Expressions followed by a comma (or nothing) are sent to the VDU drivers as one byte, taken from the least significant byte of the expression.

- The vertical bar | means ,0,0,0,0,0,0,0,0,0, and so sends the expression before it as a byte followed by nine zero bytes. Since the maximum number of parameters required by any of the VDU statements is nine, the vertical bar ensures that sufficient parameters have been sent for any particular call. Any surplus ones are irrelevant, since VDU 0 does nothing.

VDU 0

VDU 0 does nothing.

VDU 1

VDU 1 sends the next character to the printer only, if the printer has been enabled (with VDU 2 for example).

VDU 2

VDU 2 causes all subsequent printable characters, and certain control characters, to be sent to the printer as well as to the screen (subject to FX3 mask etc).

VDU 3

VDU 3 cancels the effects of VDU 2 so that all subsequent printable characters are sent to the screen only.

VDU 4

VDU 4 causes all subsequent printable characters to be printed at the current text cursor position using the current text foreground colour. Cursor control characters (e.g. carriage return and line feed) affect the text cursor and not the graphics cursor

VDU 5

VDU 5 links the text and graphics cursors and causes all subsequent printable characters to be printed at the current graphics cursor position using the current graphics foreground colour and action. Cursor control characters (e.g. carriage return and line feed) affect the graphics cursor and not the text cursor.

VDU 6

VDU 6 restores the functions of the VDU driver after it has been disabled (using VDU 21). Hence, this command causes all subsequent printable characters to be sent to the screen.

VDU 7

VDU 7 generates the bell sound.

VDU 8

VDU 8 causes either the text cursor (by default or after a VDU 4 command) or the graphics cursor (after a VDU 5 command) to be moved back one character position. It does not cause the last character to be deleted. Note that during command input, Ctrl-H acts as the Backspace key, so the last character *will* be deleted.

VDU 9

VDU 9 causes either the text cursor (by default or after a VDU 4 command) or the graphics cursor (after a VDU 5 command) to be moved on one character position.

VDU 10

VDU 10 causes either the text cursor (by default or after a VDU 4 command) or the graphics cursor (after a VDU 5 command) to be moved on one line.

VDU 11

VDU 11 causes either the text cursor (by default or after a VDU 4 command) or the graphics cursor (after a VDU 5 command) to be moved back one line.

VDU 12

VDU 12 clears either the current text viewport (by default or after a VDU 4 command) or the current graphics viewport (after a VDU 5 command) to the current text or graphics background colour respectively. In addition the text or graphics cursor is moved to its home position (see VDU 30).

VDU 13

VDU 13 causes the text cursor (by default or after a VDU 4 command) or the graphics cursor (after a VDU 5 command) to be moved to the start of the current line.

VDU 14

VDU 14 enters paged mode, and so makes the screen display wait for Shift or Scroll Lock (twice) to be pressed before displaying the next page.

VDU 15

VDU 15 cancels the effect of VDU 14 so that scrolling is unrestricted.

VDU 16

VDU 16 clears the current graphics viewport to the current graphics background colour using the graphics and action. It does not affect the position of the graphics cursor.

VDU 17,n

VDU 17 sets either the text foreground ($n<128$) or background ($n>=128$) colours to the value n. It is equivalent to COLOUR n.

VDU 18,k,c

VDU 18 is used to define either the graphics foreground or background colour and the way in which it is to be applied to the screen. The BASIC equivalent is GCOL k,c.

VDU 19,1,p,r,g,b

VDU 19 is used to define the physical colours associated with the logical colour l.

If $p <= 15$ & $p >= 0$, r, g and b are ignored, and one of the standard colour settings is used. This is equivalent to COLOUR l,p.

If $p = 16$, the palette is set up to contain the levels of red, green and blue dictated by r, g and b. This is equivalent to COLOUR l,r,g,b.

If $p = 24$, the border is given colour components according to r, g and b.

If $p = 25$, the mouse logical colour l is given colour components according to r, g and b. This is equivalent to MOUSE COLOUR l,r,g,b.

VDU 20

VDU 20 restores the default palette for the current mode and so cancels the effect of all VDU 19 commands or their BASIC keyword counterparts. It also sets the default text and graphics foreground and background colours.

VDU 21

VDU 21 stops all further text and graphics output to the screen until a VDU 6 command is received.

VDU 21

VDU 22 is used to change mode. It is equivalent to MODE n.

See *Appendix H - VDU commands* for full details of the modes available.

VDU 23,p1,p2,p3,p4,p5,p6,p7,p8,p9

VDU 23 is a multi-purpose command taking nine parameters, of which the first identifies a particular function. Each of the available functions is described below. Eight additional parameters are required in each case.

VDU 23,0,n,m|

If $n = 8$, this sets the interlace as follows:

Value	Effect
$m = 0$	Toggles the screen interlace state
$m = 1$	Sets the screen interlace state to the current *TV setting
$m = \&80$	Turns the screen interlace off
$m = \&81$	Turns the screen interlace on

If $n = 10$, then m defines the start line for the cursor and its appearance. Thus:

Bits	Effect
0-4	define the start line
5-6	define its appearance:

Bit 6	Bit 5	Meaning
0	0	Steady
0	1	Off
1	0	Fast flash
1	1	Slow flash

If $n = 11$, then m defines the end line for the cursor.

VDU 23,1,n|

This controls the appearance of the cursor on the screen depending on the value of n. Thus:

Value	Effect
$n = 0$	Stops the cursor appearing (OFF)
$n = 1$	Makes the cursor reappear (ON)
$n = 2$	Makes the cursor steady
$n = 3$	Makes the cursor flash

VDU 23,2 to 5,n1,n2,n3,n4,n5,n6,n7,n8

These define the four colour patterns. Each of the parameters $n1$ to $n8$ defines one row of the pattern, $n1$ being the top row and $n8$ the bottom row. See the chapter entitled *Graphic patterns* on page 139 for more details.

VDU 23,6,n1,n2,n3,n4,n5,n6,n7,n8

This sets the dot-dash line style used by dotted line PLOT commands. Each of the parameters $n1$ to $n8$ defines eight elements of the line style, $n1$ controlling the start and $n8$ the end. The bits in each are read from the most significant to the least significant, zero representing a space and one representing a dot. See the chapter entitled *Complex graphics* on page 127 for more details.

VDU 23,7,m,d,z|

This scrolls the current text screen. The values of m, d and z determine the area to be scrolled, the direction of scrolling and the amount of scrolling respectively. Thus:

Value	Effect
$m = 0$	Scroll the current text viewport
$m = 1$	Scroll the entire screen
$d = 0$	Scroll right
$d = 1$	Scroll left
$d = 2$	Scroll down
$d = 3$	Scroll up
$d = 4$	Scroll in the positive X direction
$d = 5$	Scroll in the negative X direction
$d = 6$	Scroll in the positive Y direction
$d = 7$	Scroll in the negative Y direction
$z = 0$	Scroll by one character cell
$z = 1$	Scroll by one character cell vertically or one byte horizontally

VDU 23,8,t1,t2,x1,y1,x2,y2;0;

This clears a block of the current text viewport to the text background colour. The parameters $t1$ and $t2$ indicate the base positions relating to the start and end of the block to be cleared respectively. The positions to which the values of t refer are shown below:

Value	Position
$t = 0$	top left of viewport
$t = 1$	top of cursor column
$t = 2$	off top right of viewport
$t = 4$	left end of cursor line
$t = 5$	cursor position
$t = 6$	off right of cursor line
$t = 8$	bottom left of viewport
$t = 9$	bottom of cursor column
$t = 10$	off bottom right of viewport

The parameters $x1$, $y1$ and $x2$, $y2$ are the x and y displacements from the positions specified by $t1$ and $t2$ respectively. They determine the start and end of the block.

VDU 23,9,n|
VDU 23,10,n|

These set the durations for the first and second flashing colours respectively. The duration is set to *n* frame periods (1/50th of a second in the standard modes). For example, VDU 23,9,10| sets the duration of the first flash colour to 10/50 or 1/5 of a second. An alternative to the VDU command is *FX9 or *FX10 described in the appendix *FX commands.

VDU 23,11|

This sets the four-colour patterns to their default values. See the chapter entitled *Graphic patterns* for more details.

VDU 23,12 to 15,n1,n2,n3,n4,n5,n6,n7,n8

These set up the simple colour patterns. A block of two-by-four pixels is defined using the eight parameters. Each pair of parameters corresponds to the colours of the pixels on a given row, *n*1 and *n*2 being the top row and *n*7 and *n*8 the bottom row. See the chapter entitled *Graphic patterns* for more details.

VDU 23,16,n|

This alters the direction of printing on the screen.

Normally when a character has been printed, the cursor moves to the right by one place, and then to the start of the row below when a character is entered in the righthand column. This movement, however, can be altered so that, for example, the cursor moves down one row after each character, and moves to the top of the next column to the right when the bottom of the screen has been reached. This effect can by produced by typing

VDU 23,16,8|

The effect on cursor movement depends on the value *n* as shown below:

Value	Effect
0	Positive X direction is right, positive Y direction is down
2	Positive X direction is left, positive Y direction is down
4	Positive X direction is right, positive Y direction is up
6	Positive X direction is left, positive Y direction is up
8	Positive X direction is down, positive Y direction is right
10	Positive X direction is down, positive Y direction is left
12	Positive X direction is up, positive Y direction is right
14	Positive X direction is up, positive Y direction is left

Altering the direction of cursor movement also affects the way in which the screen scrolls; so in the example above, when a character has been entered at the bottom righthand corner, the screen scrolls to the left by one column rather than scrolling up by one row as it usually does.

The following is the complete list of VDU commands for moving the cursor:

Command	Movement
VDU 8	Moves the cursor one place in the negative X direction
VDU 9	Moves the cursor one place in the positive X direction
VDU 10	Moves the cursor one place in the negative Y direction
VDU 11	Moves the cursor one place in the positive Y direction
VDU 13	Moves the cursor to negative X edge
VDU 30	Moves the cursor to the negative X and Y edges (home)
VDU 31,x,y	Moves the cursor to TAB(x,y)
VDU 127	Moves the cursor one place in the negative X direction, destructively

VDU 23,17,n,m|

If $n = 0$ to 3, this command sets the tint to the value m for the text foreground, text background, graphics foreground and graphics background colours respectively. It is equivalent to TINT n,m. See the chapter entitled *Screen modes* on page 107 for more details.

If $n = 4$, this command chooses which set of default colour patterns is used. $m = 0$ gives the Master 128-compatible set; $m = 1$ gives the native set. See the chapter entitled *Graphic patterns* for more details.

If $n = 5$, this command swaps the text foreground and background colours.

If $n = 6$, then the command has the format:

`VDU 23,17,x;y;0;0`

This is used to set the origin of colour patterns. By default, patterns are aligned so that the top left corner of the pattern coincides with the top left corner of the screen. Using this call, you can make the top left of the pattern coincide with any pixel on the screen, given by the coordinates (x,y).

If $n = 7$, then the command has the format:

`VDU 23,17,7,flags,dx;dy;0;0`

The bits in the flag byte have the following meanings:

Bit	Meaning if set
0	Set VDU 4 character size from dx,dy
1	Set VDU 5 character size from dx,dy
2	Set VDU 5 character spacing from dx,dy

The bit 0 option is not implemented at present.

If bit 1 is set, then dx and dy give the size in pixels of characters plotted in VDU 5 mode. The standard size of 8 by 8, and double height, 8 by 16, are optimised. Other sizes use the scaled character option of the SpriteExtend module and are therefore somewhat slower.

Bit 2 set causes dx and dy to be used to set the amount by which the VDU driver moves after each VDU 5-mode character has been printed (dx) and the amount to move down for a line feed (dy). Usually these would be set to the same values as the character size (so you would set bit 1 and 2), but they can be set independently to allow, for example, narrower than usual spacing.

VDU 23,18,0,n|

Set Teletext transparency mode. This only has an effect in a system that has a video frame buffer with a graphics frame buffer overlay, and controls whether the video is visible through the Teletext display.

Value	Effect
0	"Text" mode: the whole display is set opaque (default)
1	"Mix" mode: foreground colours, and both the foreground and background of boxed text are opaque; non-boxed background colours are all transparent
2	"Box" mode: boxed regions are opaque, others are transparent
3	"TV" mode: the whole display is set transparent

VDU 23,18,1,n|

In a Teletext mode this allows updating of the screen to be suspended or resumed. If n is 1 the screen will not be updated when characters are output. If n is 0 any suspended output is displayed in a single pass, and subsequent output causes the screen to be updated each time.

Suspending the display can allow for a significant speed increase in the rendering time for a large amount of text, for example when redrawing a complete teletext page, because each time you plot a single character, it can cause the whole of the rest of the line to be redrawn.

Note that the appearance of the display is undefined if you cause a hardware scroll while in suspend mode.

VDU 23,18,2,n|

This sets the Teletext reveal state. If *n* is 0, characters between the Conceal control code (152) and the next colour control code are replaced by spaces. If *n* is 1 all characters are displayed. The default is 0.

VDU 23,18,3,n|

This determines whether Teletext black foreground colour control codes have an effect. If *n* is 0 (the default state) control codes 128 and 144 do nothing. If *n* is 1 control code 128 selects black text and control code 144 selects black graphics.

Enabling black colour control will only have a visible effect when Teletext is overlaid over video and the transparency mode is not opaque (see VDU 23,18,0).

VDU23,19 to 24,n1,n2,n3,n4,n5,n6,n7,n8

These are reserved for future expansion.

VDU 23,25 to 26,n1,n2,n3,n4,n5,n6,n7,n8

VDU 23,25 and VDU 23,26 were used for anti-aliased fonts. Use of these calls is now deprecated, and you should use the SWIs provided by the FontManager module. See the RISC OS *Programmer's Reference Manual* for details.

VDU 23,27,m,n|

If *m* = 0, this command selects the sprite whose name is STR$*n*. It is equivalent to *SChoose *n*.

If *m* = 1, this command defines sprite *n* to contain the contents of the previously marked rectangle. It is equivalent to *SGET *n*.

VDU 23,28 to 30,n1,n2,n3,n4,n5,n6,n7,n8

These are reserved for use by applications programs.

VDU 23,32 to 255,n1,n2,n3,n4,n5,n6,n7,n8

These redefine the printable ASCII characters. The bit pattern of each of the parameters *n*1 to *n*8 corresponds to a row in the eight-by-eight grid of the character. See the chapter entitled *Outputting text* on page 55 for more details.

VDU 24,x1;y1;x2;y2

VDU 24 defines a graphics viewport. The four parameters define the left, bottom, right and top boundaries respectively, relative to the current graphics origin.

The parameters may be sent as shown, with semicolons after them. This indicates that the values are each two bytes long. Alternatively, they can be sent as eight one-byte values separated as usual by commas. The first of each pair contains the low byte for the boundary; the second contains the high byte.

For example,

VDU 24,160;300;360;800;

is equivalent to

VDU 24,160,0,44,1,104,1,32,3.

See the chapter entitled *Viewports* on page 147 for more details.

VDU 25,k,x;y;

VDU 25 is a multi-purpose graphics plotting command. It is equivalent to PLOT k,x,y. See the chapter entitled *Complex graphics* on page 127 for more details.

VDU 26

VDU 26 returns the text and graphics viewports to their default states: full screen size. In addition, it resets the graphics origin to (0,0), moves the graphics cursor to (0,0), and moves the text cursor to its home position.

VDU 27

VDU 27 has no effect.

VDU 28,lx,by,rx,ty

VDU 28 defines a text viewport. The parameters specify the boundary of the viewport; the left-most column, the bottom row, the right-most column and the top row respectively. See the chapter entitled *Viewports* for more details.

VDU 29,x;y;

VDU 29 moves the graphics origin. x and y specify the coordinates of the new position. Normally the origin is at the bottom left of the screen at (0,0): whenever a position is given as an absolute value, for example MOVE 20,80, the coordinates are taken as being relative to the graphics origin. This command, therefore, affects all movements of the graphics cursor and all subsequent graphics viewport commands. The position on the screen of any existing graphics viewport is not affected. This command is equivalent to ORIGIN x,y.

VDU 30

VDU 30 moves the text cursor to its home position.

VDU 31,x,y

VDU 31 moves the text cursor to a specified position on the screen. It is equivalent to PRINT TAB(x,y);.

26 Editing BASIC files

There are two main ways to edit BASIC files:

- A desktop editor such as Edit can be used as a BASIC program editor.
- Using the BASIC screen editor module, originally provided with RISC OS 2.

Note that BASIC files are not normal text files because for space and performance reasons most BASIC keywords are replaced by shorter *tokens*, and line numbers are in an internal format. For this reason they should only be edited by an editor that understands tokenised BASIC files.

Editing BASIC files with Edit

Edit can be used as a BASIC program editor. It automatically converts BASIC programs into text format for editing, and then *tokenises* the text back into BASIC format when they are saved.

For full details of editing files using Edit see the RISC OS *User Guide*.

Using Edit to write and edit BASIC programs

Edit can convert Text files produced in Edit to tokenised BASIC files.

Writing a new program

To write a new program, click Menu over the Edit icon on the icon bar and from the **Create** menu choose **BASIC**. You can now type your program directly into an Edit window. There is no need to include line numbers, as Edit will insert them for you when you save the file. Press Return at the end of the last line of the program.

Editing an existing program

To use Edit for working on an existing BASIC program, simply drag the program's icon from its directory onto the Edit icon on the icon bar, or hold down Shift and double-click on the program's icon.

Icon bar menu

Pressing Menu on the Edit icon bar icon displays a menu containing the Edit options. Moving to the **BASIC options** submenu displays the following options:

Editing BASIC files with Edit

- **Strip line numbers** produces a text file with no line numbers. If a reference to a line is found, an error box will appear asking whether you want to leave the number in. This option is on by default.
- **Line number increment** sets the number increment between successive lines in the program.

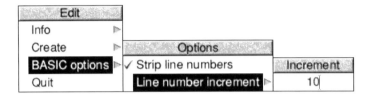

Converting to a tokenised file

Converting a text file to a tokenised file is usually quite straightforward. If there are no line numbers, Edit will start at 10 and increment by 10. If line numbers are supplied, these are used as a basis for any lines without line numbers.

If there are line numbers, Edit will **not** sort them into ascending sequence and the resulting BASIC program may behave very strangely.

If your code is incomplete, Edit will warn you about the following problems:

- Line number reference too large
- Mismatched quotes
- Mismatched brackets.

In all cases Edit will also quote the offending line number. After you have clicked on **OK**, the tokenising continues.

Attempts to tokenise a crunched program (e.g. one with the spaces removed) will generally result in a non-functioning program.

Printing a BASIC program

If you have Edit running, you can print a BASIC program on paper by dragging its icon onto a printer driver icon. Edit will perform the conversion to allow the program to be printed.

Editing BASIC files with the BASIC screen editor

The BASIC screen editor allows you to move around and change any part of a program currently loaded in the computer. It is a full-screen application that changes the screen mode, so it cannot be used in a task window on the desktop.

Entering the editor

To enter the screen editor from BASIC type

```
EDIT
```

and press Return. The editor is supplied as a module called BasicEdit inside !System and this will be automatically loaded if required.

This command enters the editor with the current BASIC program displayed.

If you have previously been editing the program, and you type

```
EDIT .
```

the editor tries to re-enter it at the point at which you left it. If you have changed the program from within BASIC, it may not be possible to maintain the position, in which case editing starts from the top of the program.

If you wish to enter the editor at a particular point, such as line 100, type

```
EDIT 100
```

The editor starts with line 100 displayed at the top of the screen. If line 100 does not exist, the editor chooses either the next line or the end of the program, whichever comes first.

You may wish to enter the editor with the first occurrence of a particular piece of text at the top of the screen. For example:

```
EDIT three
```

The editor displays the program starting with the first occurrence of the word three at the top of the screen. If the string cannot be found, the computer 'beeps' and editing starts at the top of the program.

Leaving the editor

If you want to save anything you have done before you leave the BASIC Editor, follow the instructions in the section entitled *Saving a program* on page 196. When you are ready to leave the editor and return to BASIC, press Shift-F4.

The BASIC screen

Once in the editor, your program is displayed with the line numbers at the lefthand side. If you enter the editor with no program loaded the screen is nearly blank, with just the number 10 at the top left.

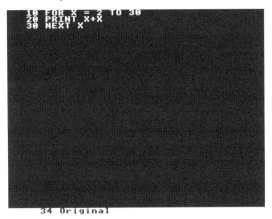

The cursor is at the beginning of the top line on the screen, just to the right of the line number. Note that the editor automatically puts a line number on the beginning of each line: there is no need for you to type them in.

The status line

The status line is at the bottom of the screen, displayed in reversed colours in order to make it stand out from your program text. It contains various useful pieces of information such as the size of your program, its name, and whether it has been modified since you entered the editor.

The status line displays the following information (if it will fit):

- Program size
- Original/Modified indicator
- Program name
- Copy if in cursor copy mode.

In addition, the status line is used for prompts such as Replace? (Y/N) which appear in the SELECTIVE REPLACE facility. See the section entitled *Searching and replacing* on page 202 for details.

Editing BASIC files

Moving the cursor

The cursor can be moved around using the four arrow keys. Note, however, that you cannot move the cursor into that area of the screen containing the line numbers. This is because in general you need never be concerned with providing line numbers for your BASIC statements. As a result, cursor movement is restricted to the area of the screen which contains program text.

Changing a line

To change a line, use the cursor keys to position the cursor on the correct line. You can then delete part or all of the line and type new text in place of the old.

Now, assume that the program looks like this:

```
10 FOR X = 2 TO 30
20 PRINT X+X
30 NEXT X
```

and that it needs to be changed to look like this:

```
10 FOR X = 2 TO 20
11 PRINT X*X
20 PRINT X+X
30 NEXT X
```

To achieve this you must change line 10 and add a new line: line 11.

Position the cursor on the 0 of 30 on line 10, press Backspace and type 2. The 30 is replaced by 20.

Adding a line

To create a new line in the middle of the program move the cursor to the line above the place where you want the new line and press Return.

In the example above, move the cursor to line 10 and press Return.

Line 11 is now created.

To complete the above program type

```
PRINT X*X
```

The program should now be complete. You may like to experiment with the Return and cursor keys to create a larger program.

Inserting lines

There are two function keys which, no matter where you are in the program, create a new line at the top or end of the program and move you there directly. These keys are Ctrl-F9 (INSERT AT START) and Ctrl-F10 (INSERT AT END).

Deleting text

There are two ways to delete single characters. The Backspace or Delete key removes the character to the left of the cursor and moves the characters to the right of the cursor back one space.

To delete the character on which the cursor is placed, hold the Shift key down and press the Backspace or Delete key. Backspace/Delete and Shift-Backspace/Delete both move the following text back a space, but Shift-Backspace/Delete leaves the cursor in the same position.

To delete all the characters from the cursor position to the end of the line, press the F11 key.

Long lines

If a statement is too long to fit on one line of the screen, it wraps around to the next line. To see this, try typing more text after one of the lines in the program. As in a BASIC program, the length of a line is limited by the BASIC Editor to 251 characters.

Saving and loading programs

Saving a program

To save a program which you have created or changed press F3 (SAVE).

A window appears into which you should type the name of the program. Once you are sure that you have typed the correct name for the program press Return or F12 (EXECUTE) to perform the save operation.

The program name need not be enclosed within quotation marks.

If you wish to save only a portion of a program you may do this by setting limits. See the section entitled *Line command* on page 199 for details of how to do this.

Loading a program

You may now wish to load in one of your own programs to experiment with before moving on to the next section. To do this press F2 (LOAD).

A window appears ready to accept the filename.

Type in the name of the program and press Return or F12 (EXECUTE).

If the current program has been modified but not saved a warning message is given.

Appending a program

You can also join one program onto the end of the current one.

To do this press Shift-F2 (APPEND) and then proceed in the same manner as for loading.

Seeing other parts of your program

Several commands are provided to help you move quickly around when you are editing a large program, such as one which is too large to be displayed on the screen at one time.

Moving vertically

If you move the cursor to the top screen line and keep pressing the ↑ key, previous statements are brought onto the screen one at a time until you reach the beginning of the program. Similarly, pressing ↓ from the bottom screen line brings the following statements onto the screen one at a time until you reach the end of the program.

To move directly to the top of your program, press Ctrl ↑ which moves the cursor to the first line of the program. Pressing Ctrl ↓ moves to the last line.

If you press Shift ↓, the next screenful of your program is displayed. In this way, you can move quickly around your program from beginning to end. Similarly, if you press Shift ↑, you can see the previous screenful. These functions are duplicated by the Page Up and Page Down keys.

If you press Ctrl-Shift ↑ or Ctrl-Shift ↓ you can move to the first or last statement on the current screen. In addition, if the cursor starts *n* characters along a statement, it remains *n* characters along. It does not go to the beginning of the statement.

Moving horizontally

Pressing the Shift → and Shift ← enables you to move sideways across the screen at twice the normal speed.

Pressing Ctrl ← takes you to the beginning of the current statement and Ctrl → takes you to the end of the current line. Pressing Ctrl-Shift → takes you to the beginning of the next statement. Pressing Ctrl-Shift ← takes you to the beginning of the previous statement.

Using two windows

You can split the screen into two windows, which lets you look at two portions of your program at the same time (this is called split window mode). To do this, press Ctrl-F4. This saves you scrolling through the program many times. To place the cursor in the other window, press Ctrl-F2 (which acts as a toggle between the two windows).

When you want to return to a single window, press Ctrl-F4 again. Note that while you are using the split window mode, the Copy key will not work.

Renumbering the program

If new lines are created in the middle of a program, the editor automatically adjusts the numbering where necessary. If this happens in a program containing a GOTO or a GOSUB to a line number as yet non-existent, then that line number is replaced by the characters @@@@.

You may at any time renumber the program yourself by pressing F8 (RENUMBER). This renumbers the program starting at line 10 with an increment of 10.

Further editing functions

Swapping case

If you have typed in some text in either upper or lower case and you want to change it to the opposite case, move to the area to be changed and press F10 (SWAP). This converts one alphabetic character at a time from lower case to upper case and vice versa.

Undoing changes to a line

If you want to abandon any changes you have made to a statement before you have left it, press Shift-F10 (UNDO). This restores the statement to the way it was before you made the changes. This only works if you have not moved the cursor off the line.

Splitting and joining lines

Occasionally, you may want to split one statement into two or more. You can do this by positioning the cursor on the character which is to be at the start of the new statement and pressing Shift-F1 (SPLIT). You can only split a statement from somewhere in the middle. As you are creating a new statement, this may cause renumbering to take place.

Editing BASIC files

There may also be occasions when you want to join two statements together. To do this, move the cursor to the first of the two statements and press Ctrl-F1 (JOIN). The editor automatically puts a colon between the two statements. If the combined length of the two statements would exceed the maximum space available, the join is not carried out and an error message is displayed.

Repeating a line

To create an exact copy of any statement immediately after it, move to the statement you wish to copy and press Shift-F8 (REPEAT). As in the case of SPLIT, this may cause renumbering to be carried out.

Marking a line

Placing the marker line

As you move about your program, there may be a statement which you wish to come back to later on. The editor provides a way of marking a statement so that you can go back to it with a single key-stroke. To mark a statement, first move to it and press F6 (TOGGLE MARK). Pressing the same key again removes the marker. A full stop appears on the screen between the line number and the start of the text, indicating that this statement has been marked. Up to four marks may be set at any time.

Finding a marker

Wherever you are in the program, pressing Shift-F6 (GOTO MARK) brings the marked statement to the top of the screen and positions the cursor there. If there is no marked line, pressing GOTO MARK displays an error; pressing Esc then allows you to continue.

Line command

These are commands which allow you to delete, move and copy either a single line or a block of lines. They can be inserted into the lefthand margin and are not executed until F12 (EXECUTE) is pressed.

For example, to delete a single line, move the cursor onto that statement, hold down the Ctrl-key and press D. The line number is removed and replaced by the letter D. To delete the line from your program, press F12 (EXECUTE). The line is removed from the screen and the cursor positioned on the previous line.

Deleting lines

If there is a block of lines which you want to delete, move to the first line in the block and press Ctrl-D twice. The line number disappears and is replaced by the letters DD. Now move to the last line in the block and press Ctrl-D twice more. Finally, press F12 (EXECUTE) to remove this block of lines from your program.

You may wish to delete from the current line to the end of the program. In this case, press Ctrl-D twice on the current line and then press Ctrl-E. The line number is replaced by DDE and the block from there to the end of the program can be removed by pressing F12 (EXECUTE).

In a similar way, you can delete from the current line to the top of the program by using Ctrl-T instead of Ctrl-E and then pressing F12 (EXECUTE).

Ctrl-E and Ctrl-T are examples of destinations and we shall encounter more of these later.

Moving a block

To move a single statement from its current position to the end of the program, move to it and press Ctrl-M followed by Ctrl-E. The line number is replaced by ME and pressing F12 (EXECUTE) moves that line to the end of the program.

Ctrl-T can be used likewise to move a statement to the top of a program.

Instead of using Ctrl-T or Ctrl-E to specify the destination as the top or the end of the program you can specify that the destination is before or after a certain line.

To move text to a position after a particular line, move to the destination and press Ctrl-A.

Alternatively you can use Ctrl-B to move text to a position before a particular line.

Blocks of lines can be moved as easily as a single line by putting MM around the block to be moved, choosing your destination, and pressing F12 (EXECUTE).

Copying lines

Whereas moving text removes it from its original position, copying text leaves the original unchanged and duplicates it elsewhere. The command to copy text is Ctrl-C instead of Ctrl-M, but otherwise the move and copy commands are the same.

Naturally, for both the move and copy commands the destination must not be within the block being moved or copied.

Denoting limits

You can limit the effect of certain operations either to one line or to a block of lines. These operations are:

- SAVE: Part of a program can be saved.
- SEARCH, SEARCH & EDIT: The search is limited to the line or block.
- SELECTIVE REPLACE, GLOBAL REPLACE: The replacement is limited to the line or block.

To limit the operation to a single line, move the cursor to that line and press Ctrl-L. To limit the operation to a block of lines, press Ctrl-L twice each on the first and last line of the block.

To limit the operation from a particular line to the top (or end) of the program, move the cursor to that line and press Ctrl-L Ctrl-L T (or Ctrl-L Ctrl-L E).

When a limit is set up, the functions which take account of it display the limit in their window.

Justifying text

The editor can indent all or part of a program automatically. To reformat a part of the program, move to the first line of the block you want to justify and press Ctrl-J twice. Then move to the last line of the block and press Ctrl-J twice. Pressing F12 (EXECUTE) justifies the block so that the indentation of each line is identical to that of the first line.

Removing line commands

To remove a line command, move to the line in question and press Ctrl-R. This deletes the line command from the screen and replaces the line number. Pressing Ctrl-R on a line which does not contain any line commands removes all line commands no matter where they are. You do not, however, have to remove a line command in order to change it: to replace the old command simply overtype it with a new one.

Ctrl-R can also be used to remove the line marker set by F6 (TOGGLE MARK); but unlike the line commands, the marker can only be removed when you are on the marked statement.

Things to notice about line commands

Line commands are not stored as part of your program text but are only held internally in the editor. There is no need, therefore, to remove line commands or the marker before saving your program.

Editing BASIC files with the BASIC screen editor

Note that copying or moving statements causes renumbering to take place automatically.

Searching and replacing

Search and edit

To search for the first occurrence of a particular piece of text, press F4 (SEARCH & EDIT). A window appears where you should enter the text to be found. When you have done this press F12 (EXECUTE) and the search is carried out. The cursor reappears on the first match within the program.

Search

As an alternative to SEARCH & EDIT you can find all occurrences of a given string and have them displayed. To do this press F7 (SEARCH) and enter the string which is to be located. Then press F12 (EXECUTE) to perform the search. Any line on which a match is found is displayed. You may then move up and down the list, choose one to look at and press Home. This line is then placed at the top of the full edit screen and you can edit it.

Global replace

To change one string for another throughout your entire program press F5 (GLOBAL REPLACE) and enter the text to be changed. You must then enter the new text, and when you are happy with it press F12 (EXECUTE) to carry out the change.

Selective replace

It is possible to perform a replace operation selectively. To do so press Shift F5 (SELECTIVE REPLACE). You must then enter both the text to be changed and the new text. Press F12 (EXECUTE) to start the search. Each match is displayed and you are prompted for either Y or N to indicate whether the replacement is to be performed or not.

Next match & previous match

It is possible to move on to the next occurrence of the text searched for in the last search operation or back to the previous one. To do this press either Shift-F7 (NEXT MATCH) or Ctrl-F7 (PREVIOUS MATCH).

Keyboard options

Pressing Shift-F3 brings up a window which allows you to select various options. This is called the Options Window. The options are displayed in three groups described below. Pressing Return allows you to cycle through the groups.

Editing BASIC files

The Tab key

This enables you to move more quickly across the screen. It moves the cursor to every third character position. At the end of a line, it takes the cursor to the beginning of the next line.

Pressing Shift-Tab moves the cursor in the opposite direction.

The options can be used to set the width of the tab movement to any value (number of characters) in the range 0 to 63.

Auto indentation

The editor can automatically line up text in a program so that each line starts beneath the first position of the line above which is not blank. This is known as auto-indentation. It can be turned on or off using the Options Window: Auto-indent (on/off).

Insert mode and overtype mode

There will be times when you want to overtype existing text rather than insert before what is already there. To do this, press Insert and you will see that the cursor has changed to an underline. This indicates that you are in overtype mode, and that text which you type in will replace existing text. To return to insert mode, press Insert again, and you will be able to insert text as before. In insert mode, a block cursor is used. In overtype mode, a line cursor is used.

When you enter the editor, the default setting (insert or overtype) is used. You can change this default using the Options Window. Your choice is retained in non-volatile memory.

Wildcard options

There are four wildcards, each of which may be customised using the options available.

- Single character (default is .).
- Multiple characters (default is |).
- Start case insensitivity: This will match both PRINT and print (default is {).
- End case insensitivity: this will match exactly what is entered. This is the normal method of searching (default is }).

Wildcards can be changed to any punctuation character, or can be disabled by using the Space Bar. Different wildcards must not use the same character.

203

Mode and colours

The editor works in 40-, 80- or 132-column modes. You can choose the default mode using the Options Window. The value is held between sessions in non-volatile memory.

Note that 256-colour modes and modes with 20-column text are not allowed. You can also set up your default choice of foreground and background colours.

User-defined keys

The editor makes extensive use of the normal function keys, but you can still program your own in the usual way via the *KEY command. To access them you must press Ctrl Shift together with the function key, and not just the function key on its own.

Full use of windows

Windows are displayed whenever input is required or information is shown.

Input windows

Valid keys and their actions are:

Keys	Effect
Tab / Return / ↓	Moves cursor to next field
Shift-Tab / ↑	Moves cursor to previous field
Esc	Cancels window, returns to editing
F12 (EXECUTE)	Validates input & executes command
Insert	Toggles insert/overtype for this window only
Backspace/Delete	Deletes character to left of cursor
Shift-Backspace/Delete	Deletes character at cursor
F11	Deletes characters from cursor to end of field
Shift-F11	Deletes all characters before cursor
Ctrl-F11	Deletes all text in this field
← / Shift ←	Moves cursor left 1 or 2 positions
→ / Shift →	Moves cursor right 1 or 2 positions
Ctrl ←	Moves cursor to beginning of field
Ctrl →	Moves cursor to end of field

Information windows

Esc	Removes window and returns to editing.

Entering data

Data can be entered in one of three ways:

- Typing in text (eg program name)
- Selecting a prompted action (eg Y/N)
- Pressing the Space Bar to cycle through a list of valid choices (eg foreground colour)

Pressing another function key whilst a window is present usually executes its function. The exceptions are those functions which manipulate the program text (eg SPLIT and JOIN).

Editing BASIC files with the BASIC screen editor

Keyboard summary

The following actions are performed directly via key presses:

Editing keys

←	Moves right
→	Moves left
↑	Moves up
↓	Moves down
Shift →	Moves right two characters
Shift ←	Moves left two characters
Shift ↑	Moves cursor up a screenful
Shift ↓	Moves cursor down a screenful
Ctrl →	Moves to the end of the statement
Ctrl ←	Moves to the beginning of the statement
Ctrl ↑	Moves to the beginning of the program
Ctrl ↓	Moves to the end of the program
Ctrl-Shift →	Moves to beginning of next statement
Ctrl-Shift ←	Moves to beginning of previous statement
Ctrl-Shift ↑	Moves to top of current screen
Ctrl-Shift ↓	Moves to bottom of current screen
Page Up	Moves cursor up a screenful
Page Down	Moves cursor down a screenful
Tab	Moves right to next tab position
Shift-Tab	Moves left to previous tab position
Home	Brings statement to top of screen
End (Copy)	Enters copy mode
Enter	Ends copy mode
Insert	Toggles insert/overtype mode
Backspace/Delete	Deletes character to left of cursor
Shift-Backspace/Delete	Deletes character at cursor position
Enter	Creates a new statement after the current one

Function keys

F1 (* COMMAND)	Perform OS command
F2 (LOAD)	Load a program
F3 (SAVE)	Save a program
F4 (SEARCH & EDIT)	Find string and edit from it
F5 (GLOBAL REPLACE)	Global search and replace

Editing BASIC files

F6 (TOGGLE MARK)	Set or remove a marker. Up to four markers allowed
F7 (SEARCH)	Find all occurrences of a string
F8 (RENUMBER)	Renumber the entire program
F9 (OLD)	Same as BASIC OLD
F10 (SWAP)	Swap case of alphabetic characters
F11 (DEL TO END OF LINE)	Delete from cursor to end of line
F12 (EXECUTE)	Execute line commands

Function keys with Shift

Shift-F1 (SPLIT)	Split statement at the cursor
Shift-F2 (APPEND)	Append a program
Shift-F3 (OPTIONS)	Present the Options Window
Shift-F4 (EXIT)	Return to BASIC. Variables will be lost if changes were made
Shift-F5 (SELECTIVE REPLACE)	Selective replace. When prompted, only Y,N, Escape and Home are valid
Shift-F6 (GOTO MARK)	Go to next marker, with program wraparound
Shift-F7 (NEXT MATCH)	Go to next occurrence of search string
Shift-F8 (REPEAT)	Copy current statement
Shift-F9 (NEW)	Same as BASIC NEW. Prompts if program has been modified
Shift-F10 (UNDO)	Undo changes to current statement
Shift-F11 (DELETE TO START OF LINE)	Delete all characters before the cursor
Shift-F12 (GOTO LINE COMMAND)	Go to next line command, with program wraparound

Function keys with Ctrl

Ctrl-F1 (JOIN)	Join two statements, with a colon separator
Ctrl-F2 (SWAP WINDOW)	Toggle between windows
Ctrl-F3	Reserved
Ctrl-F4 (SPLIT/JOIN WINDOW)	Split or join window(s)
Ctrl-F5 (HELP)	Display help window
Ctrl-F6 (INFO)	Display program information
Ctrl-F7 (PREV. MATCH)	Go to previous occurrence of search string
Ctrl-F8 (EXTEND)	Add a line to current statement
Ctrl-F9 (INSERT START)	Add a statement at beginning of program
Ctrl-F10 (INSERT END)	Add a statement at end of program
Ctrl-F11 (DELETE LINE)	Delete all text from current statement
Ctrl-F12 (GO TO LINE)	Go to selected line number

Function keys are used with Ctrl and Shift for user-defined strings.

Error messages

The editor displays the following messages. In each case, an explanation is given below the message.

```
Limit is xxxx to xxxx/Limit is xxxx only
```
A range has been set using the L or LL line commands, and this function will only operate within the range.

```
Line xxxx is too long to be edited
```
The program already contains a line which is too long.

```
Not enough room in RMA for The BASIC Editor
```
RMA initialisation failed to acquire workspace.

```
Replace? (Y/N)
```
Displayed on the status line when prompting during the SELECTIVE REPLACE operation.

```
Tab must be between 0 and 63
```
Displayed by OPTIONS.

```
The combined length of these statements would be too big
```
The two statements cannot be joined.

```
The destination must be outside the block being moved or copied
```
Raised by EXECUTE.

```
The first statement in the block to be justified must not be blank
```
Raised by EXECUTE.

```
The maximum line is 65279
```
Raised by GOTO LINE.

```
The name has been truncated
```
On saving, the program name following REM > in the first line of the program is longer than can be displayed in the window.

```
The named program is invalid
```
The user appended a program which was invalid. The editor restored the original.

```
The named program is too big
```

The user tried to load or append a program for which there was not enough room in memory.

```
The renumber has failed.Unmatched line numbers have
been replaced by @@@@
```
When trying to renumber the program one or more line number references could not be resolved.

```
The search string has no text
```
The search string must not be blank, and must not contain only wildcards.

```
The string could not be found
```
The search string could not be found.

```
There is not enough memory to update the program
```
All available memory has been used up.

```
This is not a valid mode
```
An invalid screen mode was specified in OPTIONS.

```
This is not a valid program
```
OLD was pressed with no valid BASIC program in memory, or the user tried to load an invalid program.

```
This program could not be found
```
The named program on a load or append was not in the directory.

```
This program has not been saved
```
The user is warned on a load if the program has been modified and not saved.

```
This program has not been saved
```
Press NEW again to confirm.

```
Press ESCAPE to cancel
```
The user pressed NEW but the program had been modified and not saved.

```
This statement is too long
```
The statement is too long, and needs to be shortened.

```
This statement is too long to be changed
```
Replacing or justifying would make the statement too long.

```
This statement is too long to be split
```
Even after splitting, both parts of the statement would still be too long.

```
Wildcards must not be the same
```
Raised by OPTIONS.

Editing BASIC files with the BASIC screen editor

```
You cannot load a directory
```
The filename specified in load or append is a directory.

```
You do not need to enter a destination for this command
```
Raised by EXECUTE.

```
You do not need to enter a repetition factor for this
command
```
Raised by EXECUTE.

```
You have entered a destination but no command
```
Raised by EXECUTE.

```
You have entered too many commands
```
Raised by EXECUTE.

```
You have not entered any line commands
```
Raised by GOTO LINE COMMAND when there are no line commands.

```
You have not entered any markers
```
Raised by GOTO MARKER when no markers are set.

```
You have not yet entered a search string
```
Raised by NEXT MATCH or PREVIOUS MATCH when no find string has been entered.

```
You have used the maximum number of statements. No
more can be added
```
The program already contains the maximum number of statements allowed by BASIC (65279) and the user tried to add another.

```
You must enter a destination for this command
```
Raised by EXECUTE.

```
You must enter a mode
```
No screen mode was specified within OPTIONS.

```
You must enter a program name
```
The program name was not entered for load, append or save.

```
You must enter a search string
```
The search string was not entered.

```
You must enter a tab value
```
No tab value was specified in OPTIONS.

>   You need to specify both ends of the range for this
>   command

Raised by EXECUTE.

>   You should not enter two different commands

Raised by EXECUTE.

>   *ARMBE is only valid from BASIC

The user invoked the editor from outside BASIC.

Editing BASIC files with the BASIC screen editor

Part 3 – Reference

27 Keywords

This chapter describes the BBC BASIC keywords. First, there is a short list grouping the keywords by function. Use this list if you are not sure what keywords are available for a particular task.

- **Assembly language**

    CALL, SYS, USR

- **Character/string handling**

    ASC, CHR$, INSTR(, LEFT$(, LEN, MID$(, RIGHT$(, STR$, STRING$(

- **Error handling**

    ERL, ERR, ERROR, LOCAL ERROR, ON ERROR, REPORT, REPORT$, RESTORE ERROR

- **File commands**

    BGET#, BPUT#, CLOSE#, EOF#, EXT#, GET$#, INPUT#, OPENIN, OPENOUT, OPENUP, PRINT#, PTR#

- **Graphics**

    BY, CIRCLE, CLG, CLS, COLOUR (COLOR), DRAW, ELLIPSE, FILL, GCOL, LINE, MODE, MOVE, OFF, ON, ORIGIN, PLOT, POINT, POINT(, RECTANGLE, TINT, VDU, WAIT

- **Input/Output**

    GET, GET$, INKEY, INKEY$, INPUT, INPUT LINE, LINE INPUT, MOUSE, PRINT, SPC, TAB, WIDTH

- **Logical**

    AND, EOR, FALSE, NOT, OR, TRUE

- **Numerical**

    ABS, DIV, EVAL, INT, MOD, RND, SGN, SQR, SUM, SUMLEN, SWAP, VAL

- **Program construction**

    APPEND, AUTO, CRUNCH, DELETE, EDIT, HELP, INSTALL, LIST, LISTO, LOAD, LVAR, NEW, OLD, RENUMBER, SAVE, TEXTLOAD, TEXTSAVE

- **Program statements**

    CHAIN, CLEAR, DATA, DEF, DIM, END, ENDPROC, FN, GOSUB, GOTO, LET, LIBRARY, LOCAL, OSCLI, PROC, QUIT, READ, REM, RESTORE, RETURN, RUN, STOP, TRACE

- **Sound**

    BEAT, BEATS, ENVELOPE, SOUND, STEREO, TEMPO, VOICE, VOICES

- **Structures**

    CASE, ELSE, ENDCASE, ENDIF, ENDWHILE, FOR, IF, NEXT, OF, OTHERWISE, REPEAT, THEN, UNTIL, WHEN, WHILE

- **Trigonometric**

    ACS, ASN, ATN, COS, DEG, EXP, LN, LOG, PI, RAD, SIN, TAN

- **Variables**

    ADVAL, COUNT, HIMEM, LOMEM, PAGE, POS, TIME, TIME$, TOP, VPOS

The remainder of this chapter lists the keywords alphabetically for ease of reference. It gives complete definitions of syntax, with examples.

Each keyword is listed in the index.

Syntax descriptions

In the descriptions of the syntax of each keyword, words in upper case are the keywords themselves. Most punctuation such as ',' and '=' also stands for itself, except for square brackets '[ ]' which enclose items that are optional, and ellipsis '. . .' which indicate that the item preceding them may be repeated an arbitrary number of times (including zero).

For keywords that take arguments the class of each argument is shown in *italics* and these stand for items that you need to supply. The classes used are as follows:

expression or *expr*

This is any valid numeric or string expression. The type of the expression may be qualified, e.g. *numeric-expression* or *string-expression*, and details of possible types and ranges is always given in the explanation of the keyword.

Where more than one expression is required *expression1*, *expression2* or *expr1*, *expr2* is often used to make the identification of each expression easier.

In general, wherever an integer is required, BASIC will accept a real, as long as it can be converted into an integer.

factor

This means an expression which is a single unit, i.e. a variable reference, a constant, a function call (user-defined or built-in), or a general expression enclosed in round brackets. For functions that only take a single argument the argument is always a factor, so examples of keywords using factors are:

```
SINRAD45
LENA$
STR$1234
EXP-A%
TAN(ang%+45)
RND(10)
```

It can be seen that brackets are only needed around arguments if they contain more than one element or, as in the case of RND, if the argument is optional.

relational

This is an expression that contains operators of higher precedence than the logical operator under discussion. Thus in the syntax:

```
relational AND relational
```

the *relational* expression may contain any operator except AND, OR and EOR, as these have the same or lower precedence. To use one of these operators (e.g. OR) in an argument, you will need brackets, for example:

```
(a>b OR c<d) AND f<>1
```

For a full description of operator precedence see *Arithmetic operators* on page 31

variable or var

This is a reference to any variable. Examples are a, a%, a$, a(23), a%(32), a$(i+1), $a, ?a, !a, a?1, a!1 etc. Sometimes it is qualified, e.g. *numeric variable*.

statements

This means zero or more statements, separated by colons, e.g.
```
PRINT "Hello":GOTO 100
```

Null statements are permitted in BBC BASIC, so lines such as:

```
IF GET
```

are valid. In this example, the optional THEN is omitted and there is a null THEN part. This can be useful if you want to use a function call but discard the return value.

The keywords REPEAT, THEN, ELSE, OTHERWISE and the assembly language introducer '[' do not require colons to separate them from the next statement. Also, there is no need for a colon after the PROC or FN part of a DEF statement.

pathname

This is a string expression that contains a valid RISC OS pathname, identifying a file on a filing system. This may be simply the name of a file, for example `MyFile`, in which case it will be located in the currently selected directory of the current filing system, or it may be a full pathname identifying the filing system and the full path to the file, for example `ADFS::HardDisc4.$.Examples.MyFile`.

Technical details

Some keyword descriptions contain a technical details section which gives further information on how the keyword is implemented that may be of use to advanced programmers.

History

For keywords that have been altered or extended after interpreter version 1.04 (the first version of BASIC V) a history section summarises the changes. More detailed information can be found in *Appendix I – BBC BASIC's history*.

ABS

Function returning the magnitude (absolute value) of its numeric argument, i.e. changes negative numbers into positive numbers.

Syntax

    ABS factor

Argument

Any numeric.

Result

Same as the argument if this is positive, or –(the argument) if it is negative.

Notes

The largest negative integer does not have a legal positive value, so that if a%=–2147483648, ABS(a%) yields the same value: –2147483648. However, this does not arise with floating point numbers.

Example

    diff=ABS(length1-length2)

ACS

Function returning the arc-cosine of its numeric argument.

Syntax

```
ACS factor
```

Argument

Real or integer between −1 and 1 inclusive.

Result

Real in the range 0 to π radians, being the inverse cosine of the argument.

Examples

```
ang=ACS(normvec1(1)*normvec2(1)+normvec1(2)*normvec2(2))
angle=DEG(ACS(cos1))
PRINT ACS(0.5)
```

ADVAL

Function returning buffer data or reading data from an analogue or joystick port if fitted.

Syntax

    (1) ADVAL negative-factor
    (2) ADVAL 0
    (3) ADVAL positive-factor

Argument (1)

Negative integer $-n$, where n is a buffer number between 1 and 10.

Result (1)

The number of spaces or entries in the buffer is given in the table below:

arg	Buffer name	Result
−1	Keyboard (input)	Number of characters used
−2	Serial (input)	Number of characters used
−3	Serial (output)	Number of characters free
−4	Printer (output)	Number of characters free
−10	Mouse (input)	Number of bytes used

Argument (2)

Zero.

Result (2)

An integer giving the state of joystick switches. Bit 0 is the state of the first switch, bit 1 gives the state of the second switch and so on.

This behaviour is usually implemented by the Joystick module and will only work if this module is loaded and suitable hardware is present. If this is absent, the function will result in a `Command not recognised` error.

Argument (3)

Positive integer n, where n is an analogue–digital converter channel number.

Result (3)

An integer giving the current voltage level of the analogue–digital converter channel in the range 0 to 65535.

This behaviour is usually implemented by the Joystick module and will only work if this module is loaded and suitable hardware is present. If this is absent, the function will result in a Command not recognised error.

Technical details

The ADVAL keyword uses OS_Byte 128.

Example

```
IF ADVAL(-1)=0 THEN PROCinput
```

AND

Operator performing logical AND or bitwise AND.

Syntax

relational AND *relational*

Arguments

Relational expressions, or bit values to be ANDed.

Result

The bitwise AND of the arguments. Corresponding bits in the integer arguments are ANDed to produce the result. Hence a bit in the result is one if both of the corresponding bits of the arguments are one. Otherwise it is zero.

If used to combine relational values, AND's arguments should be either TRUE (−1) or FALSE (0). Otherwise, unexpected results may occur. For example, 2 and 4 are both true (non-zero), but 2 AND 4 yields FALSE (zero).

Examples

```
a = x AND y      : REM a is set to binary AND of x and y
PRINT var AND 3 : REM print lowest 2 bits of var
IF day=4 AND month$="April" THEN PRINT "Happy birthday"
IF temp>10 AND NOT windy THEN PROCgo_out ELSE PROCstay_in
REPEAT
  a=a+1
  b=b-1
UNTIL a>10 AND b<0
isadog = feet=4 AND tails=1 AND hairy
```

APPEND

Command to append a file to a BASIC program.

Syntax

```
APPEND pathname
```

Argument

pathname is a string expression which should evaluate to the pathname of a valid file.

Purpose

The file specified is added to the end of the BASIC program currently in memory. If the file contains a BASIC program, the line numbers and any references to them in the added section are renumbered so that they start after the last line of the current program.

Examples

```
APPEND ":0.lib"
APPEND second_half$
```

ASC

Function returning the ASCII code of the first character in a string.

Syntax

ASC *factor*

Argument

String of length 0 to 255 characters.

Result

ASCII code of the first character of the argument in the range 0 to 255, or −1 if the argument is a null string.

Examples

```
x2=ASC(name$)
IF code >= ASC("a") AND code <= ASC("z") THEN PRINT "Lower
case"
```

ASN

Function returning the arc-sine of its numeric argument.

Syntax

    ASN factor

Argument

Numeric between −1 and 1 inclusive.

Result

Real in the range $-\pi/2$ to $+\pi/2$ radians, being the inverse sine of the argument.

Examples

    PRINT ASN(opposite/hypotenuse)
    angle=DEG(ASN(0.2213))

ATN

Function returning the arc-tangent of its numeric argument.

Syntax

    ATN factor

Argument

Any numeric.

Result

Real in the range $-\pi/2$ to $+\pi/2$ radians, being the inverse tangent of the argument.

Examples

    ang = DEG(ATN(sin/cos))
    PRINT "The slope is ";ATN(opposite/adjacent)

AUTO

Command initiating automatic line numbering.

Syntax

```
AUTO [start][,step]
```

Arguments

start is an integer constant in the range 0 to 65279 and is the first line to be generated automatically. It defaults to 10.

step is an integer constant in the range 1 to 65279 and is the amount by which the line numbers increase when Return is pressed. If omitted, 10 is assumed.

Purpose

AUTO is used when entering program lines to produce a line number automatically, so that you do not have to type them yourself. To end automatic line numbering use Esc. AUTO will stop if the line number becomes greater than 65279.

Examples

```
AUTO
AUTO 1000
AUTO 12,2
```

BEAT

Function returning the current beat value.

Syntax

    BEAT

Result

An integer giving the current beat value. This is the value yielded by the beat counter as it counts from zero to the number set by BEATS at a rate determined by TEMPO. When it reaches its limit it resets to zero. Synchronisation between sound channels is performed with respect to the last reset of the beat counter.

Example

    PRINT BEAT

BEATS

Function returning or statement altering the beat counter.

Syntax

as a statement:

(1) BEATS *expression*

as a function:

(2) BEATS

Arguments (1)

expression gives the value 1 higher than that which the beat counter increments to, i.e. it counts from 0 to *expression*–1. This counter is used in conjunction with the SOUND and TEMPO statements to synchronise sound outputs from different sound channels.

Result (2)

An integer giving the current value of the beat limit, as set by a BEATS statement, or 0 if no counting is currently being performed.

Examples

```
BEATS 2000
PRINT BEATS
```

BGET#

Function returning the next byte from a file.

Syntax

    BGET# *factor*

Argument

A channel number returned by an OPEN*xx* function.

Result

The ASCII code of the character read (at position PTR#) from the file, in the range 0 to 255.

Notes

PTR# is updated to point to the next character in the file. If the last character in the file has been read, EOF# for the channel will be TRUE. The next BGET# will return an undefined value and the one after that will produce an `End of file on file handle` *nn* error.

Examples

    char%=BGET# channel
    char$=CHR$(BGET#fileno)

    WHILE NOT EOF# channel
      char% = BGET# channel
      PROCprocess(char%)
    ENDWHILE

BPUT#

Statement to write a byte or a string to a file.

Syntax

    (1) BPUT#*factor*,*numeric-expression*
    (2) BPUT#*factor*,*string-expression*[;]

Arguments (1)

factor is a channel number as returned by an OPEN*xx* function.
numeric-expression is truncated to an integer 0 to 255, and is the ASCII code of the character to be sent to the file.

Arguments (2)

factor is a channel number as returned by an OPEN*xx* function.
string-expression is a string containing 0 to 255 characters. The ASCII codes of all the characters in the string are sent to the file. This is followed by a newline (ASCII value 10), unless the statement is terminated by a ; (semi-colon).

Notes

PTR# is updated to point to the next character to be written. If the end of the file is reached, the length (EXT#) increases too. It is only possible to use BPUT# with OPENUP and OPENOUT files, not OPENIN ones.

Examples

```
BPUT#outputfile,byte%
BPUT#channel,ASC(MID$(name$,pos,1))
BPUT#file,"Hello"
BPUT#chan,A$+B$;
```

BY

Optional part of MOVE, DRAW, POINT and FILL statements.

Syntax

See the above-mentioned keywords.

Purpose

The BY keyword changes the effect of certain graphics statements. In particular it indicates that the coordinates given in the statement are relative rather than absolute. For example, POINT BY 100,100 means plot a point at coordinates displaced by (100,100) from the current graphics cursor position, rather than a point which is at (100,100).

In terms of its effect at the VDU driver level, BY makes BASIC use the relative forms of the appropriate OS_Plot calls, instead of the absolute ones.

Examples

```
MOVE BY 4*x%,4*y%
POINT BY 100,0
DRAW BY x%*16, y%=4
FILL BY x%, y%
```

CALL

Statement to execute a machine code or assembly language subroutine.

Syntax

```
CALL expression[,variable...]
```

Arguments

expression is the address of the routine to be called. The parameter variables, if present, may be of any type. They are accessed through a parameter block which BASIC sets up. The format of this parameter block and of the variables accessed through it is described below.

Purpose

CALL can be used to enter a machine code program from BASIC. Before the routine is called, the ARM's registers are set up as follows:

R0	A%
R1	B%
R2	C%
R3	D%
R4	E%
R5	F%
R6	G%
R7	H%
R8	Pointer to BASIC's workspace (ARGP)
R9	Pointer to list of l-values and types of the parameters
R10	Number of parameters
R11	Pointer to BASIC's string accumulator (STRACC)
R12	BASIC's LINE pointer (points to the character after the CALL statement)
R13	Pointer to BASIC's full, descending stack
R14	Link back to BASIC and environment information pointer.

The called routine does not need to preserve any of these registers except R13.

Format of the CALL parameter block

R9 points to a list giving details of each variable passed as a parameter to CALL. For each variable, two word-aligned words are used. The first one is the l-value of the parameter. This is the address in memory in which the value of the variable is stored.

The second word is the type of variable. This list is in reverse order, so the l-value pointed to by R9 is that of the last parameter in the list. The pointer to the list is always valid, even when if the list is null (i.e. R10 contains 0). The possible types are as follows:

Type	BASIC	l-value points to
&00	?*factor*	byte-aligned byte
&04	!*factor*	byte-aligned word
&04	name%	word-aligned word
&04	name%(*n*)	word-aligned word
&05	|*factor*	byte-aligned FP value (5 bytes)
&05	name	byte-aligned FP value (5 bytes)
&05	name(*n*)	byte-aligned FP value (5 bytes)
&08	|*factor*	word-aligned FP value (8 bytes)
&08	name	word-aligned FP value (8 bytes)
&08	name(*n*)	word-aligned FP value (8 bytes)
&80	name$	byte-aligned SIB (5 bytes)
&80	name$(*n*)	byte-aligned SIB (5 bytes)
&81	$*factor*	byte-aligned byte-string (CR-terminated)
&100+&04	name%()	word-aligned array pointer
&100+&05	name()	word-aligned array pointer
&100+&08	name()	word-aligned array pointer
&100+&80	name$()	word-aligned array pointer

For types &00, &04, &05 and &08, the address points to the actual byte, the four-byte integer, the five-byte floating point value or the eight-byte floating point value.

For type &80, the address points to a five-byte 'string information block'. The first four bytes are a byte-aligned word pointing to the first character of the string itself, which is on a word boundary, followed by a byte containing the length of the string.

For types &100+*n* the value points to a word-aligned word. If the array has not been allocated, or has been made LOCAL but not DIMed, this word contains a value less than 16. Otherwise, the word points to a word-aligned list of integer subscript sizes (the values in the DIM statement plus 1) terminated by a zero word, followed by a word which contains the total number of entries in the array, followed by the zeroth element of the array. For example, consider the following program:

CALL

```
10 DIM a(10,20)
20 a = 12.3
30 a$ = "char"
40 ...
100 CALL code, a, a(), a$
```

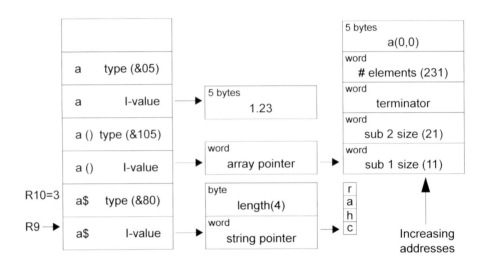

The diagram above shows the resulting parameter block and other data items when code is called. The access method into the arrays is given by the following algorithm:

```
position = 0
number = 0
REPEAT
  IF subscript(number) > array(number) THEN fault
  number = number+1
  IF number<>total THEN position = (position+subscript) *
array(number)
UNTIL no_more_subscripts
position = position*size(array)
```

This means that the last subscript references adjacent elements. For a simple two dimensional array DIM A(LIMI−1,LIMJ−1) the address of A(I,J) is

   (I*LIMJ+J)*size+base_address

MOV PC,R14 returns to the BASIC calling program. If V is set on return an error will be signalled, with R0 being treated as a pointer to a standard RISC OS error block. However, R14 also points to an array of useful values:

Offset	Name	Meaning
-&04	BASICID	BASIC identity word
&00	RETURN	Return address to BASIC

The following are words containing a word-aligned offset from ARGP (R8):

Offset	Name	Meaning
&04	STRACC	String accumulator (256 bytes long)
&08	PAGE	Current program PAGE
&0C	TOP	Current program TOP
&10	LOMEM	Current start of variable storage
&14	HIMEM	Current stack end (i.e. highest stack location)
&18	MEMLIMIT	Limit of available memory
&1C	FSA	Free space start (end of variables/stack limit)
&20	TALLY	Value of COUNT
&24	TRACEF	TRACEFILE handle (or 0 if no file being traced to)
&28	ESCWORD	Exception flag word (contains escflg, trcflg)
&2C	WIDTHLOC	Value of WIDTH−1

Branches to internal BASIC routines:

Offset	Name	Meaning
&30	VARIND	Get value of l-value
&34	STOREA	Store value into l-value
&38	STSTORE	Store string into type 128 strings
&3C	LVBLNK	Convert variable name string to l-value address and type
&40	CREATE	Create new variable
&44	EXPR	Use expression analyser on string
&48	MATCH	Lexically analyse source string to destination string
&4C	TOKENADDR	Pointer to string for given token
&50	END	End of list, a zero word

In the following (**BASIC V only**), R0..R3 contain an expanded floating point value. R9 points to a packed five-byte floating point value accessed through the | operator:

Offset	Name	Meaning
&54	9	number of extra routines
&58	FSTA	[R9] = R0..R3
&5C	FLDA	R0..R3 = [R9]
&60	FADD	R0..R3 = [R9] + (R0..R3)
&64	FSUB	R0..R3 = [R9] − (R0..R3)
&68	FMUL	R0..R3 = (R0..R3) * [R9]
&6C	FDIV	R0..R3 = [R9] / (R0..R3)
&70	FLOAT	R0..R3 = FLOAT(R0) (R0 contains an integer on entry)
&74	FIX	R0 = FIX(R0..R3) (R0 contains an integer on exit)
&78	FSQRT	R0..R3 = SQR(R0..R3)

CALL

The word at address [R14] is a branch instruction which returns you to the BASIC interpreter. The word before it, [R14,#–4] identifies that the code is running from BASIC. The current BASIC interpreter provides &BA51C005, and the bottom three nybbles (&005) denote that the calling standard follows the one shown here (to allow for possible future changes). The words which follow it contain useful addresses which are not absolute, but are offsets from the contents of the ARGP register, R8.

The first offset word, at [R14,#4], gives the location of the string accumulator, STRACC, where string results are kept. Thus if you execute

```
LDR     R0,[R14,#4]     ;Get STRACC offset from R8
ADD     R0,R8,R0        ;Add offset to ARGP
```

R0 will give the base address of the string accumulator. (Actually, the address of STRACC is also in R11 on entry, so this isn't a particularly good example.) Similarly, to load the pointer to the end of free space into R0, you would use:

```
LDR     R0,[R14,#&1C]   ;Get FSA offset from R8
LDR     R0,[R8, R0]     ;De-reference it
```

Although the word referenced through the TRACEF offset is the TRACEFILE handle, the four that follow it are also used. They contain respectively:

[TRACEF+4]	LOCALARLIST	a pointer to the list of local arrays
[TRACEF+8]	INSTALLLIST	a pointer to the list of installed libraries
[TRACEF+12]	LIBRARYLIST	a pointer to the list of transient libraries
[TRACEF+16]	OVERPTR	a pointer to the overlay structure

The first of these is probably not very useful, but the other three allow routines to access the libraries that have been loaded. For example, a 'find' routine would be able to find a procedure no matter where it was defined (which LIST IF can't do).

Libraries are stored as a word, which is a pointer to the next library (0 denoting the end of the list). The word is followed immediately by the BASIC program which forms the library.

Before an OVERLAY statement has been executed, OVERPTR contains 0. After a statement such as OVERLAY a$(), it contains a pointer to the following structure:

OVERPTR+&00	Pointer to base of OVERLAY array, i.e. a$(0)
OVERPTR+&04	Index of current OVERLAY file (or –1 if none loaded)
OVERPTR+&08	Total allowed size of OVERLAY area
OVERPTR+&0C	Start of current OVERLAY file in memory.

...

After the word offsets come the branches useful to BASIC routines. For example, to call STOREA, whose branch is at offset &34 from R14, you might use:

```
STMFD  R13!, {R14}       ;Save BASIC return address
MOV    R10, R14          ;Save pointer to branches
MOV    R14, PC           ;Return to the subsequent address
ADD    PC, R10, #&34     ;Do the 'branch'
...
LDMFD  R13!, {PC}        ;Return to BASIC
```

Note that MOV R14,PC works because of the pipeline offset, it will set R14 to point to the instruction following the ADD instruction.

If your code has a lot of branch calls, it may be convenient to set up a branch table to which you can BL:

```
STMFD  R13!, {R14}
MOV    R9, R14  ;keep environment pointer
...
BL     BASIC_STOREA
...
LDMFD  R13!, {PC}
.BASIC_VARIND     ADD PC, R9, #&30
.BASIC_STOREA     ADD PC, R9, #&34
.BASIC_STSTORE    ADD PC, R9, #&38
.BASIC_LVBLNK     ADD PC, R9, #&3C
.BASIC_CREATE     ADD PC, R9, #&40
.BASIC_EXPR       ADD PC, R9, #&44
.BASIC_MATCH      ADD PC, R9, #&48
.BASIC_TOKENADDR  ADD PC, R9, #&4C
```

The internal routines are only guaranteed to work in ARM user mode. The following functions are provided:

VARIND

Entry with R0:

R0 = Address of l-value, i.e. where to load the variable from
R9 = Type of l-value, as in CALL parameter block
R12 = LINE

Returns with R0..R3 as the value, R9 the type of the value as follows:

R9	Type	Location of value
0	String	STRACC, R2 points to end (|R2|–STRACC is length)
&40000000	Integer	R0
&80000000	Float	R0..R3 (or F0 if using BASIC64, D0 if using BASICVFP)

CALL

Uses no other registers (including stack). Unless used for the output value, R0-R3 are corrupted. Possible error if asked to take value of an array fred(): will need R12 valid for this error to be reported correctly.

When floating point values are returned/required in R0..R3, the format is as follows:

R0	=	32-bit mantissa, normalised (so bit 31 = 1)
R1	=	Exponent in excess-128 form
R2	=	Undefined
R3	=	Sign. 0 $\Rightarrow$ positive, &80000000 $\Rightarrow$ negative

This is provided for information only. We reserve the right to change this format; you should treat R0..R3 as a single item, without regard to the constituent parts.

STOREA

Entry with value in R0..R3, as appropriate to the type of value in R9. Strings must be located within STRACC – use STSTORE for strings which are not. For BASIC64, floating point values will be in F0. For BASICVFP, floating point values will be in D0.

R4	=	Address of l-value (where to store the value)
R5	=	Type of l-value (as in CALL parameter block)
R8	=	ARGP
R9	=	Type of value
R12	=	LINE (for errors)
R13	=	Stack pointer (for free space check)

Converts between integer and floating point numbers, or produces an error if conversion is impossible.

Returns with R0-R7 and R9 destroyed. BASIC64 may also destroy F0-F2, F7. BASICVFP may also destroy F0-F2, F7, D0-D15.

STSTORE

This stores a string into a string variable. Entry with:

R2	=	Length (i.e. address of byte beyond the last one)
R3	=	Address of start of string
R4	=	Address of l-value
R8	=	ARGP
R12	=	LINE (for error reporting)
R13	=	Stack pointer (for free space check)

The string must start on a word boundary and the length must be 255 or less.

Uses R0, R1, R5, R6, R7. Preserves input registers. Stack not used.

LVBLNK

This routine looks up a variable from the name pointed to by R8.

On entry:

R8	=	ARGP
R11	=	Pointer to start of name
R12	=	LINE (many errors possible, such as subscript error in array)
R13	=	Stack (may call EXPR to evaluate subscripts)

The string is processed to read one variable name and provide an address and type which can be given to VARIND.

If a valid variable name (or more precisely l-value) was found:

Z flag	=	0
R0	=	Address of l-value
R9	=	Type of l-value
R11	=	Points to next character after the end of the accepted name

If a valid variable was not found:

Z flag	=	1
C flag	=	1 if there is no way the string was a variable name (e.g. %Q)
C flag	=	0 Could be a variable but hasn't been created (e.g. A)

Other registers set up for a subsequent call to CREATE.

If the name contains BASIC keywords, for example `array%(SIN PI)`, then it must be tokenised using MATCH first.

Uses all registers except R8 and R12. For BASIC64, F0-F2 and F7 may also be used. For BASICVFP, F0-F2, F7 and D0-D15 may also be used.

CREATE

This creates a variable. Input is the failure of LVBLNK to find something. Thus we have:

R3	=	Second character of name or 0
R4	=	Points to start of the rest of the name
R8	=	ARGP
R9	=	Contains the number of zero bytes on the end
R10	=	First character of name
R11	=	Points to the end of the name
R12	=	LINE
R13	=	Stack pointer

It is recommended that CREATE is only called immediately after a failed LVBLNK.

CALL

CREATE uses all registers. Returns result as LVBLNK. The LVBLNK and CREATE routines can be combined together to provide a routine which checks for a variable to assign to, and creates it if necessary:

```
STMFD     R13!,{R14}       ;Save return address
MOV       R6,R14           ;Set R6 to info pointer
MOV       R14,PC           ;Set return address
ADD       PC,R6,#&3C       ;Look-up name (LVBLNK)
LDMNEFD   R13!,{PC}        ;Return if found
LDMCSFD   R13!,{PC}        ;Or illegal name
MOV       R14,PC           ;Set return address
ADD       PC,R6,#&40       ;Create a new var (CREATE)
LDMFD     R13!,{PC}        ;Return
```

EXPR

This evaluates an expression pointed to by R11. On entry:

R8	=	ARGP
R11	=	Pointer to start of string
R12	=	LINE
R13	=	Stack pointer

EXPR stops after reading one expression (like those in the PRINT statement).

The value is returned in the same manner as VARIND. On exit:

Z flag = 1 ⇒ the expression was a string
Z flag = 0 ⇒ the expression was a number
     N flag = 1 ⇒ expression was a floating point number
     N flag = 0 ⇒ expression was an integer
R9 = Type
R11 = Pointer to next character after the expression, which will be to the next expression (if any) if it is, for example, a comma-separated list

Uses all registers except R8 and R12. For BASIC64, F0-F2 and F7 may also be used. For BASICVFP, F0-F2, F7 and D0-D15 may also be used.

The status found in the Z and N flags on exit can be recreated by executing the instruction `TEQ R9,#0`.

One useful thing about EXPR is that it enables the machine code to call a BASIC routine. You do this by evaluating a string which has a call to a user-defined function in it. For example, the string you evaluate might be `"FNinput"`. The function could perform some task which is tedious to do in machine code, such as input a floating point number.

One slight complication is that the string to be evaluated must have been tokenised already, so you must either call MATCH described below, or store the string with the tokenised form of FN (the byte &A4).

MATCH

This routine takes a text string and tokenises it to another string. Strings passed to EXPR and LVBLNK must be tokenised first if they contain any BASIC keywords. On entry:

R1 = Points to the source string (terminated by ASCII 10 or 13)
R2 = Points to the destination string
R3 = MODE
R4 = CONSTA
R13 = Stack pointer

Note that MATCH does not need ARGP or LINE.

The MODE value is 0 for left-mode (before an = sign, or at the start of a statement) and 1 for right-mode (in an expression). The difference is in the way that BASIC tokenises the pseudo-variables. Each of these has two tokens, one for when it is used as a statement (e.g. TIME=...) and one when it is used as a function (PRINT TIME). As you will generally use MATCH to tokenise an expression string, you will use MODE = 1.

The CONSTA value is 0 if you do not want BASIC to convert integers which could be line numbers (in the range 0 to 65279) into internal format, and 1 if you do. Internal format consists of the token &8D followed by three bytes which contain the encoded line number. A property of these bytes is that they lie in the range 64 to 127, and therefore do not contain control codes or tokens.

Encoded constants are used for line numbers after GOTO, GOSUB, RESTORE, THEN and ELSE keywords. Because they are of fixed length, the program can be renumbered without having to move program lines about. Because they don't contain special characters, certain BASIC search operations (e.g. for the ELSE in a single-line IF) are speeded up.

Both MODE and CONSTA will be updated during the use of the routine. For example, GOTO will set CONSTA to &8D to read the line number, PRINT will change MODE to 1 to read an expression. The table below summarises the setting of MODE and CONSTA:

MODE	CONSTA	Meaning
0	0	Tokenise a statement
0	&8D	Used to read line number at the start of a line
1	0	Tokenise an expression
1	&8D	Tokenise an expression after GOTO etc.

CALL

The routine uses R0 to R5.

On exit, R1 and R2 are left pointing one byte beyond the terminating CR codes of the strings.

R5 contains status information, it can usually be disregarded: values greater than or equal to &1000 imply mismatched brackets. Bit 8 set implies that a number which was too large to be encoded using &8D (i.e. was greater than 65279) was found. If (R5 AND 255) = 1 then mismatched string quotes were found.

> Note: if the first item in the source string is a line number and CONSTA is set on entry, the &8D byte will not be inserted into the destination string, but a space will be left for it. It is safe for the source and destination strings to be the same, as long as the destination never becomes longer than the source (which CONSTA line numbers can do.)

TOKENADDR

This routine converts a token value into a pointer to the text string representing it. On entry:

R0   =   The token value
R12 =   Pointer to next byte of token string

The value of R12 is only used when two-byte tokens are required. No other registers are used or required.

Returns R1 as a pointer to the first character of the string, terminated by a byte whose value is &7F or greater. R0 is set to the address of the start of the token table itself. R12 will have been incremented by one if a two-byte token has been used.

FSTA

Store a four-word FP value into a five-byte variable. On entry:

R0..R3 =   Source floating pointer value
R9   =   Pointer to destination value

On exit:

R2   =   Altered (but this doesn't affect the FP value)

No errors. Stack not used.

FLDA

Load a five-byte variable into a four-word FP value. On entry:

R9   =   Pointer to source value

On exit:

R0..R3 = Loaded FP value

No errors. Stack not used.

FADD/FMUL

Add/multiply the four-word FP value in R0..R3 by the variable at [R9]. On entry:

R0..R3 = Source FP value
R9 = Pointer to five-byte variable.

On exit:

R0..R3 = Added/multiplied by [R9]
R4..R7 = Corrupted

Overflow errors possible. Stack not used.

FSUB/FDIV

Subtract R0..R3 from [R9] or divide [R9] by R0..R3, with the result in R0..R3. On entry:

R0..R3 = FP value
R9 = Pointer to five-byte variable.

On exit:

R0..R3 = [R9] minus old value or [R9] / old value
R4..R7 = Corrupted

Overflow errors possible. Divide by zero possible for FDIV. Stack not used.

FLOAT

Convert integer to four-word floating point value. On entry:

R0 = Integer

On exit:

R0..R3 = Floated version
R9 = &80000000 (floating type code)

No overflow possible. Stack not used.

FIX

Convert four-word floating point value to an integer. On entry:

CALL

R0..R3 = Floating point value

On exit:

R0 = Fixed version (rounded towards 0)
R1..R3 = Corrupted
R9 = &40000000 (integer type code)

Overflow error possible. Stack not used.

FSQRT

Take the square root of the floating point number in R0..R3. On entry:

R0..R3 = Floating point value

On exit:

R0..R3 = SQR(old value)
R0..R7 = Corrupt

Negative root error possible. Stack not used.

BBC/Master compatible calls

In BASIC V (but not BASIC VI) if the CALL statement is used with an address which corresponds to a MOS entry point on the BBC Micro/Acorn Electron/Master series machines and there are no other parameters, then BASIC treats the call as if it had been made from one of those machines. The way in which the registers are initialised is then as follows:

R0   A%
R1   X%
R2   Y%
C flag C% (bit 0)

This means that programs written to run on earlier machines using legal MOS calls can continue to work. For example, the sequence

```
  10 osbyte=&FFF4
1000 A%=138
1010 X%=0
1020 Y%=65
1030 CALL osbyte
```

will be interpreted as the equivalent SYS OS_Byte call:

```
1000 SYS "OS_Byte",138,0,65
```

This facility is provided for backwards compatibility only. You should not use it in new programs. Also, you must be careful that any machine code you assemble in a program does not lie in the address range &FFCE to &FFF7; otherwise when you call it, it might be mistaken for a call to an old MOS routine.

Examples

```
CALL invertMatrix,a()
CALL sampleWaveform,start%,end%,values%()
```

CASE

Statement marking the start of a CASE ... OF ... WHEN ... OTHERWISE ... ENDCASE construct. It must be the first statement on the line.

Syntax

```
CASE expression OF
WHEN expression [,expression...] [:statements...]
[statements]
[WHEN ...]
OTHERWISE [statements...]
[statements...]
ENDCASE
```

Arguments

expression can be any numeric or string expression. The value of *expression* is compared with the values of each of the expressions in the list following the first WHEN statement. If a match is found, then the block of statements following the WHEN down to either the next WHEN or OTHERWISE or ENDCASE is executed. Then control moves on to the statement following the ENDCASE. If there is no match, then the next WHEN is used, if it exists. OTHERWISE is equivalent to a WHEN but matches any value.

Examples

```
CASE A% OF
CASE Y*2 + X*3 OF
CASE GET$ OF
```

CHAIN

Statement to load and run a BASIC program.

Syntax

    CHAIN pathname

Argument

pathname should evaluate to the pathname of a valid BASIC file.

Notes

A filing system error may be produced if, for example, the file specified cannot be found.

When the program is loaded, all existing variables are lost (except the system integer variables and installed libraries).

Examples

    CHAIN "partB"
    CHAIN a$+"2"

CHR$

Function returning the character corresponding to an ASCII code.

Syntax

```
CHR$ factor
```

Argument

An integer in the range 0 to 255.

Result

A single-character string whose ASCII code is the argument.

Examples

```
PRINT CHR$(code)
lower$=CHR$(ASC(upper$) OR &20)
```

CIRCLE

Statement to draw a circle.

Syntax

CIRCLE [FILL] expression1,expression2,expression3

Arguments

The expressions are integers in the range −32768 to +32767. The first two values give the x and y coordinates of the centre of the circle. The third gives the radius. CIRCLE produces a circle outline, whereas CIRCLE FILL plots a solid circle. The current graphics foreground colour and action are used.

Notes

In both cases, the position of the graphics cursor is updated to lie at a position on the circumference which has an x coordinate of *expression1* + *expression3* and a y coordinate of *expression2*. The 'previous graphics cursor' position (as used by, for example, triangle plotting) will be updated to lie at the centre of the circle plotted.

Examples

```
CIRCLE 640,512,50
CIRCLE FILL RND(1278),RND(1022),RND(200)+50
```

CLEAR

Statement to remove all program variables.

Syntax

    CLEAR

Purpose

When this statement is executed, all variables are removed and so become undefined. In addition, any currently active procedures, subroutines, loops, and so on are forgotten, and LIBRARY and OVERLAY libraries are lost. The exceptions to this are the system integer variables and INSTALLed libraries which still remain.

CLG

Statement to clear the graphics viewport to the graphics background colour, using the graphics background action.

Syntax

    CLG

Examples

    CLG

    MODE 1
    GCOL 130
    VDU 24,200;200;1080;824;
    CLG

CLOSE#

Statement to close an open file.

Syntax

    CLOSE# factor

Argument

A channel number as returned by the OPEN*xx* function. If zero is used all open files on the current filing system are closed. Otherwise, only the file with the channel number specified is closed.

Notes

You should not use the CLOSE#0 form within programs, as other programs may be relying on files remaining open. You should only use it as an immediate command, and possibly in a program during its development stage.

Purpose

Closing a file ensures that its contents are updated on whatever medium is being used. This is necessary as a certain amount of buffering is used to make the transfer of data between computer and mass-storage device more efficient. Closing a file, therefore, releases a buffer for use by another file.

Examples

    CLOSE#indexFile
    CLOSE#0

CLS

Statement to clear the text viewport to the text background colour.

Syntax

    CLS

Notes

CLS also resets COUNT to zero and moves the text cursor to its home position, which is normally the top left of the text window.

Examples

    CLS

    MODE "X640 Y480 C4"
    COLOUR 129
    VDU 28,4,28,35,4
    CLS

COLOUR (COLOR)

Statement to set the text colours or alter the palette settings.

Syntax

```
(1) COLOUR expression [TINT expression]
(2) COLOUR expression,expression
(3) COLOUR expression,expression,expression
(4) COLOUR [OF expr,expr,expr] [ON expr,expr,expr]
(5) COLOUR [OF expr] [ON expr]
(6) COLOUR expr,expr,expr,expr[,expr]
```

Arguments (1)

expression is an integer in the range 0 to 255. The range 0 to 127 sets the text foreground colour. Adding 128 to this (i.e. 128 to 255) sets the text background colour. The colour is treated MOD the number of colours in the current mode. The argument is the logical colour. For a list of the default logical colours, see the chapter entitled *Screen modes* on page 107.

The optional TINT is only effective in VIDC1-style 256-colour modes. It selects the amount of white to be added to the colour. The value can lie in the range 0 to 255, with only the values 0, 64, 128 and 192 currently being used to obtain different whiteness levels. Colours in VIDC1-style 256-colour modes are in the range 0 to 63.

Arguments (2)

The first expression is an integer in the range 0 to 15 giving the logical colour number. The second expression is an integer in the range 0 to 15 giving the actual colour to be displayed when the logical colour is used. The actual colour numbers correspond to the default colours available in 16-colour modes: eight steady colours and eight flashing colours. The colour list is given in the chapter entitled *Screen modes* on page 107.

This form of the command sets the palette, so any changes are visible immediately.

Arguments (3)

The text foreground colour is set using the three expressions which are integers in the range 0 to 255 giving the amount of red, green and blue. The actual colour selected will be the closest colour available in the current mode and palette.

Arguments (4)

The text foreground colour is set using the three expressions following OF, and the text background colour is set using the three expressions following ON. In each case the expressions are integers in the range 0 to 255 giving the amount of red, green and blue, and either the ON or OFF part may be omitted. The actual colour selected will be the closest colour available in the current mode and palette.

Arguments (5)

This form allows the foreground and/or background colour to be set using colour numbers. The expression following OF is an integer giving the foreground colour number, and the expression following ON is an integer giving the background colour number.

Arguments (6)

This form of the command sets the palette. The first expression is an integer in the range 0 to 255 giving the logical colour number. The next three expressions are integers in the range 0 to 255 giving the amount of red, green and blue which are to be assigned to that logical colour. The optional fifth expression is an integer in the range 0 to 255 giving the supremacy value for this palette entry – this is used for alpha blending, and is only supported on certain types of graphics hardware.

Notes

The keyword is listed as COLOUR in programs, even if it was typed in using the alternative spelling.

In all modes the default state, before any changes to the palette, dictates that colour 0 is black and colour 63 is white.

Only colours 0 and 1 are unique in two-colour modes. After that the cycle repeats. Similarly, only colours 0, 1, 2 and 3 are distinct in the four-colour modes.

In Wimp-based programs, you should use the call `Wimp_SetPalette` to control the palette.

Technical Details

(1) sets the colour and tint using VDU 17, for (3) and (4) the colour is set using `ColourTrans_SetTextColour`, and for (5) `OS_SetColour` is used. (6) sets the palette by using VDU 19 if it has four parameters and by using PaletteV with reason code 2 if it has five.

COLOUR (COLOR)

History

(3) was added in version 1.06. (4) and (5) were added in version 1.34. The optional fifth parameter for (6) was added in version 1.39.

Examples

```
COLOUR 128+1 : REM text background colour = 1
COLOUR 1,5 : REM logical colour 1 = colour 5 (magenta)
COLOUR 1,255,255,255 : REM logical colour 1 = white
```

COS

Function returning the cosine of its numeric argument.

Syntax

COS *factor*

Argument

factor is an angle in radians.

Result

Real between −1 and +1 inclusive.

Notes

For BASIC V if the argument is outside the range −8388608 to +8388608 radians, it is impossible to determine how many πs to subtract. The error `Accuracy lost in sine/cosine/tangent` is generated. For BASIC VI the range is larger, from approximately −6E9 to +6E9 radians, and outside this range the error `Floating point exception: invalid operation` is generated.

Examples

```
PRINT COS(RAD(45))
adjacent = hypotenuse*COS(angle)
```

COUNT

Function returning the number of characters printed since the last newline.

Syntax

    COUNT

Result

Positive integer, giving the number of characters output since the last newline was generated by BASIC.

Notes

COUNT is reset to zero every time a carriage return is printed (which may happen automatically if a non-zero WIDTH is being used). It is incremented every time a character is output by PRINT, INPUT or REPORT, but not when output by VDU or any of the graphics commands. COUNT is also reset to zero by CLS and MODE.

Examples

```
REPEAT PRINT " ";
UNTIL COUNT=20
chars = COUNT
```

CRUNCH

Command to strip various spaces from a program.

Syntax

```
CRUNCH expression
```

Argument

expression is an integer in which the lowest 5-bits are significant:

Bit	Meaning
0	strips out all spaces before statements.
1	strips out all spaces within statements.
2	strips out all REM statements, except those on the first line.
3	strips out all empty statements.
4	strips out all empty lines.

Notes

The interpreter has been optimised for fully CRUNCHed programs.

`CRUNCH %10` may make a program uneditable.

If the system variable `BASIC$Crunch` exists with any value, programs run with `-quit` set will be automatically CRUNCHed with CRUNCH %1111, as will LIBRARY subprograms. OVERLAY libraries will not be CRUNCHed.

Examples

```
CRUNCH %1101
CRUNCH %10011
```

DATA

Passive statement marking the position of data in the program.

Syntax

DATA [expression][,expression], etc

Arguments

The expressions may be of any type and range, and are only evaluated when a READ statement requires them.

Notes

The way in which DATA is interpreted depends on the type of variable in the READ statement. A numeric READ evaluates the data as an expression, whereas a string READ treats the data as a literal string. Leading spaces in the data item are ignored, but trailing spaces (except for the last data item on the line) are counted. If it is necessary to have leading spaces, or a comma or quote in the data item, it must be put between quotation marks. For example:

100 DATA "   HI","A,B,", """ABCD"

If an attempt is made to execute a DATA statement, BASIC treats it as a REM. In order to be recognised by BASIC, the DATA statement, like other passive statements, should be the first item on a line.

Items in a DATA statement are not tokenised so, for example, PI/2 will generate an error if used with a numeric READ. Read the item as a string and use EVAL to get the numeric value.

Examples

DATA Jan,Feb,Mar,Apr,May,Jun,Jul,Aug,Sep,Oct,Nov,Dec
DATA 3.26,4,4.3,0

DEF

Passive statement defining a function or procedure.

Syntax

 (1) DEF FN*proc-part*
 (2) DEF PROC*proc-part*

where *proc-part* has the form *identifier*[(*parameter-list*)].

The optional parameters, which must be enclosed between round brackets and separated by commas, may be of any type. For example: `parm`, `parm%`, `parm$`. Any parameter may be preceded by RETURN to use value-result passing instead of simple value passing. In addition, whole arrays may be passed as parameters, e.g. `a()`, `a$()`.

Purpose

The DEF statement marks the first line of a user-defined function or procedure, and also indicates which parameters are required and their types. The parameters are local to the function or procedure (except for arrays), and are used within it to stand for the values of the actual parameters used when it was called.

Notes

Function and procedure definitions should be placed at the end of the program, so that they cannot be executed except when called by the appropriate PROC statement or FN function. The DEF statement should be the first item on the line. If not, it will not be found.

Examples

```
DEF FNmean(a,b)
DEF PROCinit
DEF PROCthrow_dice(d%,tries,RETURN mesg$)
DEF PROCarray_determinant(A())
```

DEG

Function returning the number of degrees of its radian argument.

Syntax

```
DEG factor
```

Argument

Any numeric value.

Result

A real equal to $180*n/\pi$ where n is the argument's value.

Examples

```
angle=DEG(ATN(a))
PRINT DEG(PI/4)
```

DELETE

Command to delete a section of the program.

Syntax

DELETE *integer*, *integer*

Arguments

Integer constants in the range zero to 65279. They give the first and last line to be deleted respectively. If the first line number is greater than the second, no lines are deleted. To delete just a single line the DELETE command is not necessary. Instead type the line number and press Return.

Examples

```
DELETE 5,22
DELETE 110,150
```

DIM

Statement declaring arrays or reserving storage.
Function returning information about an array.

Syntax

```
DIM dim-part [,dim-part] etc
```

where *dim-part* is:

(1) *identifier*[% or $](*expression*[,*expression*] etc)

or

(2) *numeric-variable expression*
(3) *numeric-variable* LOCAL *expression*

or as a function:

(4) DIM(*array*)
(5) DIM(*array*,*expression*)

Argument (1)

The *identifier* can be any real, integer or string variable name. The expressions are integers which should be greater than or equal to zero. They declare the upper bound of the subscripts; the lower bound is always zero.

This is the way to declare arrays in BASIC. They may be multi-dimensional: the bounds are limited by the amount of memory available to BASIC, with an absolute maximum total elements in all dimensions of 16,777,215 (&FFFFFE). Numeric arrays are initialised to zeros and string arrays to null strings.

Arguments (2)

The *numeric-variable* is any integer or real name. It is always global, even if it is declared locally. The *expression* gives the number of bytes of storage required minus one, and should be −1 or greater. It is limited only by the amount of free memory.

The use of this form of DIM is to reserve a given number of bytes of memory, in which to put for example, machine code. The address of the first byte reserved, which will be a multiple of four, is placed in the *numeric-variable*. The byte array is uninitialised.

If the *expression* is –1 no memory is allocated and the *numeric-variable* is set to be the address of the end of the BASIC heap (where variables are stored) at the time of request. The function END returns the same value.

Argument (3)

The *numeric-variable* is any integer or real name. The *expression* gives the number of bytes of storage required minus one, and should be –1 or greater. It is limited only by the amount of free memory.

This form of DIM reserves a given number of bytes of memory on BASIC's stack so that it can be used temporarily within a procedure or function. The memory is uninitialised, and is released when the procedure or function exits, so be careful not to store the returned address in a global variable and attempt to use it after the procedure or function exits.

If the *expression* is –1 no memory is allocated and the *numeric-variable* is set to be the value of the BASIC stack pointer at the time of the request. Together with the value returned by END or DIM –1 (see above), this can be useful for computing the free space between the top of the BASIC heap and the bottom of the BASIC stack.

Note: The stack cannot be moved while there are DIM LOCALs defined. This means that END= will return an error and any Service_Memory calls will be claimed.

Argument (4)

The *array* is the name of any previously DIMed array, or an array used as a formal parameter in a procedure or function.

Result (4)

The result of the function is the number of dimensions which that array has.

Argument (5)

The *array* is the name of any previously DIMed array or an array used as a formal parameter in a procedure or function. The expression is a number between one and the number of dimensions of the array.

Result (5)

The result of the function is the subscript of the highest element in that dimension, i.e. the value used for that subscript in the DIM statement that declared the array in the first place.

Notes

It is possible to have local arrays, whose contents are discarded when the procedure or function in which they are created returns. See LOCAL on page 326.

History

(3) was added in version 1.34.

Examples

```
DIM name$(num_names%)
DIM sin(90)
DIM matrix%(4,4)
DIM A(64), B%(12,4), C$(2,8,3)
DIM bytes% size*10+overhead
PRINT DIM(name$())
size%=DIM(name$(),1)
```

DIV

Operator performing integer division.

Syntax

factor DIV *factor*

Arguments

Integer-range numerics. Reals are converted to integers before the divide operation is carried out. The righthand side must not evaluate to zero.

Result

The (integer) quotient of the arguments is always rounded towards zero. If the signs of the arguments are the same, the quotient is positive, otherwise it is negative. The remainder can be found using MOD.

Examples

```
PRINT (first-last) DIV 10
a%=space% DIV &100
```

DRAW

Statement to draw a line to specified coordinates.

Syntax

```
DRAW [BY] expression,expression
```

Arguments

The two expressions give the coordinates of one of the end points of a straight line. The other end point is given by the current graphics cursor position. After the line has been drawn (using the graphics foreground colour and action), the graphics cursor is updated to the coordinates given in the DRAW statement.

If the keyword BY is omitted, the coordinates are absolute. That is, they give the position of the end of the line with respect to the graphics origin. If BY is included, the coordinates are relative. That means they give the position of the end of the line with respect to the current graphics cursor position.

Examples

```
DRAW 640,512 : REM Draw a line to middle of the screen
DRAW BY dx%, dy%
```

EDIT

Command to enter the BASIC screen editor.

Syntax

    EDIT

Purpose

EDIT enters the BASIC screen editor to allow you to create a new program or amend the current one. Full details of the editor are given in the chapter entitled *Editing* BASIC *files* on page 191.

ELLIPSE

Statement to draw an ellipse.

Syntax

```
ELLIPSE [FILL] expr1,expr2,expr3,expr4[,expr5]
```

Arguments

expr1 to *expr5* are integer expressions. The first two give the coordinates of the centre of the ellipse. The third expression gives the length of the semi-major axis. This is the axis parallel with the x axis if the ellipse is not rotated. The fourth expression gives the length of the semi-minor axis. This is the axis parallel with the y axis if the ellipse is not rotated.

The optional fifth expression gives the rotation of the ellipse, in radians, anti-clockwise.

ELLIPSE draws the outline of an ellipse. ELLIPSE FILL plots a solid ellipse.

Notes

The ELLIPSE statement has some (minor) restrictions about the size of its arguments: if both of the semi-axes are of length zero, then you are not allowed to specify a rotation value. If the semi-minor axis length is zero, then the rotation, if specified, must not be zero. The result of trying to draw any of these 'illegal' ellipses is a `Division by zero` error.

Examples

```
ELLIPSE 640,512,200,100
ELLIPSE FILL x%,y%,major%,minor%,ang
```

ELSE

Part of the ON GOTO/GOSUB/PROC ... ELSE or IF ... THEN ... ELSE or IF ... THEN ... ELSE ... ENDIF constructs.

Syntax

See IF and ON entries, as appropriate.

Notes

ELSE may occur anywhere in the program, but is only meaningful after an IF (multi- or single-line) or ON ... GOSUB/GOTO/PROC statement. When used as part of a multi-line IF statement, it must be the first non-space object on the line.

Examples

```
IF a=b THEN PRINT "hello" ELSE PRINT "good-bye"
IF ok ELSE PRINT "Error"
ON choice GOSUB 100,200,300,400 ELSE PRINT"Bad choice"

IF num>=0 THEN
  PRINT SQR(num)
ELSE
  PRINT "Negative number"
  PRINT SQR(-num)
ENDIF
```

END

Statement terminating the execution of a program.
Statement setting the highest address used by BASIC.
Function returning the address of the end of the BASIC heap.

Syntax

as a statement:

(1) END
(2) END = *expression*

as a function:

(3) END

Purpose (1)

The END statement terminates the execution of a program.

> Note: This statement is not always necessary in programs; execution stops when the line at the end of the program is executed. However, END (or STOP) must be included if execution is to end at a point other than at the last program line. This prevents control falling through into a procedure, function or subroutine. END is also useful in error handlers.

Purpose (2)

When used in a assignment, END sets the highest address used by BASIC when running under the Wimp. This can be used by programs running under the Wimp to claim more memory from the free pool, or alternatively to give up unrequired memory.

The expression should be an integer giving the new value for HIMEM. After the call, memory above the given address will be de-allocated and HIMEM will be set to that location. In addition, local arrays and installed libraries are cleared.

Restrictions on the use of END=

You should not use END= with INSTALLed libraries, nested within EVAL, LOCAL ERROR or DIM LOCAL, nested within assignments to local arrays, or within nested local arrays.

If there is not enough free memory to set HIMEM to the requested value, the error `Attempt to allocate insufficient memory` is given.

Purpose (3)

The END function returns the address of the end of the BASIC heap and the start of free user memory. The expression END–TOP gives the number of bytes used by the BASIC heap.

Examples

```
PRINT END
END = &10000 : REM only need 32K to RUN
```

ENDCASE

Statement marking the end of a CASE ... OF ... WHEN ... OTHERWISE ... ENDCASE construct.

Syntax

ENDCASE

Notes

ENDCASE must be the first non-space object on the line. When the statements corresponding to a WHEN or OTHERWISE statement have been executed, control then jumps to the statement following the ENDCASE. If ENDCASE itself is executed, it signals the end of the CASE statement, no matches having been made. Control then continues as normal.

ENDIF

Statement terminating an IF ... THEN ... ELSE ... ENDIF construct.

Syntax

    ENDIF

Notes

ENDIF marks the end of a block-structured IF statement. It must be the first non-space object on a line. When the statements corresponding to the THEN or ELSE statement have been executed, control jumps to the statement following the ENDIF. If ENDIF itself is executed, it signals the end of the IF statement, nothing having been executed as a result of it. Control then continues as normal.

ENDPROC

Statement marking the end of a user-defined procedure.

Syntax

    ENDPROC

Purpose

When executed, an ENDPROC statement causes BASIC to terminate the execution of the current procedure and to restore local variables and actual parameters. Any LOCAL DATA and LOCAL ERROR statements that have not been closed with RESTORE DATA or RESTORE ERROR will be restored. Local arrays and blocks of memory allocated with DIM ... LOCAL will be deleted. Any unclosed FOR ... NEXT, REPEAT ...UNTIL or WHILE ... ENDWHILE loops will be closed. Control is passed to the statement after the PROC which called the procedure.

ENDPROC should only be used in a procedure. Otherwise, when it is encountered, a Not in a procedure error message is generated.

Examples

    ENDPROC

    IF a<=0 THEN ENDPROC ELSE PROCrecurse(a-1)

ENDWHILE

Statement to terminate a WHILE ... ENDWHILE loop.

Syntax

    ENDWHILE

Notes

When an ENDWHILE is executed, control loops back to the corresponding WHILE statement. The statements forming the WHILE ... ENDWHILE loop are executed until the condition following the matching WHILE evaluates to FALSE, whereupon control jumps to the statement following the ENDWHILE.

Example

```
MODE "X640 Y480 C256"
INPUT X
WHILE X > 0
  GCOL X
  CIRCLE FILL 640,480,X
  X -= 4
ENDWHILE
```

ENVELOPE

Statement used with the SOUND statement to control the volume and pitch of a sound while it is playing.

Note: Standard RISC OS does not support the ENVELOPE command so it will have no effect unless a module that provides support for it is loaded.

Syntax

ENVELOPE *expr1,expr2,expr3,expr4,expr5,expr6,expr7,expr8, expr9,expr10,expr11,expr12,expr13,expr14*

Arguments

expr1 is the envelope number
expr2 is the length of each step and repeat flag
expr3 is the change of pitch per step in section 1
expr4 is the change of pitch per step in section 2
expr5 is the change of pitch per step in section 3
expr6 is the number of steps in section 1
expr7 is the number of steps in section 2
expr8 is the number of steps in section 3
expr9 is the attack rate (change of amplitude per step in the attack phase)
expr10 is the decay rate (change of amplitude per step in the decay phase)
expr11 is the sustain rate (change of amplitude per step in the sustain phase)
expr12 is the release rate (change of amplitude per step in the release phase)
expr13 is the attack phase target level
expr14 is the decay phase target level

Envelope number
An integer in the range 1 to 16 which specifies the envelope number that is to be defined.

Length of each step and repeat flag
This is an integer in the range 1 to 127 that determines the length in centi-seconds of each step of the pitch and amplitude envelopes. The pitch envelope normally auto-repeats but this can be suppressed by adding 128 to the value of this argument (setting bit 7).

Change of pitch per step
Number of steps
These parameters determine the pitch envelope. The pitch envelope has three sections and each section is specified with two parameters; the increment which is

an integer in the range -128 to 127, and the number of times the increment is applied during that section, that is the number of steps, which is an integer in the range 0 to 255.

Change of amplitude per step
Target levels
These parameters determine the amplitude envelope. The shape of the amplitude envelope is defined in terms of rates (increments) between levels, and is an extended form of the standard ADSR (attack, decay, sustain, release) system of envelope control. The envelope starts at zero and then climbs at the *attack rate* (an integer between -127 and 127) until it reaches the *attack phase target level* (an integer in the range 0 to 126). It then climbs or falls at the *decay rate* (an integer between -127 and 127) until it reaches the *decay phase target level* (an integer in the range 0 to 126). However, if the *decay rate* is zero the amplitude will stay at the *attack phase target level* for the duration of the sound.

The envelope then enters the sustain phase which lasts for the remaining duration of the sound. The duration is set by the SOUND statement. During the sustain phase the amplitude will remain the same or fall at the *sustain rate* (an integer between -127 and 0).

At the end of the sustain phase the note will be terminated if there is another note waiting to be played on the selected channel. If no note is waiting then the amplitude will decay at the *release rate* (an integer between -127 and 0) until the amplitude reaches zero. If the *release rate* is zero then the note will continue indefinitely, with the pitch envelope auto-repeating if bit 7 of the second parameter is zero.

Technical details

The ENVELOPE command calls OS_Word 8. For the ENVELOPE command to have any effect a module that implements OS_Word 8 must be loaded.

Example

```
ENVELOPE 1,1,4,-4,4,10,20,10,127,0,0,-5,126,126
SOUND 1,1,100,200
```

EOF#

Function returning whether the end of a file has been reached.

Syntax

    EOF#factor

Argument

A channel number returned by an OPENxx function.

Result

TRUE if the last character in the specified file has been read, FALSE otherwise. EOF for a file may be reset by positioning its pointer using the PTR# statement.

Examples

    REPEAT
      VDU BGET#file
    UNTIL EOF#file

    IF EOF#invoices PRINT "No more invoices"

EOR

Operator performing bitwise exclusive-OR (EOR).

Syntax

relational EOR *relational*

Arguments

Relational expressions, or bit values to be EORed.

Result

The logical bitwise EOR of the arguments. Corresponding bits in the arguments are EORed to produce the result. Each bit in the result is zero if the corresponding bits in the arguments are equal, and otherwise one.

Examples

```
PRINT height>10 EOR weight<20
bits = mask EOR value1
```

ERL

Function returning the last error line.

Syntax

```
ERL
```

Result

Integer between 0 and 65279. This is the line number of the last error to occur. An error line of 0 implies that the error happened in immediate mode or that there has not been an error. If an error occurs inside a procedure or function in a library, ERL is set to the line number in the library where the error occurred.

Examples

```
REPORT : IF ERL<>0 THEN PRINT " at line "; ERL
IF ERL=3245 PRINT "Bad function, try again"
```

ERR

Function returning the last error number.

Syntax

    ERR

Result

A signed integer. Errors produced by BASIC are in the range 0 to 127.

Notes

The error number 0 is classed as a fatal error and cannot be trapped by the ON ERROR statement. An example of a fatal error is that produced when a BASIC STOP statement is executed.

Examples

    IF ERR=18 THEN PRINT "Can't use zero; try again!!"

    IF ERR=17 THEN PRINT"Sure?":A$=GET$:IF INSTR("Yy",A$) THEN STOP

ERROR

Statement generating an error, or part of the ON ERROR statement.

Syntax

```
(1) ON ERROR ...
(2) ERROR [EXT] numeric-expression, string-expression
```

Purpose (1):

See ON ERROR on page 348 for details of the error handling statements.

Arguments (2)

numeric-expression evaluates to a four-byte signed integer corresponding to an error number. *string-expression* evaluates to a string associated with this error number. The error described is generated, in the same way as internal BASIC errors, so ERL will be set to the current line, ERR set to *numeric-expression* and REPORT$ set to *string-expression*. The current error handler will then be called, unless the error number is zero, in which case a fatal (untrappable) error will be generated.

If the keyword EXT is present, then BASIC terminates and the error number and string are passed to the error handler of the program that invoked BASIC. The default BASIC error handler uses this if the -quit option was given on the command line.

Examples

```
ERROR 6, "Type mismatch: number needed"
ERROR EXT ERR,REPORT$ : REM pass on the error
```

EVAL

Function which evaluates a string statement as an expression.

Syntax

    EVAL factor

Argument

A string which EVAL evaluates as a BASIC expression.

Result

EVAL can return anything that could appear on the righthand side of an assignment statement, including strings. It can also produce the same errors that occur during assignment. For example:

    Type mismatch: number needed

and

    No such function/procedure.

Examples

    INPUT hex$
    PRINT EVAL("&"+hex$)

    f$="LEFT$("
    e$=EVAL(f$+""""ABCDE""",2)")

EXP

Function returning the exponential of its argument.

Syntax

```
EXP factor
```

Argument

Numeric, which for BASIC V can range from the largest negative real (about 1.7E38) to approximately +88, and for BASIC VI can range from the largest negative real (about 1.7E308) to approximately +709.7.

Result

Positive real in the range zero to the largest positive real (about 1.7E38 for BASIC V or 1.7E308 for BASIC VI). The result is e raised to the power of the argument, where e is the constant 2.718281828, the base of natural logarithms.

Notes

EXP is the inverse of LN.

Example

```
DEF FNcosh(x)=(EXP(x) + EXP(-x))/2
```

EXT#

Pseudo-variable returning or setting the length (extent) of an open file.

Syntax

(1) EXT#*factor*
(2) EXT#*factor*=*expression*

Argument (1)

factor is a channel number, as allocated by one of the OPEN*xx* functions.

Result

Integer giving the current length of the file from 0 to, in theory 2147483648, although in practice the extent is limited by the file medium in use.

Argument (2)

factor is a channel number as allocated by one of the OPEN*xx* functions.

expression is the desired extent of the file, whose upper limit depends on the filing system. The lower limit is 0. The main use of the statement is to *shorten* a file. For example: EXT#file=EXT#file-&1000. A file may be lengthened by explicitly using PTR#, or implicitly by BPUTing to its end.

Notes

As with all the pseudo-variables, the LET keyword and the operators += and -= cannot be used with EXT#.

EXT is also used a part of the ERROR EXT ... statement; see the ERROR keyword for details.

Examples

```
IF EXT#file>90000 THEN PRINT "File full":CLOSE#file
EXT#op=EXT#op+&2000
```

FALSE

Function returning the logical value FALSE.

Syntax

```
FALSE
```

Result

The constant zero. The function is used mnemonically in logical or conditional expressions.

Examples

```
flag=FALSE

REPEAT
  CIRCLE RND(1279),RND(1024),RND(200)
UNTIL FALSE
```

FILL

Statement flood-filling an area in the current foreground colour.

Syntax

```
FILL [BY] expression,expression
```

Arguments

The two expressions give the coordinates of the point from which the flood-fill is to commence (the 'seed' point). The filled pixels are plotted using the current foreground colour and action over an area bounded by non-background colour pixels and the graphics viewport. If the seed point is in a non-background colour, then no filling takes place at all.

The graphics cursor is updated to the coordinates given,

If the keyword BY is omitted, the coordinates are absolute. That is, they give the position of the seed point with respect to the graphics origin. If BY is included, the coordinates are relative. That means they give the position of the seed point with respect to the current graphics cursor position.

Examples

```
FILL x%,y%
FILL BY dx%,dy%
```

FN

Statement introducing or calling a user-defined function.

Syntax

```
(1) DEF FNproc-part
(2) FNproc-part
```

Argument (1)

For the format of *proc-part*, see DEF above. It gives the names and types of the parameters of the function, if any. For example:

```
1000 DEF FNmin(a%,b%) IF a%<b% THEN =a% ELSE =b%
```

`a%` and `b%` are the formal parameters. They stand for the expressions passed to the function (the actual parameters) when `FNmin` is called. The result of a user-defined function is given by a statement starting with =. As the example above shows, there may be more than one = in a function. The first one which is encountered during execution terminates the function.

Argument (2)

proc-part is an identifier followed by a list of expressions (or array or RETURN variables) corresponding to the formal parameters in the DEF statement for the function. The result depends on the assignment that terminated the function, and so can be of any type and range. An example function call is:

```
PRINT FNmin(2*bananas%, 3*apples%+1)
```

Notes

User-defined functions may span several program lines, and contain all the normal BASIC statements. They may also declare local variables using the LOCAL keyword. When a function terminates any LOCAL DATA and LOCAL ERROR statements that have not been closed with RESTORE DATA or RESTORE ERROR will be restored, local arrays and blocks of memory allocated with DIM ... LOCAL will be deleted and any unclosed FOR, REPEAT or WHILE loops will be closed.

Examples

```
DEF FNfact(n%) IF n%<1 THEN =1 ELSE =n%*FNfact(n%-1)
DEF FNhex4(n%)=RIGHT$("000"+STR$~(n%),4)
REPEAT PRINT FNhex4(GET): UNTIL FALSE
```

FOR

Part of the FOR ... NEXT statement.

Syntax

FOR *variable=expression* TO *expression* [STEP *expression*]

Arguments

The variable can be any numeric variable reference. The expressions can be any numeric expressions, though they must lie in the integer range if the variable is an integer one. It is recommended that integer looping variables are used for the following reasons:

- the loops go faster
- rounding errors are avoided.

If the STEP part is omitted, the step is taken to be +1. The action of the FOR loop is as follows. The looping variable is set to the first expression. The limit expression and step, if present, are remembered for later. The statements up to the matching NEXT are executed. At this stage, the step is added to the looping variable. The termination condition is that, for positive steps, the looping variable has become greater than the limit, and for negative steps it has become less than the limit. If this condition is met, control continues at the statement after the NEXT. Otherwise, control jumps back to the statement after the FOR statement.

Notes

The statements between a FOR and its corresponding NEXT are executed at least once as the test for loop termination is performed at the NEXT rather than the FOR. Thus a loop started with FOR I=1 TO 0 executes once, with I set to 1 in the body of the loop. The value of the looping variable when the loop has finished should be treated as undefined, and should not be used before being reset by an assignment.

Examples

```
FOR addr%=200 TO 8000 STEP 4
FOR I=1 TO LEN(a$)
```

GCOL

Statement to set the graphics colours and actions.

Syntax

(1) GCOL [*expression1*,]*expression2* [TINT *expression3*]
(2) GCOL [OF [*expr1*,]*expr2*] [ON [*expr3*,]*expr4*]
(3) GCOL [*expr*,]*expr*,*expr*,*expr*
(4) GCOL [OF [*expr*,]*expr*,*expr*,*expr*] [ON [*expr*,]*expr*,*expr*, *expr*]

Arguments (1)

GCOL sets the colour and plot mode that will be used in subsequent graphics operations.

expression1, if present, is an integer between 0 and 255 which determines the plot 'action', i.e. how the graphics colour, *expression2*, will be combined with what's on the screen when plotting points, lines, etc. Its basic range is 0 to 7, as shown below:

Action	Meaning
0	Store the colour *expression2* on the screen
1	OR the colour on the screen with *expression2*
2	AND the colour on the screen with *expression2*
3	EOR the colour on the screen with *expression2*
4	Invert the current colour, disregarding *expression2*
5	Do not affect the screen at all
6	AND the colour on the screen with the NOT *expression2*
7	OR the colour on the screen with the NOT *expression2*

Although action 5 does not actually alter the screen, each pixel is accessed as though the operation was taking place, so it is no quicker than the other actions.

If you add n*16 to the action number, then colour patterns are used instead of solid colours. n is in the range 1 to 4 for the four basic patterns, or 5 for a large pattern made from the other four placed side by side. VDU 23,2 to VDU 23,5 are used to set the colour fill patterns. If the currently selected pattern is re-defined, it becomes active immediately.

If you further add 8 to the action, then where the colour pattern contains the current graphics background colour, nothing is plotted, i.e. that colour becomes transparent. For example, suppose the display is a four-colour one, and the current background colour is 129 (red).

Now, if pattern 1 was selected as the foreground colour (GCOL 16,0), a solid rectangle would be red-yellow, as pattern 1 consists of alternating red and yellow pixels. However, if the foreground colour was set using GCOL 24,0 (adding 8 to the plot action number), then a solid rectangle would appear yellow, with transparent 'holes' where the red pixels would have been plotted.

Adding 8 to the action also causes sprite plotting to use the transparency mask, if present. See the chapter entitled Sprites on page 151 for more details.

If *expression1* is omitted, 0 is used, which means that the colour given is stored onto the screen.

The colour number, *expression2*, is in the range 0 to 255. Values below 128 are used to set the graphics foreground colour. Other values set the background colour. For example, colour 129 sets the background colour to 129-128, or 1. The number is treated MOD the number of colours in the current mode, i.e. 2, 4, 16 or 64. Thus in 256-colour modes, the colour range is 0 to 63 (or 128 to 191 for background).

The TINT value, if present, is used to add one of four whiteness levels to the 64 colours available in VIDC1-compatible 256-colour modes, giving the total 256 possible hues. *expression3* is in the range 0 to 255, where currently the only significant levels are 0, 64, 128 and 192.

> Note: Wimp-based programs should use Wimp_SetColour or ColourTrans_ReturnGCOL, not GCOL.

Arguments (2)

The parameters following OF are used to set the graphics foreground colour and those following ON are used to set the graphics background colour. *expr1* and *expr3*, if specified are the plot 'action' as described above and *expr2* and *expr4* are colour numbers

Arguments (3)

The graphics foreground colour is set using the three expressions which are integers in the range 0 to 255 giving the amount of red, green and blue. The actual colour selected will be the closest colour available in the current mode and palette.

Arguments (4)

The graphics foreground colour is set using the three expressions following OF, and the graphics background colour is set using the three expressions following ON. In each case the expressions are integers in the range 0 to 255 giving the amount of red, green and blue, and either the ON or OF part may be omitted. The actual colour selected will be the closest colour available in the current mode and palette.

Technical Details

(1) uses VDU 18, (2) uses `OS_SetColour`, (3) and (4) use `ColourTrans_SetGCOL`.

History

(3) was added in version 1.06. (2) and (4) were added in version 1.34.

Examples

```
GCOL 2
DRAW 100,100    : REM Draw a line in colour 2

GCOL 4,128
CLG             : REM Invert the graphics window

GCOL 1,2        : REM OR the screen with colour 2

GCOL 18 TINT 128
```

GET

Function returning a character code from the input stream (e.g. keyboard, serial port, etc).

Syntax

    GET

Result

An integer between 0 and 255. This is the ASCII code of the next character in the buffer of the currently selected input stream (keyboard or serial port). The function will not return until a character is available, and so it can be used to halt the program temporarily.

Notes

The character entered is not echoed onto the screen. To make it appear you must explicitly PRINT it.

Examples

    PRINT "Press space to continue" :REPEAT UNTIL GET=32
    ON GET-127 PROCa, PROCb, PROCc ELSE PRINT "Illegal entry"

GET$#

Function returning a string from a file.

Syntax

GET$#*factor*

Argument

A channel number returned by an OPEN*xx* function.

Result

A string of characters read until a linefeed (ASCII 10), carriage return (ASCII 13) or the end of the file is encountered, or else the maximum of 255 characters is reached. The terminating character is not returned as part of the string.

Notes

PTR# is updated to point to the next character in the file. If the last character in the file has been read, EOF# for the channel will be TRUE.

Examples

```
string$ = GET$#channel
PRINT GET$#fileno
```

GET$

Function returning a character from the input stream (e.g. keyboard).

Syntax

    GET$

Result

A one-character string whose value would be CHR$(GET) if GET had been called instead. This is provided so you can use statements like IF GET$="*"... rather than IF CHR$(GET)="*".

Examples

    PRINT "Do you want another game?":response$ = GET$
    IF response$ = "Y" or response$ = "y" CHAIN "program"

    PRINT "Input a digit "; : PRINT GET$

GOSUB

Statement to call a subroutine.

Syntax

    (1) GOSUB expression
    (2) ON expression GOSUB expression1 [,expression2...]
    [ELSE statement]

Argument (1)

expression should evaluate to an integer between 0 and 65279, in other words a line number. If the expression is not a simple integer (e.g. 1030) it should be enclosed between round brackets. The line given is jumped to, and control is returned to the statement after the GOSUB by the next RETURN statement.

Argument (2)

expression should evaluate to an integer. If this integer is *n* then the *n*th subroutine listed after the GOSUB is jumped to. If the integer is less than 1 or greater than the number of line numbers given, the statement following the ELSE, if it is present, is executed.

Notes

Procedures should be used in preference to subroutines since they are more flexible and produce a better structured program.

The line number after GOSUB should be a constant so that RENUMBER works properly.

Examples

    10 GOSUB 2000
    20 GOSUB (2300+20*opt): REM not nice
    30 ON x% GOSUB 100,200,300 ELSE PRINT "Out of range"

GOTO

Statement to transfer control to another line.

Syntax

    (1) GOTO expression
    (2) ON expression GOTO expression1 [,expression2...][ELSE statement]

Argument (1)

expression should evaluate to an integer between 0 and 65279: a line number. If the expression is not a simple integer, it should be placed between round brackets. This line number is jumped to and execution carries on from this new line.

Arguments (2)

expression should evaluate to an integer. *expression1...* should evaluate to integer line numbers between 0 and 65279. If the first integer is n then the nth line after the GOTO is jumped to. If the integer is less than 1 or greater than the number of line numbers given, the statement following the ELSE, if it is present, is executed.

Notes

The line number after GOTO should be a constant so that RENUMBER and APPEND work properly.

Examples

    GOTO 230
    IF TIME<1000 THEN GOTO 1000
    ON x GOTO 20,50,30,160

HELP

Command giving help information.

Syntax

HELP [keyword]

Purpose

HELP displays a list of useful information about the status of BASIC. If the keyword is present, help about that particular command, statement or function is printed. In addition, HELP . prints a list of all keywords, HELP followed by a single letter prints all the keywords beginning with that letter, and HELP [prints help for the BASIC assembler.

Examples

HELP
HELP HIM.
HELP .
HELP [

HIMEM

Pseudo-variable holding address of the top of the BASIC stack.

Syntax

```
(1) HIMEM
(2) HIMEM = expression
```

Result (1)

An integer giving the address of the location above the end of user memory. The amount of user memory is given by HIMEM − LOMEM and the amount of free memory by HIMEM − END.

Argument (2)

expression should be an integer between LOMEM and the top of usable memory. It restricts the amount of memory which the current program can use for workspace stacks etc, hence giving an area where data, or machine code routines can be stored.

Notes

If HIMEM is set carelessly, running the program may produce the No room error. There must always be enough for the stack.

The INSTALL statement lowers HIMEM by the size of the library being installed.

When an attempt is made to set HIMEM, LOMEM, or PAGE to an illegal value, a warning message is displayed, and no change is made, but the program nevertheless continues to run. This means that such errors cannot be trapped using ON ERROR.

Examples

```
PRINT "Memory available = ";HIMEM - LOMEM
a%=HIMEM-1000 : HIMEM=a%
```

IF

Statement to execute statements conditionally.

Syntax

```
(1)
IF expr [THEN] [statements...]
[[ELSE][statements...]]

(2)
IF expression THEN
  [statements...]
  [ELSE [statements...]
  statements...]
ENDIF
```

Arguments (1)

expr is treated as a truth value. If it is non-zero, it is counted as TRUE and any *statements* in the THEN part are executed. If the expression evaluates to zero (FALSE), then the ELSE part *statements* are executed.

statements is either a list of zero or more statements separated by colons, or a line number. In the latter case there is an implied GOTO after the THEN (which has to be present) or ELSE.

Note: The THEN is optional before statements except before * commands. For example:

```
IF a THEN *CAT
```

not

```
IF a *CAT
```

The ELSE part matches any IF, so be wary of nesting IFs on a line. Constructs of the form:

```
IF a THEN... IF b THEN... ELSE...
```

should be avoided because the ELSE part might match either the first or second IF depending on the values of a and b. To avoid the ambiguity, use a multi-line IF of the form:

```
          IF a THEN                IF a THEN
            IF b THEN                IF b THEN
              ...                      ...
            ELSE           or        ENDIF
              ...                    ELSE REM part of IF a
            ENDIF                      ...
          ENDIF                      ENDIF
```

depending on the effect required.

However, the form:

```
IF a THEN... ELSE IF b THEN...
```

is not ambiguous and can be used with no problems.

Arguments (2)

expression is treated as a truth value. If it is non-zero, it is counted as TRUE and any statements on the line after the THEN down to either an ELSE or an ENDIF are executed. If the expression evaluates to zero (FALSE), any statements following the ELSE (if present) until the ENDIF are executed. Note that in this form, THEN must be the last thing on the line.

Examples

```
IF temp<=10 PROClow_temp
IF a%>b% THEN SWAP a%, b% ELSE PRINT "No swap"

IF B^2 >= 4*A*C THEN
  PROCroots(A,B,C)
ENDIF
IF r$ = "Y" OR r$ = "y" THEN
  PRINT "YES"
ELSE
  PRINT "NO"
  STOP
ENDIF
```

INKEY

Function returning a character code from the current input stream with time limit.
Function returning the operating system version.
Function interrogating the keyboard.

Syntax

(1) INKEY *positive-factor*
(2) INKEY -256
(3) INKEY *negative-factor* (where bit 7 is set)
(4) INKEY *negative-factor* (where bit 7 is clear)

Argument (1)

An integer in the range 0 to 32767, which is a time limit in centi-seconds.

Result (1)

The ASCII code of the next character in the current input buffer if one appears in the time limit set by the argument, or –1 if a time-out occurs.

Argument (2)

-256

Result (2)

A number indicating which version of the operating system is in the computer.

Value	Version	Value	Version
&A0	Arthur 1.20	&A6	RISC OS 3.60
&A1	RISC OS 2.00	&A7	RISC OS 3.70/3.71
&A2	RISC OS 2.01	&A8	RISC OS 3.80/4.0x
&A3	RISC OS 3.00	&A9	RISC OS 4 Select
&A4	RISC OS 3.10/3.11	&AA	RISC OS 5.xx
&A5	RISC OS 3.50		

Argument (3)

A negative integer where bit 7 is set, i.e. (*negative-factor* AND 128)=128. This is the negative INKEY code of the key being interrogated (see *Appendix D – INKEY values* on page 469 for details).

Result (3)

TRUE if the key is being pressed at the time of the call, FALSE if it is not.

Argument (4)

A negative integer, other than –256, where bit 7 is clear, i.e. (*negative-factor* AND 128)=0. This is the negative INKEY code of a key (see *Appendix* D – INKEY *values* on page 469) with 128 subtracted from it. Keys with negative INKEY codes less than or equal to *negative-factor*+128 will be interrogated.

Result (4)

255 if no key from the specified range is being pressed, otherwise the bitwise NOT of the negative INKEY code of the key being pressed.

Examples

```
DEF PROCwait(secs%)
IF INKEY(100*secs%): REM throw away result
ENDPROC

IF INKEY(-99) THEN REPEAT UNTIL NOT INKEY(-99)

IF INKEY(-256) = &AA THEN PRINT "Using RISC OS 5"

REM Scan for keys excluding Shift, Ctrl, Alt, etc.
Key% = INKEY(-16-128)
IF Key% = 255 THEN
   PRINT "No key pressed"
ELSE
   PRINT "Negative INKEY code ";NOT Key%;" key pressed"
ENDIF
```

INKEY$

Function returning a character from the input stream.

Syntax

```
INKEY$ factor
```

Argument

As INKEY (1)

Result

Where INKEY would return −1, INKEY$ returns the null string " ". In all other situations, it returns CHR$(INKEY*argument*).

Example

```
A$ = INKEY$(500)
```

INPUT

Statement obtaining a value or values from the input stream.

Syntax

INPUT is followed by an optional prompt, which, if present, may be followed by a semi-colon or comma, which causes a ? to be printed out after the prompt. This is followed by a list of variable names of any type, separated by commas. After the last variable, the whole sequence may be repeated, separated from the first by a comma. In addition the position of prompts may be controlled by the SPC, TAB and ' (single quote) print formatters (see PRINT on page 366).

Notes

Leading spaces of the input string itself are skipped, and commas are taken as marking the end of input for the current item.

Examples

```
INPUT a$ : REM Print a simple"?" as a prompt
INPUT "How many",num% : REM prompt is "How many?"
INPUT "Address &"hex$ : REM "Address &" no ? because no ,
INPUT TAB(10)"Name ",n$'TAB(10)"Address ",a$
INPUT a,b,c,d,"More ",yn$
INPUT SPC(5)"Letter",char$
```

INPUT LINE

Statement obtaining a value or values from the input stream.

Syntax

This has the same syntax as INPUT.

Result

If the input variable is a string, all the user's input is read into the variable, including leading and trailing spaces and commas. If the input variable is numeric, only a single value will be selected from the beginning of the input line.

Notes

INPUT LINE is equivalent to LINE INPUT.

Example

```
INPUT LINE ">" basic$
```

INPUT#

Statement obtaining a value or values from a file.

Syntax

INPUT#*factor* [,*variable*,*variable*...]

Arguments

factor is the channel number of the file from which the information is to be read, as obtained by an OPEN*xx* function. The variables, if present, may be of any type. The separators may be semi-colons instead of commas.

Integer variables are read as &40 followed by the two's complement representation of the integer in four bytes, most significant byte first.

5–byte real variables are read as &80 followed by five bytes. The first four bytes are the mantissa and the fifth is the exponent. The mantissa is read least significant byte (LSB) first. 31 bits represent the magnitude of the mantissa and one bit (bit 7 of the fourth byte) the sign. The exponent byte is in excess-128 form.

8–byte real variables are read as &88 followed by two 4–byte words, in IEEE Double Precision (D) format. The exponent is represented by bits 20 to 30 in the first word. The sign bit is bit 31 in the first word. The mantissa is represented by bits 0 to 19 in the first word and bits 0 to 31 in the second word.

Both BASIC V and BASIC VI can read 5– and 8–byte real formats.

String variables are read as a zero byte followed by a byte containing the string length and then the characters in the string in reverse order.

Notes

Files read using INPUT# must adhere to the format described above, which implies they should have been created using PRINT#. BASIC will perform conversion between integers and floating point values where possible.

Examples

```
INPUT#data,name$,addr1$,addr2$,addr3$,age%
INPUT#data,$buffer,len
```

INSTALL

Command to load a function or procedure library into memory.

Syntax

```
INSTALL pathname
```

Argument

pathname is a string which should evaluate to the pathname of a valid BASIC file.

Purpose

INSTALL loads the chosen function and procedure library into the top of memory and lowers the BASIC stack and value of HIMEM by an appropriate amount. The library remains in memory until you QUIT from BASIC. Any number of libraries may be installed provided that there is enough memory for them.

When searching for a procedure or function, BASIC looks in the following order: first, the current program is searched, in line-number order; next, any procedure libraries loaded using LIBRARY are searched – the most recently loaded file is searched first; then, any INSTALLed libraries are examined, again in the reverse order of loading. Finally the OVERLAY library list is searched.

The LVAR command lists (the first lines of) libraries in the order in which they are examined.

Examples

```
INSTALL "Printout"
A$ = "Library1"
INSTALL A$
```

INSTR(

Function to find the position of a substring in a string.

Syntax

    INSTR(expression1,expression2[,expression3])

Arguments

expression1 is any string which is to be searched for a substring.

expression2 is the substring required.

expression3 is a numeric in the range 1 to 255 and determines the position in the main string at which the search for the substring will start. This defaults to 1.

Result

An integer in the range 0 to 255. If 0 is returned, the substring could not be found in the main string. A result of 1 means that the substring was found at the first character of the main string, and so on. The position of the first occurrence only is returned.

Notes

If the substring is longer than the main string, 0 is always returned. If the substring is the null string, the result is always equal to *expression3*, or 1 if this is omitted.

Examples

```
REPEAT a$=GET$:UNTIL INSTR("YyNn",a$) <> 0
pos%=INSTR(com$,"*FX",10)
```

INT

Function returning the integer part of a number.

Syntax

```
INT factor
```

Argument

Any integer-range numeric.

Result

Nearest integer less than or equal to the argument. Note that this is different from rounding towards zero: whereas INT(1.5) equals 1, INT(-1.5) is equal to -2, not -1.

Examples

```
DEF FNround(n)=INT(n+0.5)
DEF FNTruncateToZero(n)=SGNn*INT(ABS(n))
size=len%*INT((top-bottom)/100)
```

LEFT$(

Function returning, or statement altering, the left part of a string.

Syntax

as a function:

(1) `LEFT$(expression1 [,expression2])`

as a statement:

(2) `LEFT$(variable [,expression1]) = expression2`

Argument (1)

expression1 is a string of length between 0 and 255 characters.

expression2, if present, gives the number of characters from the left of the string that are to be returned. If it is omitted, `LEN(expression1)` -1 is used, i.e. all but the last character of the string is returned. This is useful for stripping off unwanted trailing characters.

Result (1)

Characters from the left of *expression1*, where the length of the result is the minimum of the length of *expression1* and *expression2* (or the implied default for *expression2*).

Argument (2)

variable is the name of the string variable to be altered. The characters in the variable are replaced, starting from the lefthand character (position 1), by the string *expression2*. If the number *expression1* is present, this gives the maximum number of characters that will be overwritten in the variable. Otherwise, it is the smaller of `LEN variable` and `LEN expression2` – the length the string in *variable* can never be altered by this statement.

Examples

```
start$ = LEFT$(a$)
left_half$=LEFT$(input$,LEN(input$) DIV 2 )
LEFT$(A$) = "ABCD"
LEFT$(A$,n%) = B$
```

LEN

Function returning the length of a string.

Syntax

```
LEN factor
```

Argument

Any string of 0 to 255 characters.

Result

The number of characters in the argument string, from 0 to 255.

Notes

The function SUMLEN returns the total length of the elements in a string array.

Examples

```
REPEAT INPUT a$: UNTIL LEN(a$)<=10
IF LEN(in$) > 12 THEN PRINT "Too long"
```

LET

Statement assigning a value to a variable.

Syntax

```
LET variable = expression
```

Argument

The *variable* is any addressable object, such as a, a$, a%, !a, a?10, $a, a(1), a() and so on.

expression is any expression of the range and type allowed by the variable: for reals, any numeric; for integers, any integer-range numeric; for strings, any string of length 0 to 255 characters, and for bytes any integer in the range 0 to 255 (though an integer-range number will be treated AND &FF).

If the variable is a whole array, the righthand side obeys the rules described in the chapter entitled *Arrays* on page 47.

Notes

The LET keyword is always optional in a variable assignment, and must not be used in the assignment to a pseudo-variable. For example, LET TIME=100 is illegal.

Examples

```
LET starttime=TIME
LET a$=LEFT$(addr$,10)
LET table?i=127*SIN(RAD(i))
LET a() = 1
LET A%() = B%() + C%()
```

LIBRARY

Statement to load a function or procedure library into memory.

Syntax
```
LIBRARY pathname
```

Argument
pathname is a string which should evaluate to the pathname of a valid BASIC file.

Purpose
LIBRARY reserves an area in the BASIC heap (where variables are stored) and loads the chosen function and procedure library into this area. It remains there until the heap is cleared. Whilst the library is in memory, the current program can call any of the procedures and functions it contains. See INSTALL on page 312 for how BASIC searches for procedures or functions.

Examples
```
LIBRARY "Printout"

A$ = "Library1"
LIBRARY A$
```

LINE

Statement to draw a line between two points.

Syntax

```
LINE expression,expression,expression,expression
```

Arguments

The (integer) expressions are two pairs of coordinates between which the line is drawn. The line is drawn using the current graphics foreground colour and action, and the graphics cursor position is updated to the second pair of coordinates. It is equivalent to a MOVE followed by a DRAW.

Examples

```
LINE 100,100,600,700
LINE x1,y1,x2,y2
LINE x1,y1,x1+xoffset,y1+yoffset
```

LINE INPUT

Statement obtaining a value or values from the input stream.

Syntax

This has the same syntax as INPUT

Result

If the input variable is a string, all the user's input is read into the variable, including leading and trailing spaces and commas. If the input variable is numeric, only a single value will be selected from the input line.

Notes

LINE INPUT is equivalent to INPUT LINE

Example

```
LINE INPUT "Your message" mess$
```

LIST

Command to list the program.

Syntax

LIST [*line-range*] [IF*string*]

Arguments

line-range gives the start and end lines to be listed. Both values are optional and should be separated by a comma. The first value defaults to zero and the last to 65279.

The IF, when present, is followed by a string of characters (not in quotes). Only lines which contain this string are listed.

Notes

In the search string following the IF statement, leading spaces are included as part of the string. So the command

LIST IF PRINT

will list

100 PRINT "Single space between line number and statement."

110 PRINT "Several spaces between line number and statement"

but will ignore

120PRINT "No space between line number and statement."

The command

LIST IFPRINT

will find and list all three lines.

The string given after the IF is tokenised before it is checked against the program. Hence, LIST IF PRINT and LIST IF P. both list lines containing the PRINT keyword. However, LIST IF PR does not.

Because the string after IF is tokenised, only one version of the pseudo-variables (each of which has two tokens) can be found. This is the one acting as a function (as in PRINT TIME), rather than the statement version (as in TIME=*expression*).

Examples

`LIST`	list the whole program
`LIST 1000,`	list from line 1000 to the end
`LIST ,50`	list from the start to line 50
`LIST 10,40`	list from line 10 to 40 inclusive
`LIST IFDEF`	list all lines containing a DEF
`LIST ,100 IFfred%=`	list all lines up to line 100 containing fred%=

LISTO

Command to set the LIST indentation options.

Syntax

```
LISTO expression
```

Argument

expression should be in the range zero to 31 and is treated as a five-bit number. The meaning of the bits is as follows:

Bit	Meaning
0	A space is printed after the line number
1	Structures are indented
2	Lines are split at the : statement delimiter
3	The line number is not listed. An error is displayed at line number references
4	Keywords are listed in lower case

Examples

`LISTO 0`	Default
`LISTO 2`	All loops and conditionals indented by two characters
`LISTO %10011`	Tokens in lower case, structures indented, line numbers followed by a space.

LN

Function returning the natural logarithm of its argument.

Syntax

```
LN factor
```

Argument

Any strictly positive value: a numeric greater than zero.

Result

Real which is the log to base e (2.718281828) of the argument. For BASIC V this will be between approximately −89 and +88, and for BASIC VI this will be between approximately −744 and +709.

Notes

LN is the inverse of EXP.

Examples

```
DEF FNlog2(n)=LN(n)/LN(2)
PRINT LN(10)
```

LOAD

Command to load a BASIC program at PAGE.

Syntax

```
LOAD pathname
```

Argument

`pathname` is a string which should evaluate to the pathname of a valid BASIC file.

Notes

Any program which is currently in memory is overwritten and lost with all its variables. The static integers (A% - Z% and @%) and INSTALLed libraries are not affected.

Examples

```
LOAD adfs::GDisc.disasm
```

where `GDisc` is the name of a disc.

```
LOAD FNnextFile
```

LOCAL

Statement to declare a local variable in a procedure or function.
Statement to make current DATA pointer local.
Statement to make the error control status local.
Used with DIM to reserve a block of memory within a procedure or function.

Syntax

(1) LOCAL [*variable*] [,*variable*...]
(2) LOCAL DATA
(3) LOCAL ERROR
(4) DIM *numeric-variable* LOCAL *expression*

Arguments (1)

variables following the LOCAL may be of any type, such as a, a%, a$, $buffer, a(), and so on. The statement causes the current value of the variables cited to be stored on BASIC's stack, ready for retrieval at the end of the procedure or function. This means the value inside the procedure may be altered without fear of corrupting a variable of the same name outside the procedure. At the end of the procedure, the old value of the variable is restored.

Note: Local numerics are initialised to zero, and local strings are initialised to the null string. Arrays can be declared as being local and then dimensioned using DIM as normal.

Purpose (2)

LOCAL DATA stores the current data pointer on the stack for the duration of a loop or function/procedure call. This enables a new data pointer to be set up, using RESTORE, and for the original one to be restored with RESTORE DATA. RESTORE DATA is performed automatically on return from a function/ procedure.

Purpose (3)

LOCAL ERROR remembers the current error handler so a subsequent use of ON ERROR does not overwrite it. This error handler can later be restored using RESTORE ERROR.

Note: LOCAL ERROR can be used anywhere in a program

If LOCAL ERROR is used within a procedure or function it must be the last item to be made local.

Returning from a procedure or function call which contained a LOCAL ERROR automatically restores any stored error status.

See also ON ERROR LOCAL on page 348.

Arguments (4)

See DIM on page 266.

Examples

```
LOCAL a$,len%,price
LOCAL a(), B() : DIM a(2), B(4,5)


10 ON ERROR PROCerror
20 res = FNdivide(opp,adj)
30 END
40 DEFFNdivide(x,y)
50 LOCAL ERROR
60 ON ERROR LOCAL PRINT "attempt to divide by zero" :=0
70 =x/y : REM end of function restores previous error status
```

LOG

Function returning the logarithm to base ten of its argument.

Syntax

```
LOG factor
```

Argument

Any strictly positive value: a numeric greater than zero.

Result

Real which is the log to base ten of the argument. For BASIC V this will be in the range −38 to +38, and for BASIC VI this will be in the range −323 to +308.

Example

```
PRINT LOG(2.4323)
```

LOMEM

Pseudo-variable holding the address of the start of user memory.

Syntax

```
(1) LOMEM
(2) LOMEM = expression
```

Result (1)

The address of the start of user memory.

Argument (2)

expression is the address at which user memory starts. The expression should be in the range TOP to HIMEM to avoid corruption of the program and/or the generation of No room errors.

Notes

LOMEM should not be changed after any assignments in a program. If it is, variables assigned before the change are lost. LOMEM is reset to TOP by CLEAR (and thus by RUN).

If you attempt to set LOMEM to an illegal value, a warning message is given and LOMEM is not altered.

Examples

```
LOMEM=TOP+&400 : REM reserve 1k above TOP
PRINT LOMEM
```

LVAR

Command displaying the first line of all current libraries, all defined variables and all procedures and functions that have been called.

Syntax

LVAR

Purpose

LVAR lists all the values of BASIC variables, sizes of arrays, known procedures and functions. It also lists the first line of all libraries currently loaded. These are displayed in the same order as that in which the libraries are searched when a library procedure or function is called.

Notes

In order for LVAR to be useful, you should ensure that the first line of each library includes the full name of the library and the name of a procedure which can be called to provide details of all the routines which the library contains.

MID$(

Function returning, or statement altering, a substring of a string.

Syntax

as a function:

(1) MID$(*expression1*,*expression2*[,*expression3*])

as a statement:

(2) MID$(*variable*,*expression1*[,*expression2*]) = *expression3*

Argument (1)

expression1 is a string of length 0 to 255 characters.

expression2 is the position within the string of the first character required.

expression3, if present, gives the number of characters in the substring. The default value is 255 (or to the end of the source string).

Result (1)

The substring of the source string, of a length given in the third argument, and starting from the position specified. The result string can never be of greater length than the source string.

Argument (2)

variable is the name of the string variable which is to be altered.

expression3 evaluates to a string which provides the characters to replace those in *variable*.

expression1 is the position within the string of the first character to be replaced.

expression2, if present, gives the maximum number of characters to be replaced. The replacement stops when the end of the string variable is reached, even if there are characters in *expression3* which are unused.

MID$(

Examples

```
PRINT MID$("ABCDEFG",2,3); : REM should print "BCD"
right_half$=MID$(any$,LEN(any$) DIV 2)
MID$(A$,4,4) = B$
MID$(A$,2,5) = MID$(B$,3,6)
```

MOD

Operator performing integer modulo (remainder of division between two integers). Function returning the modulus of its array argument.

Syntax

as an operator:

(1) *factor* MOD *factor*

as a function:

(2) MOD *numeric-array*

Arguments (1)

The *factors* are integer-range numerics. The righthand side must not be zero.

Result (1)

Remainder when the lefthand argument is divided by the righthand one using integer division. The sign of the result is the same as the sign of the lefthand argument.

Argument (2)

The *numeric-array* can be any integer or floating point array.

Result (2)

The square root of the sum of the squares (the modulus) of all the elements of the array.

Examples

```
INPUT i%: i% = i% MOD max_num%
count%=count% MOD max% + 1
PRINT result% MOD 100
DEF FNrms(a())=MODa()/SQRDIM(a(),1)
```

MODE

Statement changing, or function returning, the display mode.

Syntax

as a statement:

(1) MODE *numeric-expression*
(2) MODE *string-expression*
(3) MODE *expr1,expr2,expr3[,expr4]*
(4) MODE *expr1,expr2,expr3,expr4,expr5[,expr6]*

as a function:

(5) MODE

Arguments (1)

If *numeric-expression* is an integer in the range 0 to 127, it is used to select an old-type numbered screen mode. When *numeric-expression* is between 128 and 255, the mode used is *numeric-expression*–128. Sufficient memory, however, for two copies of the screen is reserved if the configured screen size allows. This allows you to have one copy on display whilst you are updating the other, which means that smooth animation can be obtained.

Details of the numbered modes available are given in the Appendix on old-type screen modes in the RISC OS *User Guide*.

If expression is an integer greater than 255 it is treated as a pointer to a *mode selector* block and OS_ScreenMode 0 is called. See the RISC OS *Programmer's Reference Manual* for further information.

Arguments (2)

This changes the screen mode using the mode string given in *string-expression*. See Appendix E – *Specifying screen modes* for full details of the mode string syntax.

BASIC uses OS_ScreenMode 15, if available, to change mode using the provided string. On versions of RISC OS where OS_ScreenMode 15 is not available BASIC will attempt to parse the string itself, producing a *mode selector* block which is then passed to OS_ScreenMode 0.

Arguments (3)

MODE x,y,bpp[,framerate]

This builds a *mode selector* and calls OS_ScreenMode 0 to change the screen mode. The first and second expressions are integers specifying the mode width and height in pixels. The third expression gives the colour depth in bits per pixel, and may be 1, 2, 4, 6, 8, 16 or 32, where 6 selects a VIDC1-style 256 colour mode and 8 selects a 256 colour mode with a full palette. The optional fourth expression is an integer giving the frame rate in Hertz.

In the mode selector block built by this command, the value of the first expression (width) is stored at offset 4, the value of the second expression (height) is stored at offset 8, the value of the third expression is converted to the pixel depth (0, 1, 2, 3, 4 or 5) and stored at offset 12, and if the frame rate is given it is stored at offset 16, otherwise −1 is stored there. When the third expression is 8, the mode selector block is extended with extension words to set ModeFlags (VDU variable 0) to 128 and NColour (VDU variable 3) to 255 in order to select a full palette.

This form of the MODE command does not allow all possible modes to be selected, for example 4,096 and 65,536 colour modes cannot be specified, and the pixel layout cannot be set to a non-default value. Use the MODE (2) or MODE (4) forms of the command for more flexibility.

Arguments (4)

MODE x,y,ModeFlags,NColour,Log2bpp[,framerate]

This builds a *mode selector* and calls OS_ScreenMode 0 to change the screen mode. The first and second expressions are integers specifying the mode width and height in pixels and are stored at offsets 4 and 8 in the mode selector block. The third expression specifies the value of ModeFlags (VDU variable 0), and the fourth expression the value of NColour (VDU variable 3), and these are stored as extension words at offset 20 of the mode selector block. The fifth expression gives the value of Log2BPP (VDU variable 9) and is stored at offset 12. The optional sixth expression gives the frame rate and this is stored at offset 16 of the mode selector if specified, otherwise −1 is stored at this offset.

See *Appendix E – Specifying screen modes* for a table listing the valid combinations of ModeFlags, NColour and Log2bpp.

Result (5)

An integer describing the current screen mode.

MODE

- If the value is between 0 and 255 inclusive, the current mode is a numbered mode, and the returned value corresponds directly to the mode number. Note that if a shadow mode had been requested by adding 128 to the mode number, this is not reflected in the value returned by the MODE function. For example, if you typed MODE 129, the MODE function would return 1. It is still recommended however that you use 255 as the upper range limit, as that will provide consistency with other interfaces which are capable of using mode numbers in that range.

- If the value is not between 0 and 255, then it is the address of a mode selector block which describes the current mode. This is true even if the mode was selected via a mode string (internally the OS will convert the string to an equivalent mode selector block). Note that the content of this block is only valid until the next mode change. If you intend to save and restore the current mode then you must make a copy of the block.

Be careful when checking the MODE value; mode selectors may be located in the high end of the memory map (above &7FFFFFFF). In BASIC this will be treated as a negative number, so a simple check of the form IF MODE < 256 THEN ... will not suffice.

Notes

Changing mode also does the following:

- sets COUNT to zero
- sets the text and graphics viewports to their defaults of the whole screen
- clears the screen to the current text background colour
- homes the text cursor
- moves the graphics cursor to (0,0)
- resets the logical-physical colour map (palette) to the default for the new mode
- resets the colour-fill patterns to their defaults for the new mode sets the dot pattern for dotted lines to &AA and the repeat length to 8
- resets VDU 5 magnification.

History

(2) was added in version 1.06, but implemented by calling *WimpMode. Support for passing a mode selector in (1) was also added in version 1.06. (3) was added in version 1.34. (4) was added in version 1.73, which also improved (2) so that it does not affect the Wimp mode.

Examples

```
MODE 0
MODE m%+128
MODE "X640 Y480 C256"
MODE 640,480,VDU0,VDU3,VDU9:REM keep current colour format
PRINT MODE
```

MOUSE

Statement interrogating and controlling the mouse position and button status.

Syntax

(1) MOUSE *variable1,variable2,variable3[,variable4]*
(2) MOUSE ON [*expression*]
(3) MOUSE OFF
(4) MOUSE COLOUR *expr,expr,expr,expr*
(5) MOUSE TO *expression,expression*
(6) MOUSE STEP *expression[,expression]*
(7) MOUSE RECTANGLE *expr,expr,expr,expr*

Arguments (1)

The first two variables are assigned the x and y positions of the mouse as values in the range −32768 to 32767. The third variable is assigned a value giving the status of the mouse buttons as follows:

Value	Status
0	No buttons pressed
1	Right button only pressed
2	Middle button only pressed
3	Middle and right buttons pressed
4	Left button only pressed
5	Left and right buttons pressed
6	Left and middle buttons pressed
7	All three buttons pressed

If present, the last variable is assigned the time of a monotonic (always increasing) centi-second timer, which can act as a time-stamp for making sure that button-press events are processed in order, and for detecting double clicks, etc.

Argument (2)

MOUSE ON causes the mouse pointer to be displayed. The optional numeric expression is the pointer shape to be used in the range 1 to 4. If it is omitted, 1 is used.

If bit 7 of the pointer shape number is set, i.e. the expression is in the range &81 to &84, then the mouse pointer will be unlinked from the mouse. That is, movements of the physical mouse will not affect the screen pointer. Instead, you can use POINT TO *x,y* to position the pointer.

Purpose (3)

MOUSE OFF disables the mouse pointer, removing it from the screen.

Arguments (4)

MOUSE COLOUR sets the colour components of the mouse pointer logical colour given in the first expression to the red, green and blue values given in the second, third and fourth expressions. Pointer logical colours are in the range 1 to 3. Colour 0 is always transparent.

Arguments (5)

MOUSE TO moves the mouse (and pointer) to the (x,y) position given by the first and second numeric arguments.

Arguments (6)

MOUSE STEP controls the speed of movement of the mouse pointer compared to the speed of the movement of the actual mouse device. If there is one argument, it is used as a multiplier for both the x and y movements. If there are two, the first is used for x and the second for y. The arguments can be negative to reverse the usual directions.

Arguments (7)

MOUSE RECTANGLE sets a bounding rectangle outside which the mouse cannot move. The arguments are the left, bottom, right and top of the rectangle in graphics units. If the mouse pointer is outside the box when this command is given, it will be moved to the nearest point within it.

Examples

```
MOUSE xpos%,ypos%,button%
MOUSE ON 2
MOUSE OFF
MOUSE COLOUR Col%,red%,green%,blue%
MOUSE TO 100,100
MOUSE STEP 3,2
MOUSE RECTANGLE 640,512,1023,1279
```

MOVE

Statement to set the position of the graphics cursor.

Syntax

    MOVE [BY] expression,expression

Arguments

The expressions are x and y coordinates of the new position for the graphics cursor.

If the keyword BY is omitted, the coordinates are absolute. That is, they give the position of the cursor with respect to the graphics origin. If BY is included, the coordinates are relative. That means they give the new position of the cursor with respect to the current graphics cursor position.

MOVE is equivalent to PLOT 4; MOVE BY is equivalent to PLOT 0.

Examples

    MOVE 0,0 : REM Goto the origin
    MOVE BY 4*dx%,4*dy%

NEW

Command to remove the current program, and to initialise the computer so that it is ready to receive a new program.

Syntax

NEW

Purpose

The NEW command does not destroy the program, but merely sets a few internal variables as if there were no program in the memory. The effect of NEW may be undone using the OLD command, providing no program lines have been typed in, or variables created, between the two commands. BASIC does an automatic NEW whenever it is entered.

NEXT

Part of the FOR ... TO ... NEXT structure.

Syntax

```
NEXT [variable][,[variable]...]
```

Arguments

The variables are of any numeric type, and if present should correspond to the variable used to open the loop. See the FOR entry for a description of the mechanism of the FOR ... NEXT loop.

Notes

The variables after the NEXT should always be specified as this enables BASIC to detect improperly nested loops. If the loop variable given after a NEXT does not correspond to the innermost open loop, BASIC closes the inner loops until a matching looping variable is found. In order for the indentation produced by LISTO 2 to be useful, you should only close one loop per NEXT statement.

Examples

```
NEXT a%
NEXT        : REM close one loop
NEXT j%,i%  : REM close two loops
NEXT ,,,    : REM close four loops
```

NOT

Function returning the bitwise NOT of its argument.

Syntax

NOT *factor*

Argument

An integer-range numeric.

Result

An integer in which all the bits of the argument have been inverted: ones have changed to zeros and zeros have changed to ones. If the argument is a truth value, NOT can be used in a logical statement to invert the condition. In this case, the truth value should only be one of the values –1 (TRUE) and 0 (FALSE).

Examples

```
IF NOT ok THEN PRINT "Error in input"
inv%=NOT mask%
REPEAT UNTIL NOT INKEY(-99)
```

OF

Part of the CASE ... OF ... WHEN ... OTHERWISE ... ENDCASE statement.

Syntax

```
CASE expression OF
```

Argument

expression may yield any type of value: integer, floating point, or string.

Notes

The OF keyword must be the last item on the line. See the CASE keyword on page 248 for more details.

Examples

```
CASE n% OF
CASE LEFT$(answer$) OF
```

OFF

Statement to remove the cursor from the screen.

Syntax

OFF

Purpose

The OFF statement switches off the flashing text cursor until it is re-enabled by the ON statement, or until cursor copying is used.

Examples

OFF

OLD

Command to retrieve a program after NEW has been typed.

Syntax

OLD

Purpose

The OLD command retrieves a program lost by NEW or Break providing no new program lines have been entered, or variables defined. When you recover the previous program using OLD, you may notice that the first line number has changed. In particular, it is now its old value MOD 256. So if the first line used to be 1000, it will now be 232. You can remedy this slight problem using the RENUMBER command to reduce the value of the line numbers.

ON

Statement to restore the text cursor on to the screen.

Syntax

ON

Purpose

The ON statement re-enables the text cursor after it has been removed with an OFF statement.

Example

ON

ON ERROR

Statement defining or cancelling an error handler.

Syntax

```
(1) ON ERROR [LOCAL] statements
(2) ON ERROR OFF
```

Purpose (1)

The ON ERROR statement introduces an error handler. When an error occurs after an ON ERROR has been executed, control passes to the first statement of the ON ERROR line. The program continues from there. Note that all of the error handler code has to be on the ON ERROR line, so complex error handlers should use a procedure, for example:

```
10 ON ERROR PROCerr_handler
```

Usually, before the error handler is called, BASIC will forget about all active procedures, functions and loops, in effect reverting to the 'top-level' of the program. However, if the LOCAL keyword is used on the ON ERROR line, then the nesting level current when the ON ERROR is executed will be re-entered when the error occurs. Thus error handlers which are useful within loops and other constructs may be written.

See also LOCAL ERROR on page 326 and RESTORE ERROR on page 383.

Purpose (2)

ON ERROR OFF cancels any active error handler, so that this default action is used when an error occurs:

```
TRACE OFF
IF QUIT THEN
  ERROR EXT ERR,REPORT$
ELSE
  RESTORE
  IF ERL THEN
    REM Equivalent to PRINT REPORT$+" at line "+STR$(ERL)
    CALL !ERRXLATE:PRINT $STRACC
  ELSE
    REPORT:PRINT
  ENDIF
  END
ENDIF
```

An automatic ON ERROR OFF is performed when fatal errors are generated.

Examples

```
ON ERROR IF ERR=17 STOP : REM trap just Escape
ON ERROR LOCAL PRINT"Bad arguments" : ENDPROC
```

OPENIN

Function opening an existing file for input only.

Syntax

```
OPENIN pathname
```

Argument

A string which evaluates to a valid pathname.

Result

An integer acting as a channel number for the file. All subsequent operations on file (e.g. BGET#, PTR#, EOF# etc.) use the channel number, sometimes called a handle, as an argument.

OPENIN opens a file for input only. The file must exist prior to the call. If it doesn't, a channel number of 0 is returned. Only read-type operations are allowed on the file. For example, you can get characters from it, but not put them. You can move PTR# freely within the file, but not outside of it. A file may be opened for reading several times. However, you can't OPENIN and OPENOUT (or OPENUP) the same file.

Examples

```
in_file%=OPENIN "Invoices"
data%=OPENIN(":0"+data$)
```

OPENOUT

Function for opening a new file for input and output.

Syntax

```
OPENOUT pathname
```

Argument

A string which evaluates to a valid pathname.

Result

An integer acting as a channel number for the file. All subsequent operations on file (e.g. BGET#, PTR#, EOF# etc.) use the channel number, sometimes called a handle, as an argument.

OPENOUT creates and opens a file for input and output. Read- and write-type operations are allowed on the file. You can both get characters from, and write characters to, the file. You can move PTR# freely within the file, and extend the file by moving PTR# outside of the file (beyond EXT#). You can also shorten the file by assigning to EXT#. Once you OPENOUT a file, it can't be opened again unless it is closed first. Trying to OPENOUT an open file gives an error.

Examples

```
out_file%=OPENOUT "Customers"
data%=OPENOUT(":datadisc."+data$)
```

OPENUP

Function for opening an existing file for input and output (update).

Syntax

```
OPENUP pathname
```

Argument

A string which evaluates to a valid pathname.

Result

An integer acting as a channel number for the file. All subsequent operations on file (e.g. BGET#, PTR#, EOF# etc.) use the channel number, sometimes called a handle, as an argument.

OPENUP opens a file, which must exist already, for input and output. Read- and write-type operations are allowed on the file. You can both get characters from, and write characters to, the file. You can move PTR# freely within the file, and extend the file by moving PTR# outside of the file (beyond EXT#). You can also shorten the file by assigning to EXT#. Once you OPENUP a file, it can't be opened again unless it is closed first. Similarly, trying to OPENUP an open file gives an error.

Examples

```
random_file%=OPENUP("records")
```

OR

Operator performing bitwise OR of its arguments.

Syntax

relational OR *relational*

Arguments

Any integer-range numerics.

Result

An integer obtained by ORing together the corresponding bits in the arguments. The arguments may be interpreted as bit-patterns, in which case a bit in the result is set to one if either or both of the corresponding bits in the arguments are one. Alternatively, they may be interpreted as logical values, in which case the result is TRUE if either or both of the arguments are TRUE.

Examples

```
PRINT a% OR &AA55
IF a<1 OR a>10 THEN PRINT "Bad range"
```

ORIGIN

Statement to move the graphics origin.

Syntax

    ORIGIN expression,expression

Arguments

The expressions are integer numerics in the range −32768 to +32767. They are the absolute coordinates of the new graphics origin: the position of the point (0,0). These coordinates are always given with respect to the bottom left corner of the screen.

The graphics origin is used by all commands which plot graphics, such as MOVE, LINE, PLOT, CIRCLE, and so on, and also by VDU 24 which sets a graphics viewport.

Example

    ORIGIN 640,512 : REM Set origin to the centre of screen

OSCLI

Statement to pass a string to the operating system.

Syntax

OSCLI *expression*

Argument

expression should be a string of between 0 and 255 characters. It is passed to the operating system OS_CLI routine to be executed.

Notes

The difference between passing a string to the operating system via a * command and via OSCLI is that the former makes no attempt to process the text following it, whereas the latter evaluates the text as a BASIC string expression. Thus you can say:

OSCLI "LOAD file "+STR$~buffer%

but not (usefully)

*"LOAD file "+STR$~buffer%

Many extensions to BBC BASIC on 6502-based BBC Microcomputer operating systems used 'internal' BASIC routines called from OSCLI commands. BBC BASIC provides extra information when using * or OSCLI to allow such software to be ported to the BASIC built into RISC OS. (Note that this does not happen for SYS "OS_CLI","fred").

Information is passed in registers R0 to R5, because the high user-mode registers are not conveniently readable from other modes:

R0	contains CLI string pointer
R1	contains &BA51Cxxx
R2	pointer to BASIC's workspace (ARGP)
R3	BASIC's LINE pointer (points to the current statement)
R4	pointer to BASIC's full, descending stack
R5	environment information pointer

Note that by the time a module's * command handler is invoked these registers will have been overwritten, which means that any module wishing to use them will need to claim CLIV and take a copy.

OSCLI

The value in R1 should be inspected by any routine in order to validate that the call is, indeed, from BASIC (it is also a good idea to check R2 to R5 for valid addresses); this value is also at address [R5,#–4]. The current BASIC interpreter provides &BA51C005, and the bottom three nybbles (&005) denote that the calling standard follows the one shown here (to allow for possible future changes to which registers are passed).

Registers R2 to R5 contain information about BASIC's environment corresponding to the information passed in registers R8, R12, R13 and R14 by the CALL statement. Further information can be found in the section describing CALL on page 234. The value in LINE (R3) should not be relied on, except that it is sufficient for BASIC to produce the correct line number in case of an error.

If a handler wishes to call any of the internal BASIC routines then it must ensure it is executing in user mode and transfer the state information to the correct registers. When BASIC is eventually returned to at the end of the SWI OS_CLI call, its (user-mode) registers must not have been altered.

Examples

```
OSCLI "CAT"
OSCLI "LOAD "+file$+" "+STR$buff%:REM get file in buffer
```

OTHERWISE

Part of the CASE ... OF ... WHEN ... OTHERWISE ... ENDCASE statement.

Syntax

See CASE on page 248.

Notes

The OTHERWISE statement is executed only when the previous WHEN statements have failed to match the value of the CASE expression. OTHERWISE matches any values. If it is present, all statements following it will be executed until the matching ENDCASE is encountered. It must be the first statement on a line.

Examples

```
OTHERWISE PRINT "Bad input"
OTHERWISE PROCdraw(x,y) : PROCwait
```

OVERLAY

Statement setting up a list of overlay libraries.

Syntax

```
OVERLAY string-array
```

Argument

string-array is a one-dimensional array which should contain the pathnames of the libraries to be overlaid. Elements containing a null string will be ignored.

Purpose

When the OVERLAY statement is executed, BASIC reserves enough space in the BASIC heap (where variables are stored) for the largest of the files given in the array. Then, when it can't find a PROC or FN definition anywhere else, it will go through the list, loading the libraries in order until the definition is found or the end of the array is met.

Once a definition has been found, that library stays in memory (and so the other definitions in it may be used) until the next time a definition can't be found anywhere. The search process then starts again, so the current overlay library will be overwritten with the first one in the list. Once BASIC has found a definition, it will remember which file it was in (or more precisely, which element of the array held the pathname), so that file will be loaded immediately the next time the definition is required and it is not in memory.

Because of the way one area of memory is used to hold each of the overlay files (and only one at any one time), you are not allowed to call a procedure whose definition is in an overlay library if one of the overlay definitions is currently active. Another way of putting this is that you can't nest overlay calls.

If you know that a given overlay file will never be needed again in the program, you can speed up the search through the overlay list by setting the no-longer-required elements of the array to the null string. You can also add new names to the end of the array, as long as none of the new library files is bigger than the largest one specified in the original OVERLAY statement.

You can execute OVERLAY more than once in a program. Each time it is called, the memory set aside for the previous set of files will be lost, and a new block based on the size of the new ones will be allocated.

Example

```
DIM lib$(2)
lib$() = "Import","Printout","Export"
OVERLAY lib$()
```

PAGE

Pseudo-variable holding the address of the program.

Syntax

```
(1)  PAGE
(2)  PAGE = expression
```

Result (1)

An address which is an unsigned number. PAGE is the location at which the current BASIC program starts.

Argument (2)

expression is an integer in the range *n* to HIMEM, where *n* is the limit of BASIC's own workspace, which is &8F00 for BASIC V and &9700 (2 kbytes higher) for BASIC VI (this could change in later versions of BASIC). PAGE should be on a word boundary. By changing PAGE, you can have several BASIC programs residing in the machine at once.

Notes

If you attempt to set PAGE to an invalid address, a warning message is given and PAGE is not altered.

Example

```
PAGE = HIMEM - &4000
```

PI

Function returning the value of π.

Syntax

```
PI
```

Result

The constant 3.141592653589793.

Examples

```
DEF FNcircum(r)=2*PI*r
```

PLOT

Statement performing an operating system PLOT function.

Syntax

```
PLOT expression1,expression2,expression3
```

Arguments

expression1 is the plot number in the range from 0 to 255. For example, 85 is the plot number for an absolute triangle plot in the foreground colour.

The second and third expressions are the x and y coordinates respectively, in the range −32768 to +32767.

See *Appendix G – Plot codes* on page 483 for a full list of PLOT codes.

Examples

```
PLOT 85,100,100 : REM Draw a triangle
PLOT 69,x,y : REM Plot a single point
```

Keywords

POINT

Statement to plot a single point or move the on-screen pointer.

Syntax

```
(1) POINT [BY] expression,expression
(2) POINT TO expression,expression
```

Arguments (1)

The expressions are integers giving the coordinates at which the point will be plotted. The point is plotted using the current graphics foreground colour and action, and the graphics cursor is updated to these coordinates.

If the keyword BY is omitted, the coordinates are absolute. That is, they give the position of the point with respect to the graphics origin. If BY is included, the coordinates are relative. That means they give the position of the point with respect to the current graphics cursor position.

Arguments (2)

The expressions are integers giving the coordinates at which the on-screen pointer will be placed if it is not linked to the mouse position. If the pointer is linked to the mouse this command is ignored. See MOUSE for more details about unlinking the pointer from the mouse.

Examples

```
POINT 320,600
POINT X%+4, Y%+4
POINT BY 100,0
POINT TO 640,512
```

POINT(

Function retuning the logical colour of a graphics pixel.

Syntax

POINT(*expression,expression*)

Arguments

The expressions are the coordinates of the pixel whose colour is required.

Result

This is an integer identifying the colour of the pixel or −1 if the point specified lies outside the current graphics viewport.

Note that the value returned is in the range 0 to 63 for the 256-colour modes. The function TINT(x,y) will read the tint of the given coordinate, returning a value in the range 0 to 255.

In modes with less than 256 colours POINT returns the logical colour number in the range 0 to *n*, where *n* is one less than the number of logical colours in the current mode. For example, *n* is 15 in a 16-colour mode.

In 256-colour modes the value returned will be between 0 and 63 and the TINT function will be required to find the tint of the pixel.

In modes with more than 256 colours POINT returns the colour number of the pixel, the format of which depends on the number of bits per pixel (which can be determined by reading VDU 9, Log2BPP), and the colour format (which can be determined from bits 12-15 of VDU 0, ModeFlags). For example, in a 32-bit per pixel mode with a TBGR format (Log2BPP=5, ModeFlags=0) the lowest 8 bits of the returned number is the amount of red, the next 8 bits are the amount of green and the next 8 bits are the amount of blue.

Example

```
REPEAT Y%+=4:UNTIL POINT(640,Y%)<>0
```

POS

Function returning the x-coordinate of the text cursor.

Syntax

    POS

Result

An integer between 0 and *n*, where *n* is the width of the current text viewport minus one. This is the position of the text cursor which is normally given relative to the lefthand edge of the text viewport. If the cursor direction has been altered using VDU 23,16,... then it is given relative to the negative x edge of the screen which may be top, bottom, left or right.

Notes

Even in VDU 5 mode, POS returns the position of the text cursor. You should therefore keep track of the horizontal position explicitly in programs which must operate in VDU 5 mode (e.g. Wimp-based programs). COUNT still works as expected in VDU 5 mode.

Examples

    old_x%=POS
    IF POS<>0 THEN PRINT

PRINT

Statement printing information on the output stream(s) (e.g. screen, printer, etc).

Syntax

The items following PRINT may be string expressions, numeric expressions, and print formatters. By default, numerics are printed in decimal, right justified in the print field given by @% (see below). Strings are printed left justified in the print field. The print formatters have the following effects when printing numbers:

;	Do not right justify (print leading spaces before) numbers in the print field. Set numeric printing to decimal. Semi-colon stays in effect until a comma is encountered. Do not print a new line at the end if this is the last character of the PRINT statement.
, (comma)	Right justify numbers in the print field. Set numeric printing to decimal. This is the default print mode. Comma stays in effect until a semi-colon is encountered. If the cursor is not at the start of the print field, print spaces to reach the next one.
~ (tilde)	Print numbers as hexadecimal integers, using the current left/right-justify mode. Tilde stays in effect until a comma or semi-colon is encountered.
' (single quote)	Print a new line. Retain current left/right-justify and hexadecimal/decimal modes.
TAB (	If there is one argument, for example, TAB (n), print (n_COUNT) spaces. If the cursor is initially past position n (i.e. COUNT>n), print a new line first. If there are two arguments, for example, TAB (10, 20), move directly to that tab position. Left/right-justify and hexadecimal/decimal modes are retained.
SPC *factor*	Print the given number of spaces. For example SPC5 outputs five spaces. Right-justify and hexadecimal/decimal modes are retained.
space	Print the next item, retaining left/right-justify and hexadecimal/decimal modes.

When strings are printed the descriptions above apply, except that hexadecimal mode does not affect the string. Also no trailing spaces are printed after a string unless it is followed by a comma. This prints enough spaces to move to the start of the next print field.

The print formatters TAB, SPC and ' may also be used in INPUT statements.

Formatting numbers

The format in which numbers are printed, and the width of print fields are determined by the value of the special system integer variable, @%. This can be set as an integer or in a special way using a string expression.

Setting @% using a format string

The value of @% is specified in ANSI printf format, as follows:

`@%="expression"`

where *expression* takes the form *[+]Ax.y* or *[+]Ax,y*, and must be in quotes.

A defines the format, and can take the following values:

- G (General format). In G format, *x* defines the field width and *y* defines the number of digits to be printed. Note that if *x* is less than 0.01, printing reverts to E format.
- E (Exponent format). In E format, *x* defines the field width and *y* defines the number of significant figures to be printed after the decimal point. Note that E format allows 3 digits for the exponent, and an optional minus sign. This will leave up to three trailing spaces if the exponent is positive and only one or two digits long.
- F (Fixed format). In F format, *x* defines the number of figures (exactly) to be printed after the decimal point and *y* defines the field width.

The optional + sign is a switch affecting the STR$ function. If supplied, it forces STR$ to use the format determined by @%. If it is not supplied, STR$ uses a default format equivalent to `@%="+G0.10"`.

The dot or comma between *x* and *y* selects the character to be used as the decimal point. Note that there must not be any spaces in the definition of @%.

The BASIC interpreter supports partial setting of @%, which means you do not have to supply all the arguments. See the examples of @% below.

Examples of @%

`@%="G10.9"` is the default setting. It is a General format, with a field width of 10 and a precision of 9 digits; for example 12.3456789. STR$ uses its default.

`@%="+E10.3"` is an Exponent format, with a field width of 10, and 3 digits after the decimal point; for example 1.24E1. STR$ uses this format instead of its default.

`@%="F7.4"` is a Fixed format, with a field width of 7, and 4 digits after the decimal point; for example 12.3457. STR$ uses its default.

`@%="+"` forces STR$ to use the current format.

`@%="G"` changes to G format. STR$ uses its default.

`@%="10"` sets the field width for the current format to 10, and forces STR$ to use its default.

`@%=".5"` just sets the precision for the current format to 5 digits, and forces STR$ to use its default.

`@%="+,"` changes the decimal point to be a comma and forces STR$ to use the current format.

Setting @% as an integer

You can set the variable @% to an integer value to produce the same results (this is the only method possible in BASIC 1.04 and earlier). The value of @% is specified using a hexadecimal word four bytes long, as follows:

`@%=&wwxxyyzz`

- Byte 4 (*ww*), which can be 1 or 0, corresponds to the + STR$ switch. If this byte is 1, STR$ uses the format specified by the rest of @%. If it is 0, STR$ uses its default value of &00000A00.
- Byte 3 (*xx*) can be 0, 1 or 2 to select the G, E or F format with a dot as decimal point, or &80, &81 or &82 to select G, E or F format with a comma as decimal point
- Byte 2 (*yy*), which can take values from 1 to 10, determines the number of digits printed. In General format, this is the number of digits which may be printed before reverting to Exponent format (1 to 10); in Exponent format it gives the number of significant figures to be printed after the decimal point (1 to 10). In fixed format it gives the number of digits (exactly) that follow the decimal point.
- Byte 1 (*zz*), which is in the range 0 to 255, gives the print field width for tabulating using commas.

When the value of @% is read, it returns an integer in the above format.

Examples of @%

`@%=&0000090A` uses General format with up to nine significant digits in a field width of ten characters. Note that General format reverts to Exponent format when the number is less than 0.1. This is the default setting of @%.

`@%=&0101030A` uses Exponent format. Three significant digits are printed, in a field of ten characters. These numbers look like `1.23E0` or `1.10E-3`, etc. In addition, STR$ uses this format instead of its default (which is &00000A00).

`@%=&00020407` uses Fixed format with four decimal places in a tab field width of seven. Numbers are printed out in the form `1.23`, `923.10`, etc.

`@%=&00820407` is the same as the previous example but using a comma for the decimal point. Numbers will look like `4,56` or `821,20`, etc.

Notes

Setting byte two to 10, e.g. `&0A0A`, shows the inaccuracies which arise when trying to store certain numbers in binary. For example:

PRINT 7.7

prints 7.699999999 when @%=&0A0A.

Examples

```
PRINT "Hello there";
PRINT a,SIN(RAD(a)),x,y''p,q;
PRINT TAB(10,3)"Profits"SPC(10);profits;
```

PRINT#

Statement printing information to an open file.

Syntax

```
PRINT#factor [,expression,expression...]
```

Arguments

factor is the channel number of a file opened for output or update. The expressions, if present, are any BASIC integer, real or string expressions. They are evaluated and sent to the file specified with the corresponding type information.

Integers are written as &40 followed by the two's complement representation of the integer in four bytes, most significant byte first.

5-byte real variables are written as &80 followed by five bytes. The first four bytes are the mantissa and the fifth is the exponent. The mantissa is written least significant byte (LSB) first. 31 bits represent the magnitude of the mantissa and one bit (bit 7 of the fourth byte) the sign. The exponent byte is in excess-128 form. BASIC V only prints real numbers in 5-byte real format.

8-byte real variables are written as &88 followed by two 4-byte words, in IEEE Double Precision (D) format. The exponent is represented by bits 20 to 30 in the first word. The sign bit is bit 31 in the first word. The mantissa is represented by bits 0 to 19 in the first word and bits 0 to 31 in the second word. BASIC VI only prints real numbers in 8-byte real format. You need 1.05 series (rather than 1.04) to read this information back.

Strings are written as &00 followed by a one byte count of the length of the string, followed by the characters in the string in reverse order.

Example

```
PRINT#file,name$+":",INT(100*price+.5),qnty%
```

PROC

Statement introducing or calling a user-defined procedure.

Syntax

```
(1) DEF PROCproc-part
(2) PROCproc-part
(3) ON expr PROCproc1 [,PROCproc2...] [ELSE statement]
```

Argument (1)

proc-part has the form *identifier[(parameter-list)]*. It gives the name of the procedure (the *identifier*) and the names and types of the optional parameters, which must be enclosed in brackets and separated by commas.

Argument (2)

The second form is used when the procedure is actually invoked, and this time the parameter list comprises expressions of types corresponding to the parameters declared in the DEF PROC statement. The expressions are evaluated and assigned (locally) to the parameter variables. Control returns to the calling program when an ENDPROC is executed.

Argument (3)

expr should evaluate to an integer. If this integer is *n* then the *n*th procedure listed is called. If the integer is less than 1 or greater than the number of line numbers given, the statement following the ELSE, if it is present, is executed.

Examples

```
DEF PROCdelay(n)
LOCAL t%
t%=TIME:REPEAT UNTIL TIME-t%>=n*100:ENDPROC

IF ?flag=0 THEN REPEAT PROCdelay(0.1): UNTIL ?flag
```

PTR#

Pseudo-variable accessing the pointer of a file.

Syntax

(1) PTR#*factor*
(2) PTR#*factor* = *expression*

Argument (1)

factor is a channel number, as returned from an OPEN*xx* function.

Result (1)

An integer giving the position of the next byte to be read or written relative to the start of the file. The minimum value is 0 and the maximum value depends on the filing system in use.

Arguments (2)

factor is as (1). The expression is an integer giving the desired position of the sequential pointer in the file. Files opened for input may only have their PTR# value set to between 0 and the EXT# of the file.

Examples

```
PRINT PTR#file;"bytes processed"
PTR#chan%=rec_len%
```

QUIT

Statement to leave BASIC.
Function returning -quit status.

Syntax

as a statement:

(1) QUIT [*expression*]

as a function:

(2) QUIT

Argument (1)

QUIT as a statement leaves the BASIC interpreter. If the optional *expression* is specified the system variable Sys$ReturnCode is set to the value of *expression*, which should be an integer.

Result (2)

QUIT as a function returns TRUE or FALSE. If the interpreter was invoked using the -quit flag, then it will return TRUE. If -quit was not specified on the command line, then the function returns FALSE.

History

The optional expression for (1) was added in BASIC version 1.34.

RAD

Function returning the radian value of its argument.

Syntax
```
RAD factor
```

Argument
A number representing an angle in degrees.

Result
A real giving the corresponding value in radians: $factor*\pi/180$.

Examples
```
(sin%+i%*5)=SIN(RAD(i%))
PRINT RAD(theta)-PI/2
```

READ

Statement reading information from a DATA statement.

Syntax

```
READ [variable] [,variable...]
```

Argument

Any variables should correspond in type to the items in the DATA statement being read. In fact, a string READ item is able to read any type of DATA and interpret it as a string constant after stripping leading spaces. A numeric READ item tries to evaluate its DATA; so in the latter case, the DATA expression should yield a suitable number. Note that items in a DATA statement are not tokenised so, for example, PI/2 will generate an error if used with a numeric READ. For cases like this the item can be read as a string and EVAL used to get the numeric value.

Examples

```
READ n%
READ a$, fred%, float
```

RECTANGLE

Statement to draw a rectangle or copy/move a rectangular area of the screen or set the mouse bounding box.

Syntax

(1) RECTANGLE [FILL] *exp1*,*exp2*,*exp3*[,*exp4*]
(2) RECTANGLE [FILL] *exp1*,*exp2*,*exp3*[,*exp4*] TO *exp5*,*exp6*
(3) MOUSE RECTANGLE *exp1*,*exp2*,*exp3*,*exp4*

Arguments (1)

exp1 and *exp2* are integer expressions in the range −32768 to +32767. They are the coordinates of one of the corners of the rectangle.

exp3 is the width of the rectangle. It is also the height (giving a square) unless *exp4* is given, in which case this is the height.

Purpose (1)

RECTANGLE draws the outline of a rectangle which is aligned with the x and y axes. RECTANGLE FILL plots a solid axes-aligned rectangle. The rectangles are drawn using the current graphics foreground colour and action.

RECTANGLE leaves the graphics cursor at the starting position. However, with RECTANGLE FILL, the graphics cursor is updated to the position of the opposite corner to the one specified.

Arguments (2)

The first four arguments define a rectangular area of the screen, as for the first usage described above.

exp5 and *exp6* give the position to which the lower left corner of the source rectangle is copied or moved.

Purpose (2)

RECTANGLE ... TO copies the original rectangular area defined to the new position, hence making a second copy of a rectangular screen area. Pixels in the source that are outside of the current graphics viewport are drawn in the current graphics background colour.

RECTANGLE FILL ... TO moves the original rectangular area defined to the new position, replacing the old area with the current graphics background colour. In both cases the new position is allowed to overlap with the rectangular area.

Purpose (3)

To set a bounding box for the mouse pointer. See MOUSE for details.

Examples

```
RECTANGLE 500,500,-200,-100
RECTANGLE FILL bl%(1),bl%(2),width%,height%
RECTANGLE 400,400,60,60 TO 460,400
RECTANGLE FILL x,y,size,size TO xnew,ynew
```

REM

Statement indicating a remark.

Syntax

```
REM rest-of-line
```

Argument

rest-of-line can be absolutely anything; it is ignored by BASIC. The purpose of a REM is to provide comments to make the program clear to any reader.

Example

```
REM find the next prime
```

RENUMBER

Command to renumber the program lines.

Syntax

```
RENUMBER [start][,step]
```

Arguments

start is an integer constant in the range 0 to 65279 and is the first line number. It defaults to 10.

step is an integer constant in the range 1 to 65279 and is the amount by which the line numbers increase. If omitted, 10 is assumed.

Purpose

RENUMBER resequences the lines in the program so that the first line is *start* and the line numbers increase in steps of *step*. It also changes line numbers within the program, such as after RESTOREs, so that they match the new line numbers. If the line used in a RESTORE cannot be found, the message

```
Failed with nnnn on line llll
```

is given, where *nnnn* is the line number which was referenced but which does not appear in the program, and *llll* is the line on which the reference was made.

RENUMBER needs some workspace, and if there is not enough room to change the line numbers successfully, a RENUMBER space error is generated.

Examples

```
RENUMBER
RENUMBER 1000,20
```

REPEAT

Statement marking start of a REPEAT ... UNTIL loop.

Syntax

```
REPEAT
```

Purpose

The statements following REPEAT are repeatedly executed until the condition following the matching UNTIL evaluates to FALSE. The statements may occur over several program lines, or may all be on the same line separated by colons. The second approach is useful in immediate statements. The statements are executed at least once.

Examples

```
REPEAT UNTIL INKEY-99 : REM wait for SPACE

REPEAT
  a%+=1:c%=c% >> 1
UNTIL c%=0
```

Keywords

REPORT

Statement printing the message of the last error encountered.

Syntax

```
REPORT
```

Notes

If no error has occurred the BASIC version string (e.g. "ARM BBC BASIC V (C) Acorn 1989") will be printed instead.

If an error occurs in a library, the error message is suffixed with the name of the library, for example `Mistake in "MyLib"`. The name that will be printed is everything that follows REM or REM> on the first line of the library.

Examples

```
REPORT:PRINT " at line ";ERL;END
REPORT:PRINT " error!!"'':END
```

REPORT$

Function returning the message of the last error encountered as a string.

Syntax

```
REPORT$
```

Notes

See the Notes for REPORT on page 381.

Examples

```
PRINT REPORT$
ERROR ERR,REPORT$
```

RESTORE

Statement setting the DATA pointer.
Statement restoring DATA pointer from the stack.
Statement to restore saved error status.

Syntax

```
(1) RESTORE [[+] expression]
(2) RESTORE DATA
(3) RESTORE ERROR
```

Argument (1)

expression is a line number. If it is absent, the DATA pointer is reset to the first DATA statement in the program, and the next item READ comes from there. If the line number is present, the DATA pointer is set to the first item of data on or after the line specified, so that subsequent READs access that particular data item (and those which follow).

If *expression* is preceded by a + sign, then it is interpreted as an *offset* from the line containing the RESTORE statement and should be a positive number. +1 means the line after the one containing the RESTORE, +2 means the line after that, and so on. The main use of this is in libraries, where references to actual line numbers are not allowed (and RESTORE on its own restores to the start of the main program, not the library).

Purpose (2)

The second form of RESTORE loads a DATA pointer from the stack that was previously saved using LOCAL DATA. By using these two statements as a pair, you can prevent any RESTOREs in a procedure or function from changing the DATA pointer used by the main program.

Purpose (3)

RESTORE ERROR restores the error status previously saved using LOCAL ERROR. If an error status has not been saved then a fatal error arises.

The error status is restored automatically on return from a procedure or function, and when one of the loop-terminating constructs is encountered (UNTIL, ENDWHILE and NEXT).

Examples

```
RESTORE
RESTORE 1000
RESTORE +10
RESTORE DATA

10 LOCAL ERROR
20 REPEAT
30   ON ERROR LOCAL PRINT"Negative value"
40   INPUT x
50   PRINT "Square root of x = ";SQR(x)
60 UNTIL x=0
70 RESTORE ERROR
```

RETURN

Statement returning control from a subroutine.
Modifier in formal parameter list.

Syntax

    (1) RETURN
    (2) RETURN parameter

Purpose (1)

RETURN returns control to the statement following the most recent GOSUB. If there are no GOSUBs currently active, a `Not in a subroutine` error occurs.

Purpose (2)

When used in DEF PROC or DEF FN, RETURN indicates value-and-result parameter passing (as distinct from value passing, the default) when applied to a parameter. Note that there must be a space between RETURN and the parameter name.

Examples

```
DEF PROCSwapIfDisordered(RETURN A, RETURN B)
  IF A>B SWAP A,B
ENDPROC
```

RIGHT$(

Function returning, or statement altering, the right-most character(s) of a string.

Syntax

as a function:

(1) `RIGHT$(expression1[,expression2])`

as a statement:

(2) `RIGHT$(variable[,expression1]) = expression2`

Argument (1)

expression1 should be a string of length 0 to 255 characters.

If *expression2* is present, it should be a numeric giving the number of characters from the right of the string to be returned, also in the range 0 to 255. If it is omitted, a default of 1 is used.

Result (1)

A string consisting of the *n* right-most character(s) from the source string, where *n* is *expression2* or 1. If *n* is greater than the length of the source string, the whole source string is returned.

Argument (2)

variable is the name of the string variable to be altered. The righthand characters in *variable* are replaced by the string *expression2*.

If present, *expression1* gives the maximum number of characters which will be replaced: the number of characters altered is the lesser of *expression1* and LEN*expression2*. *expression1* defaults to 255.

Examples

```
PRINT RIGHT$(any$,4)
year$=RIGHT$(date$,2)
RIGHT$(birthday$) = "May"
RIGHT$(name$,4) = "Mary"
```

Keywords

RND

Function returning a random number.

Syntax

(1) RND
(2) RND(*expression*)

Result (1)

A four-byte signed random integer between −2147483648 and +2147483647

Result (2)

expression < 0

expression should be an integer. This reseeds the random number generator, and the function returns the integer part of the argument as a result. Reseeding the generator with a given seed value always produces the same sequence of random numbers.

expression = 0

This uses the same seed as the last RND(1) call and returns the same random number rounded between 0 and 1.

expression = 1

This returns a random real number between 0 and 1.

expression > 1

The expression, *n*, should be an integer. The result is an integer between 1 and *n* inclusive.

Note that there should be no space before the opening bracket.

Examples

```
dummy=RND(-TIME) : REM reseed the generator 'randomly'
x%=RND(1280)  : y%=RND AND &3ff
prob=RND(1)
lastProb=RND(0)
r%=RND
```

RUN

Command to execute the current program.

Syntax

RUN

Purpose

RUN executes the program in memory, if one is present, after clearing all variables and resetting LOMEM.

SAVE

Command to save a program as a file.

Syntax

```
SAVE [pathname]
```

Argument

If present, *pathname* should evaluate to a string which is a valid pathname. The current BASIC program is stored (without variables, etc) on the medium under this name.

SAVE can be used without an expression, in which case the name is taken from the first line of the program which should have the format:

```
10 REM > filename
```

For example:

```
10 REM > Game1
```

Examples

```
SAVE "Version1"
SAVE "$.BASIC.Games.Adventure"
SAVE FNprogName
SAVE
```

SGN

Function returning the sign of its argument.

Syntax

```
SGN factor
```

Argument

Any numeric.

Result

- −1 for negative arguments
- 0 for zero-valued arguments
- +1 for positive arguments

Examples

```
DEF FNsquare(th)=SGN(SIN(th))
IF SGN(a)<>SGN(b) THEN ...
```

SIN

Function returning the sine of its argument.

Syntax

SIN *factor*

Argument

A numeric representing an angle in radians.

Result

A real in the range −1 to 1, being the sine of the argument.

Notes

For BASIC V if the argument is outside the range −8388608 to +8388608 radians, it is impossible to determine how many πs to subtract. The error `Accuracy lost in sine/cosine/tangent` is generated. For BASIC VI the range is larger, from approximately −6E9 to +6E9 radians, and outside this range the error `Floating point exception: invalid operation` is generated.

Examples

```
PRINT SIN(RAD(135))
opp=hyp*SIN(theta)
```

SOUND

SOUND

Statement generating a sound or suppressing/allowing subsequent sound generation.

Syntax

    (1)   SOUND ON
    (2)   SOUND OFF
    (3)   SOUND *expr1,expr2,expr3,expr4[,expr5]*

Purpose (1) and (2)

SOUND ON is the default setting. It allows sounds to be produced by subsequent use of the SOUND (3) statements. SOUND OFF suppresses sounds and means that subsequent SOUND (3) statements have no effect.

Arguments (3)

expr1 is the channel number
expr2 is the amplitude
expr3 is the pitch
expr4 is the duration
expr5, if present, is the delay.

Channel
A two-byte integer giving the channel number to be used. It has the range 1 to 8.

Amplitude
This is an integer in one of two different ranges. The range −15 to 0 is a simple volume (amplitude), −15 being the loudest and zero being the quietest (no sound). The range 256 (&100) to 511 (&1FF) is a logarithmic volume range, a difference of 16 providing a doubling or halving of the volume.

Pitch
This is treated as an integer. In the range 0 to 255, the note middle C has a pitch value of 53; a difference in the parameter of 48 corresponds to a difference in pitch of one octave. In other words, there are four pitch values per semi-tone. In the range 256 (&100) to 32767 (&7FFF), the note middle C has a pitch value of &4000, and a difference in the value of &1000 corresponds to a difference in pitch of one octave.

Duration
The last compulsory SOUND parameter is also treated as a two-byte integer. It gives the duration of the note in twentieths of a second. A value of 255 gives a note with an infinite duration: one that does not stop unless the sound queue is flushed in some way. A value greater than 255 is treated as a duration in 20ths of a second.

Delay
This is the number of beat counts from the last beat counter reset before the sound is produced. See BEATS on page 230 and TEMPO on page 408 for more details. If this parameter is omitted, the sound is produced immediately. A value of −1 synchronises the new note with the last scheduled sound.

Examples

```
SOUND OFF
SOUND 1,-15,255,10
SOUND &102,&140,&2400,200
SOUND 3,300,300,100,200
```

SPC

Print formatter to generate spaces in PRINT and INPUT statements.

Syntax

    SPC factor

Argument

A one-byte integer between 0 and 255. It gives the number of spaces to be printed.

Examples

    PRINT SPC 10;
    INPUT SPC(7)"How many",a$

SQR

Function returning the square-root of its argument.

Syntax

SQR *factor*

Argument

Any non-negative numeric.

Result

A real which is the argument's square-root.

Examples

```
DEF FNlen(x1,y1,x2,y2)=SQR((x2-x1)^2+(y2-y1)^2)
disc=SQR(b*b-4*a*c)
```

STEP

Part of the FOR and MOUSE statements.

Syntax

    (1) FOR variable=expr TO expr [STEP expr]
    (2) MOUSE STEP expression[,expression]

Purpose (1)

See FOR on page 293.

Purpose (2)

See MOUSE on page 338.

STEREO

Statement setting the stereo position of a sound channel.

Syntax

```
STEREO expression1,expression2
```

Arguments

expression1 is the channel number which should be between 1 and the number of active channels (the maximum being 8).

expression2 is a value giving the stereo position. It can take any value between −127 (meaning that the sound is fully to the left) and +127 (meaning that the sound is fully to the right). The default value of each channel is 0, giving central (mono) production.

If the number of physical channels is eight, only the channel specified is programmed. Otherwise, the following occurs, where *chan* is *expression1*:

No of channels	Channels programmed
1	*chan* to eight
2	*chan* and every alternate channel up to eight
4	*chan* and *chan*+4 if *chan*+4 is less than or equal to eight

Examples

```
STEREO 4,-60
STEREO n%, stereo%
```

STOP

Statement producing the fatal error Stopped to terminate the program.

Syntax

    STOP

Purpose

The STOP statement gives the fatal (untrappable) error message Stopped. It differs from END, as the latter produces no message. It may be used as a debugging aid to halt the program at a given point so that the current values of the program's variables can be determined.

Example

    IF NOT ok THEN PRINT"Bad data":STOP

STR$

Function returning the string representation of its argument.

Syntax

    STR$[~] factor

Argument

Any numeric for decimal conversion, any integer for hexadecimal conversion. Decimal conversion is used when the tilde (~) is absent, hex conversion when it is present.

Result

Decimal or hex string representation of the argument, depending upon the absence or presence of the tilde.

Notes

The string returned by STR$ is usually formatted in the same way as the argument would be printed with @% set to &A00. However, if the most significant byte of @% is non-zero, STR$ returns the result in exactly the same format as it would be printed, taking the current value of @% into account. See also PRINT.

Examples

```
DEF FNhex4(a%)=RIGHT$("000"+STR$~(a%),4)
DEF FNdigits(a)=LEN(STR$(a))
dp=INSTR(STR$(any_val),".")
```

STRING$(

Function returning multiple copies of a string.

Syntax

    STRING$(expression1,expression2)

Arguments

expression1 is an integer, n, in the range 0 to 255.

expression2 should be a string of length 0 to (255 DIV n) characters.

Result

A string comprising n concatenated copies of the source string, of a length n*LEN(expression2).

Examples

    PRINT STRING$(40,"_"); :REM underline across the screen
    pattern$=STRING$(20,"<-->")

SUM

Function returning the arithmetic sum or string concatenation of an array.

Syntax

SUM *array*

Argument

array is the name of an array.

Result

If the argument is an integer or floating point array, it is an integer or floating point value of the sum of all the elements in the array.

If the argument is a string array, it is the string which contains each of the elements of the array concatenated. This must be less than 256 characters in all.

Examples

```
A() = 1 : PRINT "There are ";SUM(A())" elements."
DEF FNmean(a())=SUMa()/DIM(a(),1)
```

SUMLEN

Function returning the length of the string concatenation of an array.

Syntax

    SUMLEN *string-array*

Argument

string-array is the name of a string array.

Result

The sum of the lengths of all the elements in the array. Thus

    SUMLENa$()=LENSUMa$()

except that the former is not limited to a maximum of 255 characters.

Examples

    DEF FNmeanlen(a$())=SUMLENa$()/DIM(a(),1)

SWAP

Statement exchanging the value of two variables or arrays.

Syntax

SWAP *variable1,variable2*

Arguments

The arguments are variables or array names. Simple variables must be of assignment-compatible types, i.e. both string or numeric. Arrays must be of identical type elements (both integer, floating point or string), but can be of differing sizes.

Purpose

The SWAP statement exchanges the contents of the two variables or arrays. In the case where arrays are swapped, the number of subscripts and their upper limits are also swapped. For example, if you have

DIM A(10),B(20,20)

SWAP A(),B()

then after the SWAP, it would be as if the arrays had been DIMed:

DIM A(20,20),B(10)

All of the elements of the arrays are also swapped, though no actual movement of data is involved so this is a very quick operation.

Examples

```
SWAP A%, B%
SWAP forename$, surname$
SWAP arr(i%), arr(i%+gap%)
SWAP array1$(), array2$()
SWAP a, B%
SWAP A$, $A%
SWAP matrix(), vector()
```

SYS

Statement for calling operating system routines.

Syntax

SYS expr1 [,[exprn]...] [TO [var1][,[var2]...] [;flags]]

Arguments

expr1 defines which operating system routine is to be called. It may evaluate to a number giving the routine's SWI number, or to a string which is the name of a routine. BASIC uses the SWI OS_SWINumberFromString to convert from a string to number, so the case of the letters in the string must match exactly that of the SWI name.

The optional list of expressions following this, up to a maximum of ten, is passed to the routine via registers R0 to R9. If the expression evaluates to a numeric, it is converted to an integer and placed directly in a register. If the expression evaluates to a string, the string is placed on BASIC's stack, beginning at a word boundary and terminated with a null character. A pointer to it is put in the register. Any expressions not given (indicated by adjacent commas , ,) default to zero.

The optional TO is followed by a variable list. Each variable is assigned any value returned by the routine in the registers R0 to R9 respectively. If the variable to assign to is numeric, the integer in the register is converted to an appropriate format and stored in it. If the variable to assign to is a string, the register is treated as a pointer to a string terminated by ASCII 0, 10 or 13 and this string is assigned to the variable. The strings given on input can be overwritten, but should not be extended. As with the input expressions, output variables may be omitted using adjacent commas in the list.

flags is an optional variable, to which the processor flag bits are returned. The value stored in the *flags* value is a binary number of the form %NZCV, where the letters stand for the result flags of the ARM status register.

Purpose

SYS provides access to the routines supplied by the operating system for entering and outputting characters, error handling, sprite manipulation, and so on. Details of these operating system routines is beyond the scope of this book, but can be found in the RISC OS *Programmer's Reference Manual*.

History

Prior to BASIC 1.05, only R0 to R7 could be used with SYS, and calling a SWI which alters R8 would result in a crash.

In BASIC version 1.54 and later, returned registers containing zero will be converted to an empty string if the variable to assign to is a string, whereas in earlier versions of the interpreter this will potentially cause the program to fail.

Examples

```
SYS "OS_ReadMonotonicTime" TO time
SYS "OS_SpriteOp",28,,"MYSPRITE",,3
SYS "Font_FindFont",,"Homerton.Medium",12*16,12*16 TO f%

10 SYS 0,0,42 : REM output a *
20 OS_Write% = 0
30 SYS OS_Write%, 42
40 END
```

TAB(

Print formatter to position text cursor in PRINT and INPUT statements.

Syntax

```
(1)  TAB(expression)
(2)  TAB(expression1,expression2)
```

Argument (1)

A numeric in the range 0 to 255. It expresses the desired x-coordinate of the cursor. This position is obtained by printing spaces. A new line is generated first if the current position is at or to the right of the required one. COUNT is updated appropriately. This form is useful for tabulating on both the screen (even in VDU 5 mode) or printed output.

Arguments (2)

expression1 is the desired x coordinate;

expression2 is the desired y coordinate.

The position is reached using the VDU 31 command. Both coordinates must lie within the current text viewport, otherwise, no cursor movement will take place. COUNT is no longer correct. This form is only useful when positioning the cursor on the screen as it uses control codes which will not be sent to a printer.

Examples

```
PRINT TAB(10) "Product";TAB(20) "Price"
INPUT TAB(0,10)"How many eggs",eggs%
```

TAN

Function returning the tangent of its argument.

Syntax

TAN *factor*

Argument

A real number interpreted as an angle in radians.

Result

A real giving the tangent of the angle.

Notes

For BASIC V if the argument is outside the range −8388608 to +8388608 radians, it is impossible to determine how many πs to subtract. The error `Accuracy lost in sine/cosine/tangent` is generated. For BASIC VI the range is larger, from approximately −3E9 to +3E9 radians, and outside this range the error `Floating point exception: invalid operation` is generated.

Examples

```
opp=adj*TAN(RAD(theta))
```

TEMPO

Function returning or statement altering the beat counter rate.

Syntax

as a statement:

(1)　TEMPO *expression*

as a function:

(2)　TEMPO

Argument (1)

expression is a scaled fractional number, in which the 12 least-significant bits are the fractional part. Thus a value of &1000 corresponds to a tempo of one tempo beat per centi-second; doubling the value (&2000) causes the tempo to double (two tempo beats per centi-second), halving the value (&800) halves the tempo (one beat every two centi-seconds).

The tempo determines the rate at which the beat counter increases.

Result (2)

A number giving the current tempo.

Examples

```
TEMPO &2000
PRINT TEMPO
DEF FNtempo=TEMPO/&1000
DEF PROCtempo(t) TEMPO t*&1000:ENDPROC
```

TEXTLOAD

Command to load a BASIC file at PAGE.

Syntax

TEXTLOAD *pathname*

Argument

pathname is a string that should evaluate to a valid pathname. The file can be a BASIC program, or a BASIC program that was saved as a text file (see TEXTSAVE). If a text file is loaded which has lines without line numbers, TEXTLOAD automatically renumbers it.

Notes

Any program which is currently in memory is overwritten and lost with all its variables. The static integers (A% - Z% and @%) and INSTALLed libraries are not affected.

Files loaded with this command must end in a linefeed, otherwise the last line will be ignored and you will get a "Line too long" error.

Examples

TEXTLOAD "adfs::GDisc.disasm"

where GDisc is the name of a disc.

TEXTLOAD FNnextFile

TEXTSAVE

Command to save a BASIC program to a text file.

Syntax

    (1) TEXTSAVE *pathname*
    (2) TEXTSAVEO *expression, pathname*

Argument (1)

pathname is a string that should evaluate to a valid pathname. The current BASIC program is stored as a text file under this name.

Arguments (2)

expression should be in the range zero to 31, and is treated as a 5-bit binary number. TEXTSAVEO is similar to TEXTSAVE, but when it converts the program to text, it uses the LISTO-type option specified by *expression* to format the output to the file given by *pathname*. See LISTO on page 323 for details of the possible options.

Examples

```
TEXTSAVE "Version1"
TEXTSAVEO 8, "Version2" : REM strips out line numbers
```

Keywords

THEN

Optional part of a single line IF ... THEN ... ELSE statement and compulsory part of multi-line IF ... THEN ... ELSE ... ENDIF statement.

Syntax

See IF on page 304.

Examples

```
IF a>3 THEN PRINT "Too large"   : REM THEN optional
IF mem THEN HIMEM = HIMEM - &2000
IF A$="Y" THEN 1200 ELSE GOTO 1400

MODE "X640 Y480 C4"
IF colour$ = "red" THEN
  COLOUR 1
  CLS
ELSE
  COLOUR 0 : CLS
ENDIF
```

TIME

Pseudo-variable reading or altering the value of the centi-second clock.

Syntax

```
(1) TIME
(2) TIME = expression
```

Result (1)

An integer giving the number of centi-seconds that have elapsed since the last time the clock was set to zero.

Argument (2)

expression is an integer value used to set the clock. TIME is initially set to the lowest four bytes of the five–byte clock value maintained by the operating system. Assigning to the TIME pseudo-variable alters the system centi-second timer (the one which is read and written by OS_Words 1 and 2 respectively). There is, however, an additional system clock which is monotonic: it always increases in value with time, and cannot be reset by software. TIME does not affect this timer.

Notes

Setting the clock is not recommend in Wimp programs since it could cause unexpected behaviour in other programs that use the clock.

Examples

```
DEF PROCdelay(n) T%=TIME+n*100:REPEAT UNTIL TIME>=T%
```

TIME$

Pseudo-variable accessing the real-time clock.

Syntax

```
(1) TIME$
(2) TIME$ = expression
```

Result (1)

TIME$ returns a string of the format:

```
Fri,24 May 1984.17:40:59
```

The date and time part are separated by a full stop ' . ', and the language used for the day and month names will depend on the current territory.

Argument (2)

The *expression* should be a string specifying the date, the time, or both. Punctuation and spacing are crucial and should be as shown in the examples below. Note that the conversion of month names will be done in the language of the current territory.

Examples

```
PRINT TIME$
TIME$="Tue,01 Jan 1972"
TIME$="21:12:06"
TIME$="Tue,01 Jan 1972.21:12:06"
```

Note that the day of the week is automatically calculated from the date, so that any three characters may be entered at the start of the date, for example

```
TIME$="xxx,19 Aug 1987"
```

TINT

Part of the COLOUR or GCOL statements for use in 256-colour modes, or a statement on its own, or a function.

Syntax

    (1) COLOUR expr [TINT expression]
    (2) GCOL [expr,] expr [TINT expression]
    (3) TINT expression, expression
    (4) TINT(expression, expression)

Arguments (1) and (2)

For usages (1) and (2), see COLOUR (COLOR) on page 256 and GCOL on page 294 respectively.

Arguments (3)

The TINT statement takes two expressions. The first is a number in the range 0 to 3 which indicates which type of colour's tint value is being set:

Number	Colour affected
0	Text foreground
1	Text background
2	Graphics foreground
3	Graphics background

The second expression is a number in the range 0 to 255. This gives the amount of white to add to the basic colour. Currently, only the top two bits of this number are significant, so 0, 64, 128 and 192 give distinct tint values.

The two lines below are equivalent:

    GCOL 34 TINT 128
    GCOL 34 : TINT 2,128

Result (4)

The two expressions within the brackets give the coordinates of the point whose tint is required. The result is the tint for that pixel, currently one of the values 0, 64, 128 or 192. If the pixel is outside the graphics window, 0 is returned, so POINT() should be used to check that the point is valid first.

Notes

If you are using a 256-colour mode with a full palette it is possible to convert the values returned by POINT and TINT into the logical colour number used by the palette, but the mapping is not straightforward. It can be found as follows:

```
p% = POINT(x,y)
t% = TINT(x,y)
lc% = (p% AND 33)<<2 OR (p% AND 14)<<3 OR (p% AND 16)>>1 OR t%>>6
```

Examples

```
COLOUR 1+J% TINT N%
GCOL 128+63 TINT 255 : REM solid white
GCOL 3 TINT TINT(x,y) : REM NB two uses at once!
t=TINT(0,0)
```

TO

Part of the FOR ... NEXT statement.

Syntax

See FOR on page 293.

TOP

Function returning the address of the end of the program.

Syntax

    TOP

Result

TOP gives the address of the first byte after the BASIC program. The length of the program is equal to TOP–PAGE. LOMEM is usually set to TOP (or the first word above if TOP isn't on a word boundary), so this is where the variables start.

Example

    PRINT TOP

TRACE

Statement to initiate or terminate line/procedure tracing.
Function returning the handle of a trace file.

Syntax

as a statement:

(1)   TRACE [STEP] *expression*
(2)   TRACE [STEP] ON
(3)   TRACE [STEP] PROC
        TRACE [STEP] FN
(4)   TRACE OFF
(5)   TRACE TO *pathname*
(6)   TRACE CLOSE
(7)   TRACE ENDPROC

as a function:

(8)   TRACE

Argument (1)

expression is a line number. All line numbers below this line number are printed out when they are encountered during the execution of the program.

Argument (5)

pathname is the name of the file to which TRACE output is directed.

Result (8)

If TRACE TO has been used to direct trace output to a file then the handle of this file is returned, otherwise zero is returned.

Purpose

TRACE causes line numbers or procedure and function names to be printed as they are encountered. In cases (1), (2) and (3), if STEP is present, BASIC will wait for a key to be pressed before continuing after each traced item.

(1)   TRACE *expression* traces only those lines with a line number below the value of *expression*.

(2) TRACE ON is the same as TRACE 65279, i.e. all line numbers are printed as they are met.

(3) TRACE PROC traces procedures and functions only. TRACE FN can also be used and has the same effect.

(4) TRACE OFF disables tracing, as does the default error handler.

(5) TRACE TO sends the output from TRACE to a specified file.

(6) TRACE CLOSE stops output to a named file (the interpreter closes the file before exit). Note that errors found when writing to this file will cause it to be closed.

(7) TRACE ENDPROC traces the exit of procedures and functions.

(8) The function TRACE returns either zero, or a file handle. It allows output other than line numbers to be sent to the trace file, as in the last example below.

History

(5), (6) and (8) were added in version 1.05, (7) was added in version 1.34.

Examples

```
IF debug THEN TRACE 9000
TRACE STEP PROC
IF debug THEN TRACE OFF
IF TRACE THEN BPUT#TRACE,"X is "+STR$X
```

TRUE

Function returning the constant −1.

Syntax

```
TRUE
```

Result

TRUE always returns −1, which is the number yielded by the relational operators when the condition is true. For example, 1+1<3 gives TRUE as its result.

Examples

```
debug=TRUE
IF debug PRINT"debug in operation"
```

TWIN

Obsolete command previously used to enter the Twin text editor.

Syntax

```
TWIN
TWINO expression
```

Purpose

The TWIN keyword is no longer supported by BASIC, although it is still recognised. Its purpose was to convert the current program to text and call the Twin editor (a programmer's editor sold by Acorn Computers as a separate product). TWINO was similar, except that it converted the program to text using the LISTO-type option that follows the command.

Since the Twin editor is no longer supported, using this command will result in a `Mistake` error.

UNTIL

Statement to terminate a REPEAT loop.

Syntax

```
UNTIL expression
```

Argument

expression can be any numeric expression which can be evaluated to give a truth value. If it is zero (FALSE), control passes back to the statement immediately after the corresponding REPEAT. If the expression is non-zero (TRUE), control continues to the statement after the UNTIL.

Examples

```
DEF PROCirritate
REPEAT VDU 7:UNTIL FALSE
ENDPROC

REPEAT PROCmove:UNTIL gameOver
```

USR

Function returning the value of R0 after executing a machine code routine.

Syntax

USR *factor*

Argument

The address of the machine code to be called. Calls to the 6502-based BBC Microcomputer operating systems are handled by USR for compatibility.

Result

An integer, being the contents of R0 on return to BASIC.

Notes

USR is similar to CALL except that it returns a result and cannot be passed any parameters. On entry to the routine, R0..R14 are as for CALL. See page 234 for details.

As with CALL, in BASIC V (but not BASIC VI) if the USR statement is used with an address which corresponds to a MOS entry point on the BBC Micro/Acorn Electron/Master series machines, then BASIC treats the call as if it had been made from one of those machines. See BBC/*Master compatible calls* on page 246 for further information.

Example

DEF FNmachinecode =USR(start_of_code)

VAL

Function returning the numeric value of a decimal string.

Syntax

```
VAL factor
```

Argument

A string of length zero to 255 characters.

Result

The number that would have been read if the string had been typed in response to a numeric INPUT statement. The string is interpreted up to the first character that is not a legal numeric one (0 to 9, E, -, +, and .).

Example

```
date=VAL(date$)
```

VDU

Statement sending bytes to the VDU drivers.

Syntax

as a statement:

(1) VDU [expr [, or ; or | or expr]...[; or |]

as a function:

(2) VDU expression

Arguments (1)

Any expressions may be followed by a comma, a semi-colon, a vertical bar, or nothing.

Expressions followed by a semi-colon are sent as two bytes (low byte first) to the operating system VDU drivers.

Expressions followed by a comma (or nothing) are sent to the VDU drivers as one byte, taken from the least significant byte of the expression.

The vertical bar means ,0,0,0,0,0,0,0,0, and so sends the expression before it as a byte followed by nine zero bytes. Since the maximum number of parameters required by any of the VDU statements is nine, the vertical bar ensures that sufficient parameters have been sent for any particular call. Any surplus ones are irrelevant, since VDU 0 does nothing.

> Note: For the meanings of the VDU codes, see the chapter entitled VDU *control* on page 177.

Argument (2)

expression is an integer giving the number of a VDU variable. See *Appendix H – VDU variables* for the list of valid VDU variables.

Result (2)

The value of the specified VDU variable.

History

(2) was added in version 1.34

Examples

```
VDU 24,400;300;1000;740; : REM set up a graphics window
VDU 7 : REM Emit a beep
VDU 23,9,200|23,10,200| : REM Slow down the flash rate
TextColour = VDU 155 : REM Get the text foreground colour
```

VOICE

Statement assigning a named sound algorithm to a sound channel.

Syntax

VOICE *numeric-expression, string-expression*

Arguments

numeric-expression is a number between 1 and 8 identifying a sound channel and *string-expression* gives the name of the sound algorithm (voice) that should be assigned to that channel. A list of installed voices can be found by using the *VOICES command.

Notes

This statement is equivalent to the *CHANNELVOICE command.

Examples

VOICE 1,"StringLib-Steel"

VOICES

Statement specifying the number of sound channels to be used.

Syntax

```
VOICES expression
```

Argument

expression is the number of channels to be used. The maximum number allowed is eight. Any number between 1 and 8 can be specified, but the number which the computer is to handle must be a power of two and so the computer rounds up the number you give to either one, two, four or eight.

Notes

Due to the way the sound system works, increasing the number of active channels will result in a decrease in volume for each channel. Additionally, older computers may experience a significant decrease in performance when many channels are active. It is therefore considered good practice to minimise the number of active channels.

Examples

```
VOICES 4
VOICES n%*2
```

VPOS

Function returning the y-coordinate of the text cursor.

Syntax

VPOS

Result

An integer between 0 and n, where n is the height of the current text viewport minus one. This is the position of the text cursor which is normally given relative to the top edge of the text viewport. If the cursor direction has been altered using VDU 23, 16, ... then it is given relative to the negative y edge of the screen which may be top, bottom, left or right.

Notes

Even in VDU 5 mode, VPOS returns the position of the text cursor. You should therefore keep track of the vertical position explicitly in programs which must operate in VDU 5 mode (e.g. Wimp-based programs).

Examples

```
DEF FNmyTab(x%)
PRINT TAB(x%,VPOS);: =""

IF VPOS>10 THEN PRINT TAB(0,10);
```

WAIT

Statement to wait for the end of the current display frame.

Syntax

```
WAIT
```

Purpose

To enable a program to synchronise animation effects with the scanning of the display hardware. Waiting until the end of the frame maximises the amount of time available in which to draw objects before the display of the next frame begins.

Examples

```
MODE "X640 Y480 C2"
a=0
REPEAT
  POINT 1279,500+200*SINa
  a+=RAD5
  WAIT:RECTANGLE FILL 0,300,1279,400 TO -4,300
UNTIL FALSE
```

WHEN

Part of the CASE ... OF ... WHEN ... OTHERWISE ... ENDCASE statement.

Syntax

```
WHEN expression [,expression...] [:statements]
[statements]
```

Arguments

WHEN is followed by a list of expressions separated by commas. These expressions should evaluate to the same type as that of the expression following the corresponding CASE statement. If the value of the expression following the CASE statement matches that of any of the list following the WHEN, *statements* are executed and control is then passed to the statement following the ENDCASE.

Notes

WHEN must be the first non-space object on a line. A CASE statement can contain any number of WHEN statements, but only the statements of the first one which contains a matching value will be executed. To match any value, an OTHERWISE should be used.

Examples

```
WHEN 1 : PROCload
WHEN 2,4,6,8 : PRINT "Even" : remainder= 0
WHEN "Y","y","YES","Yes","yes" : PROCgame
```

WHILE

Statement marking the start of a WHILE ... ENDWHILE loop.

Syntax

```
WHILE expression
```

Arguments

expression can be any numeric which can be evaluated to give a truth value. If it is zero (FALSE), control passes forward to the statement immediately after the corresponding ENDWHILE. If it is non-zero, control continues until the ENDWHILE statement is reached, then loops back to the WHILE statement, and *expression* is re-evaluated.

Notes

The statements making up the body of the WHILE ... ENDWHILE loop are never executed if the initial value of expression is FALSE.

Examples

```
WHILE TIME < 1000
  PROCdraw
ENDWHILE

WHILE flag : PROCmainloop : ENDWHILE
```

WIDTH

Statement setting the line width for BASIC output, and function returning same.

Syntax

```
(1) WIDTH
(2) WIDTH expression
```

Result (1)

WIDTH returns the current print width, i.e. the last value used in a WIDTH statement described below (or 0 by default).

Argument (2)

expression should be a positive integer. Expressions in the range 1 to 2147483627 cause BASIC to print a new line and reset COUNT to zero every time COUNT exceeds that number. If the expression is 0, BASIC stops generating auto-newlines, which is the default.

Examples

```
WIDTH 0: REM 'infinite width'
WIDTH 40: REM newline every 40 characters horizontally
PRINT WIDTH
```

WIDTH

28 * Commands

This chapter describes the full syntax of the four * commands that can be used to start BBC BASIC.

All four commands take the same options, and the only difference between them is that they each start BASIC with a different way of handling floating point numbers.

*BASIC

The command to enter the BASIC V interpreter.

Syntax

    *BASIC [options]

Purpose

To activate the BASIC interpreter.

The *options* control how the interpreter will behave when it starts, and when any program that it executes terminates. If no option is given, BASIC simply starts with a message of the form:

    ARM BBC BASIC V (C) Acorn 1989

    Starting with 651516 bytes free

The number of bytes free in the above message will depend on the amount of free RAM available to BASIC, determined by the size of the **Next** slot set by the *WimpSlot command. The first line is also used for the default REPORT message, before any errors occur.

One of three options may follow the *BASIC command to cause a program to be loaded, and, optionally, executed automatically. Alternatively, you can use a program that is already loaded into memory by passing its address to the interpreter. Each of these possibilities is described in turn below.

In all cases where a program is specified, this may be a tokenised BASIC program, as created by a SAVE command, or a textual program, which will be tokenised (and possibly renumbered) automatically.

    *BASIC -help

This command causes BASIC to print some help information describing the options documented here. Then BASIC starts as usual.

    *BASIC [-chain] filename

If you give a *filename* after the *BASIC command, optionally preceded by the keyword -chain, then the named file is loaded and executed. When the program stops, BASIC enters immediate mode, as usual.

`*BASIC -quit filename`

This behaves in a similar way to the previous option. However, when the program terminates, BASIC quits automatically, returning to the environment from which the interpreter was originally called. If you have a variable BASIC$Crunch defined, it also performs a CRUNCH %1111 on the program (see the description of the CRUNCH command on page 261). This is the default action used by BASIC programs that are executed as * commands. In addition, the function QUIT returns TRUE if BASIC is called in this fashion.

`*BASIC -load filename`

This option causes the file to be loaded automatically, but not executed. BASIC remains in immediate mode, from where the program can be edited or executed as required.

`*BASIC @start,end`

This acts in a similar way to the -load form of the command. However, the program that is 'loaded' automatically is not in a file, but already in memory. Following the @ are two addresses. These give, in hexadecimal, the address of the start of the in-core program, and the address of the byte after the last one. The program is copied to PAGE and tokenised if necessary.

Note that the in-core address description is fixed format. It should be in the form:

`@xxxxxxxx,xxxxxxxx`

where *x* means a hexadecimal digit. Leading zeros must be supplied. The command line terminator character must come immediately after the last digit. No spaces are allowed.

`*BASIC -chain @start,end`

This behaves like the previous option, but the program is executed as well. When the program terminates, BASIC enters immediate mode.

`*BASIC -quit @start,end`

This option behaves as the previous one, but when the BASIC program terminates, BASIC automatically quits. The function QUIT will return TRUE during the execution of the program.

Examples

```
*BASIC
*BASIC -quit shellProg
*BASIC @000ADF0C,000AE345
*BASIC -chain fred
```

*BASIC64

The command to enter the BASIC VI interpreter.

Syntax

```
*BASIC64 [options]
```

Purpose

This has exactly the same purpose as the `*BASIC` command, and takes the same options, the only difference being that it enters the BASIC VI interpreter instead of the BASIC V interpreter.

If no option is given, BASIC VI simply starts with a message of the form:

```
ARM BBC BASIC VI (FPA) (C) Acorn 1989

Starting with 581628 bytes free.
```

The text in brackets on the first line of the message shows whether the FPA or VFP version of BASIC VI has been started. This will depend on the type of CPU in your computer. The number of bytes free will depend on the amount of free RAM available to BASIC, determined by the size of the **Next** slot set by the `*WimpSlot` command.

Examples

```
*BASIC64
*BASIC64 -quit shellProg
*BASIC64 @000ADF0C,000AE345
*BASIC64 -chain fred
```

*BASICFPA

The command to enter the FPA variant of the BASIC VI interpreter.

Syntax

    *BASICFPA [options]

Purpose

This has exactly the same purpose as the *BASIC64 command, and takes the same options, the only difference being that it specifically enters the FPA variant of the BASIC VI interpreter.

If no option is given, BASIC VI simply starts with a message of the form:

    ARM BBC BASIC VI (FPA) (C) Acorn 1989

    Starting with 581628 bytes free.

The number of bytes free in the above message will depend on the amount of free RAM available to BASIC, determined by the size of the **Next** slot set by the *WimpSlot command.

Examples

    *BASICFPA
    *BASICFPA -quit shellProg
    *BASICFPA @000ADF0C,000AE345
    *BASICFPA -chain fred

*BASICVFP

The command to enter the VFP variant of the BASIC VI interpreter.

Syntax

    *BASICVFP [options]

Purpose

This has exactly the same purpose as the *BASIC64 command, and takes the same options, the only difference being that it specifically enters the VFP variant of the BASIC VI interpreter.

If no option is given, BASIC simply starts with a message of the form:

    ARM BBC BASIC VI (VFP) (C) Acorn 1989

    Starting with 581628 bytes free.

The number of bytes free in the above message will depend on the amount of free RAM available to BASIC, determined by the size of the **Next** slot set by the *WimpSlot command.

Examples

    *BASICVFP
    *BASICVFP -quit shellProg
    *BASICVFP @000ADF0C,000AE345
    *BASICVFP -chain fred

29 ARM assembler

Assembly language is a programming language in which each statement translates directly into a single machine code instruction or piece of data. An assembler is a piece of software which converts these statements into their machine code counterparts.

Writing in assembly language has its disadvantages. The code is more verbose than the equivalent high-level language statements, more difficult to understand and therefore harder to debug. High-level languages were invented so that programs could be written to look more like English so we could talk to computers in our language rather than directly in its own.

There are two reasons why, in certain circumstances, assembly language is used in preference to high-level languages. The first reason is that the machine code program produced by it executes more quickly than its high-level counterparts, particularly those in languages such as BASIC which are interpreted. The second reason is that assembly language offers greater flexibility. It allows certain operating system routines to be called or replaced by new pieces of code, and it allows greater access to the hardware devices and controllers.

Finding out more

For more details of writing in assembly language see the *Acorn Assembler* manual.

For more details of RISC OS see the RISC OS *Programmer's Reference Manual*.

For more details of the ARM instruction set, see the list of Recommended Books on page 447.

Using the BASIC assembler

The assembler is part of the BBC BASIC language. Square brackets '[' and ']' are used to enclose all the assembly language instructions and directives and hence to inform BASIC that the enclosed instructions are intended for its assembler. However, there are several operations which must be performed from BASIC itself to ensure that a subsequent assembly language routine is assembled correctly.

Initialising external variables

The assembler allows the use of BASIC variables as addresses or data in instructions and assembler directives. For example variables can be set up in BASIC giving the numbers of any SWI routines which will be called:

```
OS_WriteI = &100
...
[
...
SWI OS_WriteI+ASC">"
...
```

Reserving memory space for the machine code

The machine code generated by the assembler is stored in memory. However, the assembler does not automatically set memory aside for this purpose. You must reserve sufficient memory to hold your assembled machine code by using the DIM statement. For example:

```
1000 DIM code% 99
```

The start address of the memory area reserved is assigned to the variable code%. The address of the last memory location is code%+99. Hence, this example reserves a total of 100 bytes of memory. In future examples, the size of memory reserved is shown as *required_size*, to emphasise that you must substitute a value appropriate to the size of your code.

Memory pointers

You need to tell the assembler the start address of the area of memory you have reserved. The simplest way to do this is to assign P% to point to the start of this area. For example:

```
DIM code% required_size
...
P% = code%
```

P% is then used as the program counter. The assembler places the first assembler instruction at the address P% and automatically increments the value of P% by four so that it points to the next free location. When the assembler has finished assembling the code, P% points to the byte following the final location used. Therefore, the number of bytes of machine code generated is given by:

```
P% - code%
```

It is important to ensure that the number of bytes generated does not exceed the size of the space that was reserved, otherwise the generated code will overwrite other data in the BASIC heap and cause the program to fail. The assembler will check this for you if you set L% to the address of the end of the reserved memory (i.e. `code%` + `required_size`) and set bit 3 of the directive OPT, which is described in more detail below.

Offset assembly

The method described so far assumes that you wish subsequently to execute the code at the location at which it was assembled, or that your code is position independent.

The position in memory at which you load a machine code program may be significant. For example, it might refer directly to data embedded within itself, or expect to find routines at fixed addresses. Such a program only works if it is loaded in the correct place in memory. However, it is often inconvenient to assemble the program directly into the place where it will eventually be executed. This memory may well be used for something else whilst you are assembling the program. The solution to this problem is to use a technique called 'offset assembly' where code is assembled as if it is to run at a certain address but is actually placed at another.

To do this, set O% to point to the place where the first machine code instruction is to be placed and P% to point to the address where the code is to be run.

To notify the assembler that this method of generating code is to be used, the directive OPT, which is described in more detail below, must have bit 2 set.

It is however usually easy, and always preferable, to write ARM code that is position independent, in which case offset assembly is not required, or can be used with P% set to 0.

Implementing passes

Normally, when the processor is executing a machine code program, it executes one instruction and then moves on to the one following it in memory. You can, however, make the processor move to a different location and start processing from there instead by using one of the 'branch' instructions. For example:

```
.result_was_0
...
        BEQ result_was_0
```

The fullstop in front of the name `result_was_0` identifies this string as the name of a 'label'. This is a directive to the assembler which tells it to assign the current value of the program counter (P%) to the variable whose name follows the fullstop.

BEQ means 'branch if the result of the last calculation that updated the PSR was zero'. The location to be branched to is given by the value previously assigned to the label `result_was_0`.

The label can, however, occur after the branch instruction. This causes a slight problem for the assembler since when it reaches the branch instruction, it hasn't yet assigned a value to the variable, so it doesn't know which value to replace it with. The same issue will apply to instructions such as LDR and STR which refer to labels that come after the instruction.

You can get around this problem by assembling the source code twice. This is known as two-pass assembly. During the first pass the assembler assigns values to all the label variables. In the second pass it is able to replace references to these variables by their values.

It is only when the text contains no forward references of labels that just a single pass is sufficient.

These two passes may be performed by a FOR...NEXT loop as follows:

```
DIM code% required_size
L%=code% + required_size
FOR pass% = 0 TO 10 STEP 10
   P% = code%
   [
   OPT pass%
   ...              further assembly language statements and assembler directives
   ]
NEXT pass%
```

Note that the pointer(s), in this case just P%, must be set at the start of both passes.

The OPT directive

The OPT is an assembler directive whose bits have the following meaning:

Bit	Meaning
0	Assembly listing enabled if set
1	Assembler errors enabled
2	Assembled code placed in memory at O% instead of P%
3	Check that assembled code does not exceed memory limit L%

Bit 0 controls whether a listing is produced. It is up to you whether or not you wish to have one or not.

ARM assembler

Bit 1 determines whether or not assembler errors are to be flagged or suppressed. For the first pass, bit 1 should be zero since otherwise any forward-referenced labels will cause the error 'Unknown or missing variable' and hence stop the assembly. During the second pass, this bit should be set to one, since by this stage all the labels defined are known, so the only errors it catches are 'real ones' – such as labels which have been used but not defined.

Bit 2 allows 'offset assembly', i.e. the program may be assembled into one area of memory, pointed to by O%, whilst being set to run at the address pointed to by P%.

Bit 3 checks that the assembled code does not exceed the area of memory that has been reserved (i.e. none of it is held in an address greater than the limit value held in L%). Using L% in this way is recommended.

Saving machine code to file

Once an assembly language routine has been successfully assembled, you can then save it to file. To do so, you can use the *Save command. In our above examples, code% points to the start of the code; after assembly, P% points to the byte after the code. So we could use this BASIC command:

```
OSCLI "Save "+outfile$+" "+STR$~(code%)+" "+STR$~(P%)
```

after the above example to save the code in the file named by outfile$. An alternative method is to use the SWI OS_File to save the file:

```
SYS "OS_File",10,outfile$,&FFD,,code%,code%+P%
```

The advantage with this method is that it gives the file a type, in this case &FFD ("Data"), but if you are using the assembler to create an assembly language program that can be executed directly you may want to use &FF8 ("Absolute") or &FFC ("Utility"), or &FFA ("Module") if you are assembling a relocatable module.

Executing a machine code program

From memory

From memory, the resulting machine code can be executed in a variety of ways:

```
CALL address
USR address
```

These may be used from inside BASIC to run the machine code at a given address.

From file

The commands below will load and run the named file, using either its filetype (such as &FF8 for absolute code) and the associated `Alias$@LoadType_XXX` and `Alias$@RunType_XXX` system variables, or the load and execution addresses defined when it was saved.

```
*name
*RUN name
*/name
```

We strongly advise you to use file types rather than load and execution addresses.

Format of assembly language statements

The assembly language statements and assembler directives should be between the square brackets.

There are very few rules about the format of assembly language statements; those which exist are given below:

- Each assembly language statement comprises an assembler mnemonic of one or more letters followed by a varying number of operands.
- Instructions should be separated from each other by colons or newlines.
- Any text following a full stop '.' is treated as a label name.
- Any text following a semicolon ';', or backslash '\', or 'REM' is treated as a comment and so ignored (until the next end of line or ':').
- Spaces between the mnemonic and the first operand, and between the operands themselves are ignored.

The BASIC assembler contains the following directives:

`DCB` *int*	Define 1 byte of memory from LSB of *int* (EQUB, =)
`DCW` *int*	Define 2 bytes of memory from *int* (EQUW)
`DCD` *int*	Define 4 bytes of memory from *int* (EQUD)
`DCS` *str*	Define 0 – 255 bytes as required by string expression *str* (EQUS)
`DCFS` *float*	Define 4 bytes of memory from *float* in IEEE Single precision format (EQUFS)
`DCFD` *float*	Define 8 bytes of memory from *float* in IEEE Double precision format (EQUFD)
`DCFE` *float*	Define 12 bytes of memory from *float* in IEEE Double Extended precision format (EQUFE)
`ALIGN`	Align P% (and O%) to the next word (4 byte) boundary
`ADR` *reg,addr*	Assemble instruction to load *addr* into *reg*

ARM assembler

- The first four operations initialise the reserved memory to the values specified by the operand. In the case of DCS the operand field must be a string expression. In all other cases it must be a numeric expression. EQUB (and =), EQUW, EQUD, EQUS, EQUFS, EQUFD and EQUFE are synonyms for these directives.

- The ALIGN directive ensures that the next P% (and O%) that is used lies on a word boundary. It is used after, for example, a DCS to ensure that the next instruction is word-aligned. Any unused bytes are set to zero.

- ADR assembles a single instruction – typically but not necessarily an ADD or SUB – with reg as the destination register. It obtains addr in that register. It does so in a PC-relative (i.e. position independent) manner where possible.

Recommended Books

One or more of these books will be useful if you are writing a lot of ARM assembler.

- ARM Architecture Reference Manual, Second Edition, edited by David Seal : Addison-Wesley, 2000, 816 pages, ISBN 0-201-73719-1.
  This book is also known as the 'ARM ARM' and is an essential reference for anyone working at a low level with the ARM processor, but its style makes it unsuitable as introductory reference.
  The paper version has not been re-issued since architecture 5TE, but the electronic version receives updates a few times per year. It is available in PDF format free of charge from ARM's website, although you do need to register first. The manual had a major reworking after architecture 6, when the 'UAL' assembler syntax was introduced, and it is now distributed in separate editions for profile 'M' CPUs and other CPUs. The final pre-UAL version of the manual is also still available. See:
  ARMv8-A *Architecture Reference Manual*
  http://infocenter.arm.com/help/topic/com.arm.doc.ddi0487b.a/index.html
  ARMv7-AR *Architecture Reference Manual*
  http://infocenter.arm.com/help/topic/com.arm.doc.ddi0406c/index.html
  ARMv5 *Architecture Reference Manual* (includes pre-UAL architecture 6)
  http://infocenter.arm.com/help/topic/com.arm.doc.ddi0100i/index.html
  Note that the above URLs were correct at the time of publication but are subject to change.

- ARM 7500FE Data Sheet, document number ARM DDI 0077B, ARM Ltd, 1996, 365 pages, and CL-PS7500FE Advance Data Book, document number 447500-001, Cirrus Logic, 1997, 251 pages. These include the official documentation of the final hardware implementation of the FPA, so represent the best and most easily-obtained reference for that part of the instruction set. Note that these instructions are not included in the ARM ARM.

Recommended Books

- Intel XScale Core Developer's Manual, Intel Corporation, 2004, 220 pages. The definitive reference for the XScale coprocessor 0.
- ARM Assembly Language: Fundamentals and Techniques, William Hohl, CRC Press, 2009, 371 pages, ISBN 978-1439806104.
  Despite the publication date, this reportedly only describes architectures up to 4T.
- ARM Assembly Language – an Introduction, J.R. Gibson : Lulu Enterprises, 2007, 244 pages, ISBN 978-1847536969.
- ARM System-on-Chip Architecture, 2nd Edition, Prof. Steve Furber : Addison-Wesley, 2000, 432 pages, ISBN 978-0201675191.
  By one of the original designers of the ARM, this is now showing its age, and only covers up to architecture 5TE.
- The ARM RISC Chip – A Programmer's Guide, A. van Someren and C. Atack – Wokingham, UK: Addison-Wesley, 1993, 400 pages, ISBN 0201624109.
  This is a good introduction to the ARM although the book is now rather dated and only covers up to architecture 3.
- Archimedes Assembly Language: A Dabhand Guide, second edition, M. Ginns – Manchester, UK: Dabs Press, 1988, 368 pages, ISBN 1870336208.
  Out of print and difficult to obtain, but useful as it specifically refers to using RISC OS and the built-in BBC BASIC assembler.
- ARM Assembly Language Programming, P.J. Cockerell – Computer Concepts/MTC, 1987, ISBN 0951257900.
  Out of print and difficult to obtain. Only covers architecture 2a, of historic interest.

Part 4 – Appendices

Appendix A – Numeric implementation

Before you can perform any arithmetic operations, you need to know how the computer handles numbers, and what limitations there are on their use.

This appendix describes the different types of numbers you can use with BBC BASIC, tells you how they are stored and manipulated, and explains what limitations this places on your programs.

Numeric types

You can use the following numeric types with BBC BASIC:

Integers

These are whole numbers, which can be represented exactly by the computer, for example:

    1
    2
    1024

Floating point numbers

These are real numbers expressed as a decimal fraction, for example:

    1.3
    123.45
    1.2345E2

Fixed point numbers

These are real numbers expressed as a decimal fraction, but with a fixed number of places after the decimal point. For example:

    1.3333
    1.2346
    123.4568

are fixed point numbers accurate to four decimal places.

Numeric types

The most important factor governing numeric types is the amount of memory used to store them. For the purposes of this description, we will only consider integers and floating point numbers.

BASIC VI uses the following storage sizes for numeric types:

Numeric type	Storage size
Integers	4 bytes (32 bits)
Floating point numbers	8 bytes (64 bits)

Remember that BASIC V only supports integers and 5–byte reals (we shall use the term *n–byte reals* to mean n–byte floating point numbers). The following figures show how the storage for each numeric type is organised.

Integer

BASIC V floating point number

BASIC VI (FPA) floating point number

BASIC VI (VFP) floating point number

Effects of storage size

The storage size of a numeric type affects the following things:

- the speed with which numbers of that type are processed by the computer;
- the amount of memory left for your program;
- the range of numbers of that type which can be represented by the computer;
- the accuracy with which numbers of that type can be represented by the computer.

For example, integers occupy less space than real numbers, and are handled much more quickly. 8–byte reals use more memory than 5–byte reals, and are therefore more accurate. The computer can represent larger numbers in the 8–byte format.

The effect on memory usage is very important if, for instance, your program uses arrays of real numbers. Consider an array with 100 elements in, each element being a 5–byte real. This will occupy 500 bytes of memory, whereas it would occupy 800 bytes if the elements were 8–byte reals. This is a trivial example, but the effects can become severely limiting if you use very large arrays.

The following two subsections explain range and accuracy of representation in more detail.

Effects of storage size

Range

The greater the storage size of a given numeric type, the greater the range of numbers of that type that the computer can represent. For instance, integers are stored in 4 bytes or 32 bits. The maximum positive integer that the computer can represent is given by

2 ^ (32 – 1) – 1

which means 2 raised to the power of 31, minus 1, and is equal to 2147483647

The maximum positive real number that the computer can represent depends on which type of real number you specify. For instance, the maximum positive 5-byte real that the computer can represent is

1.7×10^{38}

Accuracy

The accuracy of a number is determined by how many significant figures of the number that the computer can show. The computer can show all the significant figures in an integer (as long as it is within the representable range). However, it must lose some of the significant figures of a floating point number.

For instance, the value of PI shown to three significant figures is 3.14. Shown to six significant figures, it is 3.14159. BASIC VI can show up to 17 significant figures of a floating point number, but this does not mean it is completely accurate. PI has an infinite number of digits after the decimal point, and so the computer can only print an approximation to it, by chopping off the trailing digits.

The table below summarises the numerical representation of BBC BASIC.

	Range		Accuracy	Stored in
Integers	–2147483648 to	2147483647	absolute	4 bytes
5–byte reals	$\pm 1.7 \times 10^{38}$ to	$\pm 1.5 \times 10^{-39}$	11 sig figs	5 bytes
8–byte reals	$\pm 1.7 \times 10^{308}$ to	$\pm 1.5 \times 10^{-323}$	17 sig figs	8 bytes

The rest of this appendix explains the two methods used by BASIC VI for implementing 8-byte floating point arithmetic to IEEE standard 754. BASIC V uses a software floating point implementation for its 5-byte reals, and is not IEEE 754 compliant.

What is floating point arithmetic?

Floating point arithmetic is the process by which real numbers are manipulated, as a result of your instructions to the computer. For example, a computer cannot add two numbers together in the way we can. It must first convert the numbers into binary form, and then add them using Boolean operations.

Every arithmetic operation can be reduced, at the lowest level, to a group of Boolean operations. It is more convenient, however, to represent these groups by a set of mnemonics, called the *floating point instruction set*. Different generations of ARM hardware have used two different floating point instruction sets. The first of these was the FPA instruction set, but this has been superseded by the VFP instruction set, introduced in 2001.

Implementation

The three different BASIC modules (BASIC, BASIC64, BASICVFP) each implement floating point arithmetic in different ways.

BASIC

The BASIC module, which contains the BBC BASIC V interpreter, uses the 5-byte floating point format for real numbers. Because this is a non-standard format which is not directly supported by any ARM hardware, all arithmetic operations are implemented in software.

BASIC64

The BASIC64 module contains a version of the BBC BASIC VI interpreter which uses the 8-byte IEEE 754 double-precision format for real numbers. The design and implementation of the interpreter allows it to take advantage of the FPA floating point co-processor; thus all real arithmetic is implemented in terms of the FPA instruction set as opposed to using software routines like in the BASIC V interpreter. On machines with FPA hardware this results in better performance than that available with BASIC V.

Unfortunately the FPA instruction set was not very popular with manufacturers; the newest CPU which provides a hardware implementation of FPA is the ARM7500FE from 1996. On the vast majority of RISC OS machines, BASIC64 is dependent on the floating point emulator module (FPEmulator), which hooks onto the Undefined Instruction processor vector and provides a software implementation of the FPA instruction set. On a machine without FPA hardware, real arithmetic performed in BASIC64 will be many times slower than the equivalent code executed in the BASIC V interpreter.

Implementation

BASICVFP

Like BASIC64, the BASICVFP module contains a version of the BBC BASIC VI interpreter which uses IEEE 754 double-precision floating point. However instead of using the obsolete FPA instruction set, it is tailored for the newer VFP instruction set. Introduced by ARM in 2001, the VFP instruction set quickly gained traction with manufacturers, to the extent that almost all general-purpose ARM cores released after 2005 include hardware support for it.

Unfortunately the many differences between FPA and VFP, combined with the fact that FPA usage has been deep-set in the design of some of BASIC64's public interfaces, means that it would be prohibitively difficult to produce a version of BASIC64 which uses VFP and provides good performance while still retaining full compatibility with existing BASIC64 programs. Therefore the BASICVFP module was developed as an alternative, allowing key areas to be re-designed so that the best performance could be attained on modern CPUs.

Key differences between BASIC64 and BASICVFP are as follows:

- The memory representation of floating-point values is subtly different. FPA stores double-precision floats with the sign and exponent in the first word, while VFP stores them with the sign and exponent in the second word. This may cause compatibility issues with software which uses the '|' indirection operator, but for compatibility with BASIC data files, INPUT# and PRINT# still read and write floating-point values using the FPA word ordering.

- The routines exposed by the CALL environment information pointer (e.g. VARIND) all use VFP double-precision registers to accept and return floating point values instead of FPA registers. This may cause compatibility issues with assembler routines.

- If you wish to write VFP assembler routines in BASIC or BASIC64, you will have to manually register with the VFPSupport module in order to be granted a VFP context (without a VFP context, the VFP instructions are disabled). If you are using BASICVFP however, you can just use the context that BASICVFP provides, there is no need for your code to create a context of its own.

If you do want to create your own VFP context in BASICVFP, you must be careful not to leave it active while the BASIC interpreter is running, its usage must be restricted to just your assembler routines.

When using BASICVFP's VFP context, be careful when changing the control bits in the FPSCR. For example, enabling Short Vector mode in an assembler routine and then returning to BASIC without disabling it again is likely to result in memory corruption or a crash.

Appendix A – Numeric implementation

Other key points about the BASICVFP implementation are:

- The current version of the module is still reliant on the FPA instruction set for some operations, e.g. for implementing the TAN and COS trigonometric functions. Future versions of the module may replace these with native VFP versions. This will offer increased speed, but is also likely to result in some minor differences in numerical accuracy.

- By default, the DCFD assembler mnemonic will store its argument using the FPA word ordering. This provides consistency with the other BASIC interpreters. For correct operation with VFP assembler, you must use the '.vfp' suffix, i.e. 'DCFD.vfp'. 'DCFD.fpa' can also be used if you want to be explicit about use of FPA word ordering. These suffixes are supported in all versions of BASIC which support VFP/NEON assembler.

- BASICVFP does not use hardware floating-point exception traps; instead it checks for floating-point exceptions manually in software. The primary reason for this is that many modern VFP implementations do not support hardware trapping of floating point exceptions. This does mean however that some care is needed when writing VFP assembler – you must either enable hardware trapping (if supported) or check for exceptions in software.

- Where supported, BASICVFP will make use of the VFP Short Vector mode to accelerate whole-array operations which operate on floating point arrays. BASICVFP is also capable of using the Advanced SIMD ("NEON") instruction set to accelerate operations on integer arrays.

Currently BASICVFP is only supported on machines which provide a VFP implementation in hardware, but it is expected that future enhancements to the VFPSupport module will allow it to provide a full software implementation of the VFP instruction set, allowing BASICVFP to be used on older machines.

If you need to detect which type of floating point is being used by BASIC this can be done by writing a value with the '!' operator and inspecting its format in memory, for example:

```
10 DIM A% 8
20 |A%=-1
30 CASE !A% OF
40   WHEN &80000000:PRINT "BASIC V"
50   WHEN &BFF00000:PRINT "BASIC VI (FPA)"
60   WHEN &00000000:PRINT "BASIC VI (VFP)"
70   OTHERWISE PRINT "Unknown"
80 ENDCASE
```

Implementation

Appendix B – Minimum abbreviations

Keyword	Abbr.	Version	Token byte(s)
ABS	ABS	I	&94
ACS	ACS	I	&95
ADVAL	AD.	I	&96
AND	A.	I	&80
APPEND	AP.	V	&C7 &8E
ASC	ASC	I	&97
ASN	ASN	I	&98
ATN	ATN	I	&99
AUTO	AU.	I	&C7 &8F
BEAT	BEAT	V	&C6 &8F
BEATS	BEA.	V	&C8 &9E
BGET	B.	I	&9A
BGET$	BGET$	V	&9A &24
BPUT	BP.	I,V	&D5
BPUT$	BPUT$	V	&D5 &24
BY	BY	V	&42 &59 (not tokenised)
CALL	CA.	I	&D6
CASE	CASE	V	&C8 &8E
CHAIN	CH.	I	&D7
CHR$	CHR$	I	&BD
CIRCLE	CI.	V	&C8 &8F
CLEAR	CL.	I	&D8
CLG	CLG	I	&DA
CLOSE	CLO.	I	&D9
CLOSE#	CLOSE#	I	&D9 &23
CLS	CLS	I	&DB
COLOR	C.	III	&FB
COLOUR	C.	I	&FB
COS	COS	I	&9B
COUNT	COU.	I	&9C
CRUNCH	CR.	V	&C7 &90
DATA	D.	I	&DC
DEF	DEF	I	&DD
DEG	DEG	I	&9D
DELETE	DEL.	I	&C7 &91

Keyword	Abbr.	Version	Token byte(s)
DIM	DIM	I,V	&DE
DIV	DIV	I	&81
DRAW	DR.	I	&DF
EDIT	ED.	IV	&C7 &92
EDITO	ED.O	IV	&C7 &92 &4F
ELLIPSE	ELL.	V	&C8 &9D
ELSE	EL.	I,V	&8B / &CC
END	END	I,V	&E0
ENDCASE	ENDC.	V	&CB
ENDIF	ENDIF	V	&CD
ENDPROC	E.	I	&E1
ENDWHILE	ENDW.	V	&CE
ENVELOPE	ENV.	I	&E2
EOF	EOF	I	&C5
EOF#	EOF#	I	&C5 &23
EOR	EOR	I	&82
ERL	ERL	I	&9E
ERR	ERR	I	&9F
ERROR	ERR.	I,V	&85
EVAL	EV.	I	&A0
EXP	EXP	I	&A1
EXT	EXT	I,IV,V	&A2
EXT#	EXT#	I,V	&A2 &23
FALSE	FA.	I	&A3
FILL	FI.	V	&C8 &90
FN	FN	I	&A4
FOR	F.	I	&E3
GCOL	GC.	I,V	&E6
GET	GET	I	&A5
GET$	GE.	I,V	&BE
GET$#	GET$#	V	&BE &23
GOSUB	GOS.	I	&E4
GOTO	G.	I	&E5
HELP	HE.	V	&C7 &93
HIMEM	H.	I	&D3 / &93
IF	IF	I,V	&E7
INKEY	INKEY	I	&A6
INKEY$	INK.	I	&BF
INPUT	I.	I	&E8
INPUT#	INPUT#	I	&E8 &23
INPUT LINE	INPUT LINE	I	&E8 &20 &86

Appendix B – Minimum abbreviations

Keyword	Abbr.	Version	Token byte(s)
INSTALL	INS.	V	&C7 &9F
INSTR(	INS.	I	&A7
INT	INT	I	&A8
LEFT$(	LE.	I,V	&C0
LEN	LEN	I	&A9
LET	LET	I	&E9
LIBRARY	LIB.	V	&C8 &9B
LINE	LINE	I,V	&86
LINE INPUT	LINE INPUT	V	&86 &20 &E8
LIST	L.	I,IV	&C7 &94
LISTO	L.O	I,V	&C7 &94 &4F
LN	LN	I	&AA
LOAD	LO.	I	&C7 &95
LOCAL	LOC.	I,V	&EA
LOCAL ERROR	LOCAL ERROR	V	&EA &20 &85
LOG	LOG	I	&AB
LOMEM	LOM.	I	&D2 / &92
LVAR	LV.	V	&C7 &96
MID$(	M.	I,V	&C1
MOD	MOD	I,V	&83
MODE	MO.	I,V	&EB
MOUSE	MOU.	V	&C8 &97
MOVE	MOVE	I	&EC
NEW	NEW	I	&C7 &97
NEXT	N.	I	&ED
NOT	NOT	I	&AC
OF	OF	V	&CA
OFF	OFF	I,V	&87
OLD	O.	I	&C7 &98
ON	ON	I,V	&EE
ON ERROR	ON ERROR	V	&EE &20 &85
OPENIN	OP.	I	&8E
OPENOUT	OPENO.	I	&AE
OPENUP	OPENUP	II	&AD
OR	OR	I	&84
ORIGIN	OR.	V	&C8 &91
OSCLI	OS.	II	&FF
OTHERWISE	OT.	V	&7F
OVERLAY	OV.	V	&C8 &A3
PAGE	PA.	I	&D0 / &90
PI	PI	I	&AF

Keyword	Abbr.	Version	Token byte(s)
PLOT	PL.	I	&F0
POINT	POINT	V	&C8 &92
POINT(	PO.	I	&B0
POS	POS	I	&B1
PRINT	P.	I	&F1
PRINT#	PRINT#	I	&F1 &23
PROC	PROC	I	&F2
PTR	PTR	I	&CF / &8F
PTR#	PTR#	I	&CF &23
QUIT	Q.	V	&C8 &98
RAD	RAD	I	&B2
READ	READ	I	&F3
RECTANGLE	REC.	V	&C8 &93
REM	REM	I	&F4
RENUMBER	REN.	I	&C7 &99
REPEAT	REP.	I	&F5
REPORT	REPO.	I	&F6
REPORT$	REPO.$	V	&F6 &24
RESTORE	RES.	I,V	&F7
RESTORE DATA		V	&F7 &20 &DC
RESTORE ERROR		V	&F7 &20 &85
RETURN	R.	I,V	&F8
RIGHT$(	RI.	I,V	&C2
RND	RND	I	&B3
RUN	RUN	I	&F9
SAVE	SA.	I,V	&C7 &9A
SGN	SGN	I	&B4
SIN	SIN	I	&B5
SOUND	SO.	I,V	&D4
SPC	SPC	I	&89
SQR	SQR	I	&B6
STEP	S.	I,V	&88
STEREO	STER.	V	&C8 &A2
STOP	STOP	I	&FA
STR$	STR$	I	&C3
STRING$(	STRI.	I	&C4
SUM	SUM	V	&C6 &8E
SUMLEN	SUMLEN	V	&C6 &8E &A9
SWAP	SW.	V	&C8 &94
SYS	SYS	V	&C8 &99
TAB(	TAB(	I	&8A

Appendix B – Minimum abbreviations

Keyword	Abbr.	Version	Token byte(s)
TAN	T.	I	&B7
TEMPO	TE.	V	&C8 &9F
TEXTLOAD	TEXTL.	V	&C7 &9B
TEXTSAVE	TEXTS.	V	&C7 &9C
THEN	TH.	I,V	&8C
TIME	TI.	I,IV	&D1 / &91
TIME$	TI.$	IV	&D1 &24 / &91 &24
TINT	TINT	V	&C8 &9C
TO	TO	I,V	&B8
TOP	TOP	I	&B8 &50
TRACE	TR.	I,V	&FC
TRUE	TRUE	I	&B9
TWIN	TWIN	V	&C7 &9D
TWINO	TW.	V	&C7 &9E
UNTIL	U.	I	&FD
USR	USR	I	&BA
VAL	VAL	I	&BB
VDU	V.	I	&EF
VOICE	VOICE	V	&C8 &A1
VOICES	VO.	V	&C8 &A0
VPOS	VP.	I	&BC
WAIT	WA.	V	&C8 &96
WHEN	WHEN	V	&C9
WHILE	W.	V	&C8 &95
WIDTH	WI.	I	&FE

Where more than one version number is given, the second one indicates that the keyword was employed in a new way in that version.

The two token values for the pseudo-variables LOMEM, HIMEM, PAGE, PTR and TIME are the statement and function tokens respectively.

The two values for ELSE are the token used in a single-line IF statement and the token used in multi-line IF statement respectively.

Appendix C – Error messages

Note that error numbers 20 to 24 cannot be formed in BASIC VI.

Error number	Error message
0	Corruption of stack
	Error control status not found on stack for RESTORE ERROR
	Incorrect in-core file description
	INSTALL cannot be used in a program
	Invalid LISTO option
	Line numbers larger than 65279 would be generated by this renumber
	Line too long
	LIST found line number reference
	Missing incore name
	No room
	No room to do this renumber
	Silly!
	Stopped
	Unknown setting of exception control
	VFP internal mismatch
1	Bad FP precision
	No such mnemonic
	No such suffix on EQU
2	Assembler limit reached
	Bad address offset
	Bad coprocessor opcode
	Bad immediate constant
	Bad shift
	Bad VFP/NEON floating point immediate constant
	Label/offset must be word aligned

Error number	Error message
3	Bad register
	Duplicate register in multiply
	Too many registers in list
	VFP scalar must not change in register list
	VFP scalar offset out of range
4	Missing =
	Missing = in FOR statement
	Mistake
5	Missing ,
6	Array type mismatch as parameter
	Can't assign to array of this size
	Can't SWAP arrays of different types
	Type mismatch between arrays
	Type mismatch: array needed
	Type mismatch: number needed
	Type mismatch: numeric array needed
	Type mismatch: numeric variable needed
	Type mismatch: string array needed
	Type mismatch: string needed
	Type mismatch: string variable needed
7	Not in a function
8	Too low a value for $<number>
9	Missing "
10	Arrays cannot be redimensioned
	Bad DIM statement
	Can't DIM negative amount
	DIM() function needs an array
	Impossible dimension
	No end of dimension list)
	No room to do matrix multiply with source(s) the same as destination
11	Attempt to allocate insufficient memory
	No room for program
	No room for this DIM
	No room for this dimension

Appendix C – Error messages

Error number	Error message
	Unreferenced local array in END=
12	Items can only be made local in a function or procedure
13	Not in a procedure
14	Reference array incorrect
	Undimensioned array
	Unknown array in DIM() function
	Unknown array
15	Incorrect number of subscripts
	Subscript out of range
16	Syntax error
17	Escape
18	Division by zero
19	String too long
20	Number too big for arc Sine or arc Cosine
	Number too big
21	Negative root
22	Logarithm range
23	Accuracy lost in Sine/Cosine/Tangent
24	Exponent range
25	Bad MODE
26	Can't use array reference here
	Unknown or missing variable
27	Missing (
	Missing)
	Missing [
	Missing]
	Missing {
	Missing }
28	Bad Binary
	Bad Hex
	Hex number too large
29	No such function/procedure
30	Bad call of function/procedure

467

Error number	Error message
31	Arguments of function/procedure incorrect
	Invalid array actual parameter
	Invalid RETURN actual parameter
32	Not in a FOR loop
33	Can't match FOR
34	Bad FOR control variable
35	The step cannot be zero
36	Missing TO
37	No room for function/procedure call
38	Not in a subroutine
39	ON syntax
40	ON range
41	No such line
42	DATA pointer not found on stack for RESTORE DATA
	Out of data
43	Not in a REPEAT loop
44	Too many nested structures
45	Missing #
46	Not in a WHILE loop
47	Missing ENDCASE
48	CASE..OF statement must be the last thing on a line
	OF missing from CASE statement
49	Missing ENDIF
50	Bad MOUSE variable
51	Too many input expressions for SYS
	Too many output variables for SYS
52	Bad program used as function/procedure library
	Can't install library
	No room for library
53	Bad screen depth
54	END= not allowed within DIM LOCAL
55	Invalid arithmetic operation

Appendix D – INKEY values

In the following tables the key names shown in the **Key** column correspond to the those printed on a standard UK-layout keyboard. Where the Acorn Archimedes keyboard had different labels these are shown in square brackets.

INKEY values by functional group

Alphanumeric keys

Key	INKEY number
0	-40
1	-49
2	-50
3	-18
4	-19
5	-20
6	-53
7	-37
8	-22
9	-39
A	-66
B	-101
C	-83
D	-51
E	-35
F	-68
G	-84
H	-85
I	-38
J	-70
K	-71
L	-87
M	-102
N	-86
O	-55
P	-56
Q	-17

INKEY values by functional group

Key	INKEY number
R	-52
S	-82
T	-36
U	-54
V	-100
W	-34
X	-67
Y	-69
Z	-98

Punctuation keys

Space Bar		-99
#	[\\]	-121
'		-80
,		-103
-		-24
.		-104
/		-105
;		-88
=		-94
[		-57
\\		-95
]		-89
`		-46

Action keys

Esc		-113
Tab		-97
Return		-74
Caps Lock		-65
Backspace		-48
Print Screen	[Print]	-33
Scroll Lock		-32
Pause	[Break]	-45
Insert		-62
Delete		-90
Home		-63
End	[Copy]	-106
Page Up		-64
Page Down		-79

Appendix D – INKEY values

Key	INKEY number
↑	-58
←	-26
→	-122
↓	-42
Left flag/logo	-126
Right flag/logo	-127
Right menu	-128

Modifier keys

Key	INKEY number
Shift (either/both)	-1
Ctrl (either/both)	-2
Alt (either/both)	-3
Shift (left/right-hand)	-4/-7
Ctrl (left/right-hand)	-5/-8
Alt (left/right-hand)	-6/-9

Function keys

Key	INKEY number
F1	-114
F2	-115
F3	-116
F4	-21
F5	-117
F6	-118
F7	-23
F8	-119
F9	-120
F10	-31
F11	-29
F12	-30

Numeric keypad keys

Key	INKEY number
Num Lock	-78
0	-107
1	-108
2	-125
3	-109
4	-123
5	-124
6	-27
7	-28

INKEY values by functional group

Key	INKEY number
8	-43
9	-44
+	-59
-	-60
.	-77
/	-75
*	-92
Enter	-61

Mouse buttons

Select (Left)	-10
Menu (Middle)	-11
Adjust (Right)	-12

Extra keys, not present on standard UK keyboards

Only found on the Archimedes keyboard:

Keypad #	-91

Found on some small keyboards that do not have function keys:

Fn	-13

The key to the left of the Backspace key on some international keyboards (and the Archimedes keyboard):

Extra key [£]	-47

The key to the left of the right-hand Shift key on some international keyboards:

Extra key	-96

Found on Japanese and Korean layout keyboards:

No convert	-110
Kana	-112

Found on Japanese layout keyboards:

Convert	-111

Appendix D – INKEY values

INKEY values by number

Key	INKEY number
Shift (either/both)	-1
Ctrl (either/both)	-2
Alt (either/both)	-3
Shift (left/right-hand)	-4/-7
Ctrl (left/right-hand)	-5/-8
Alt (left/right-hand)	-6/-9
Select mouse button (Left)	-10
Menu mouse button (Middle)	-11
Adjust mouse button (Right)	-12
Fn	-13
Q	-17
3	-18
4	-19
5	-20
F4	-21
8	-22
F7	-23
-	-24
←	-26
Keypad 6	-27
Keypad 7	-28
F11	-29
F12	-30
F10	-31
Scroll Lock	-32
Print Screen [Print]	-33
W	-34
E	-35
T	-36
7	-37
I	-38
9	-39
0	-40
↓	-42
Keypad 8	-43
Keypad 9	-44
Pause [Break]	-45
`	-46
(Extra key left of Backspace) [£]	-47
Backspace	-48

INKEY values by number

Key	INKEY number
1	-49
2	-50
D	-51
R	-52
6	-53
U	-54
O	-55
P	-56
[	-57
↑	-58
Keypad +	-59
Keypad -	-60
Keypad Enter	-61
Insert	-62
Home	-63
Page Up	-64
Caps Lock	-65
A	-66
X	-67
F	-68
Y	-69
J	-70
K	-71
Return	-74
Keypad /	-75
Keypad .	-77
Num Lock	-78
Page Down	-79
'	-80
S	-82
C	-83
G	-84
H	-85
N	-86
L	-87
;	-88
]	-89
Delete	-90
Keypad #	-91
Keypad *	-92
=	-94
\	-95

Appendix D – INKEY values

Key	INKEY number
(Extra key left of right-hand Shift)	-96
Tab	-97
Z	-98
Space Bar	-99
V	-100
B	-101
M	-102
,	-103
.	-104
/	-105
End [Copy]	-106
Keypad 0	-107
Keypad 1	-108
Keypad 3	-109
No convert	-110
Convert	-111
Kana	-112
Esc	-113
F1	-114
F2	-115
F3	-116
F5	-117
F6	-118
F8	-119
F9	-120
# [\]	-121
→	-122
Keypad 4	-123
Keypad 5	-124
Keypad 2	-125
Left flag/logo	-126
Right flag/logo	-127
Right menu	-128

INKEY values by number

Appendix E – Specifying screen modes

The MODE keyword provides several different ways for specifying the screen mode to be selected. This appendix provides more detail on two of these methods, specification by mode string and by mode variables.

Mode Strings

MODE *string-expression*

Mode strings consist of a list of space or comma separated attributes. For example, "X640 Y480 C256" to describe a 256 colour 640 × 480 pixel mode.

In addition to the standard attributes described below, the string may start with a mode number. If this is the case then the additional attributes will act as modifiers on the base attributes of that mode. For example, "28 C16M" for a 16 million colour version of mode 28.

Attributes

The following attributes are currently defined:

Attribute	Details
X	Mode X resolution in pixels, e.g. X1024
Y	Mode Y resolution in pixels, e.g. Y768
C	Number of colours: C2 = 2 colours (1bpp) C4 = 4 colours (2bpp) C16 = 16 colours (4bpp) C64 = 64 colours (VIDC1 style 256 colour mode) (8bpp) C256 = 256 colours (8bpp) C4K/C4T = 4096 colours (16bpp 4:4:4:4) C32K/C32T = 32768 colours (16bpp 1:5:5:5) C64K/C64T = 65536 colours (16bpp 5:6:5) C16M = 16 million colours (32bpp 8:8:8:8)
G	Number of greys/colours: G2 = 2 greys (1bpp) G4 = 4 greys (2bpp)

Mode Strings

	G16 = 16 greys (4bpp)
	G256 = 256 greys (8bpp)
	G16M = 16 million colours (24bpp packed)
F	Frame rate in Hz, e.g. F60
EX	X eigen factor (0-3), e.g. EX1
EY	Y eigen factor (0-3), e.g. EY1
T	Teletext mode with given number of colours, e.g. T16
TX	Teletext mode width in characters, e.g. TX40
TY	Teletext mode height in characters, e.g. TY25
L	Pixel layout
	LTBGR = Traditional VIDC format with red in low bits
	LTRGB = Red/blue swapped
	LABGR = VIDC format with alpha channel
	LARGB = Red/blue swapped with alpha channel

Notes

Specifying the same attribute more than once, or specifying conflicting attributes (e.g. both C and G attributes) is an invalid string and will result in an error.

Likewise, it is illegal to omit a required attribute. E.g. for a standard mode the X, Y and C, G or T attributes must be provided unless a mode number has been provided, in which case these attributes are optional as the default values will be taken from the definition of that mode.

For colour depths which have no space for a transparency/alpha channel (e.g. C64K, G16M) it is an error to specify a pixel layout which contains alpha. If the pixel layout is to be specified then only the LTBGR or LTRGB layouts can be used.

For Teletext modes the number of colours given by the T attribute selects the pixel depth of the underlying frame buffer and must be at least 16, but you can still only actually use 16 colours in Teletext.

In Teletext modes the X and Y attributes select the size of the underlying frame buffer and the TX and TY attributes select the number of Teletext characters that are displayed within it. Depending on the OS version and platform you are using a character is either 8 × 10 or 16 × 20 pixels in size, and the Teletext screen will either be centred within the frame buffer or scaled to fill it.

Not all versions of RISC OS support all attributes:

- RISC OS 3.5 only understands the X, Y, C, G, F, EX and EY attributes. 4096 & 64K colour, and 24bpp packed are not supported, and neither is specifying a base mode number
- RISC OS Select adds support for 64K colour modes, the T, TX and TY attributes, and specifying a base mode number

Appendix E – Specifying screen modes

- RISC OS 5.22 supports all features except 24bpp packed modes and all attributes except T, TX and TY
- T, TX and TY support is introduced in RISC OS 5.24.

Mode Variables

MODE x,y,ModeFlags,NColour,Log2bpp[,framerate]

The following table lists all the combinations of ModeFlags, NColour and Log2bpp that can be used to select a valid screen mode, and gives the equivalent mode string in each case.

ModeFlags	NColour	Log2BPP	Result	String	Support
&0000	1	0	1bpp paletted	C2	RISC OS 3.50
&0100	1	0	1bpp grey paletted	G2	RISC OS 3.50
&0000	3	1	2bpp paletted	C4	RISC OS 3.50
&0100	3	1	2bpp grey paletted	G4	RISC OS 3.50
&0000	15	2	4bpp paletted	C16	RISC OS 3.50
&0100	15	2	4bpp grey paletted	G16	RISC OS 3.50
&0000	63	3	8bpp semi-paletted	C64	RISC OS 3.50
&0080	255	3	8bpp paletted	C256	RISC OS 3.50
&0180	255	3	8bpp grey paletted	G256	RISC OS 3.50
&0000	4095	4	16bpp 4:4:4:4 TBGR	C4K	RISC OS 5.22
&4000	4095	4	16bpp 4:4:4:4 TRGB	C4K LTRGB	RISC OS 5.22
&8000	4095	4	16bpp 4:4:4:4 ABGR	C4K LABGR	RISC OS 5.22
&C000	4095	4	16bpp 4:4:4:4 ARGB	C4K LARGB	RISC OS 5.22
&0000	65535	4	16bpp 1:5:5:5 TBGR	C32K	RISC OS 3.50
&4000	65535	4	16bpp 1:5:5:5 TRGB	C32K LTRGB	RISC OS 5.22
&8000	65535	4	16bpp 1:5:5:5 ABGR	C32K LABGR	RISC OS 5.22
&C000	65535	4	16bpp 1:5:5:5 ARGB	C32K LARGB	RISC OS 5.22
&0080	65535	4	16bpp 5:6:5 BGR	C64K	RISC OS 5.22
&4080	65535	4	16bpp 5:6:5 RGB	C64K LTRGB	RISC OS 5.22
&0000	16777215	6	24bpp 8:8:8 BGR	G16M	Not yet
&4000	16777215	6	24bpp 8:8:8 RGB	G16M LTRGB	Not yet
&0000	-1	5	32bpp 8:8:8:8 TBGR	C16M	RISC OS 3.50
&4000	-1	5	32bpp 8:8:8:8 TRGB	C16M LTRGB	RISC OS 5.22
&8000	-1	5	32bpp 8:8:8:8 ABGR	C16M LABGR	RISC OS 5.22
&C000	-1	5	32bpp 8:8:8:8 ARGB	C16M LARGB	RISC OS 5.22
&0007	15	2	4bpp Teletext	T16	RISC OS 5.24

Notes

- The 24bpp 8:8:8 modes are shown for completeness, but at the time of writing RISC OS does not support such modes.

- There are other possible values of ModeFlags that allow modes with different colour formats, such as YCbCr or CMYK, to be specified, but at the time of writing there is no support in RISC OS for graphics to be drawn in such modes.
- The eigen factors cannot be specified by this method.

Appendix F – Default palettes

Two-colour mode

    0 = black
    1 = white

Four-colour modes

    0 = black
    1 = red
    2 = yellow
    3 = white

16-colour modes

    0 = black
    1 = red
    2 = green
    3 = yellow
    4 = blue
    5 = magenta
    6 = cyan
    7 = white
    8 = flashing black-white
    9 = flashing red-cyan
    10 = flashing green-magenta
    11 = flashing yellow-blue
    12 = flashing blue-yellow
    13 = flashing magenta-green
    14 = flashing cyan-red
    15 = flashing white-black

256-colour modes

In 256-colour modes the default palette is set to match the colours available in VIDC1-style 256-colour modes. This means that the bits of each colour number map to the physical palette as follows:

Bit	Meaning
0	Tint bit 0 (red+green+blue bit 0 and 4)
1	Tint bit 1 (red+green+blue bit 1 and 5)
2	Red bit 2 and 6
3	Blue bit 2 and 6
4	Red bit 3 and 7
5	Green bit 2 and 6
6	Green bit 3 and 7
7	Blue bit 3 and 7

For example, colour number 149 is composed as follows: 149 = %10010101, so the tint bits are %01, the red bits are %11001100, the green bits are %00000000 and the blue bits are %10001000. This means that the default palette entry uses a physical colour with a red value of %11011101, a green value of %00010001 and a blue value of %10011001 and the colour appears as a purple shade.

Appendix G – Plot codes

The groups of PLOT codes are as follows:

Range	Hex	Description
0 - 7	(&00 - &07)	Solid line including both end points
8 - 15	(&08 - &0F)	Solid line excluding final points
16 - 23	(&10 - &17)	Dotted line including both end points
24 - 31	(&18 - &1F)	Dotted line excluding final points
32 - 39	(&20 - &27)	Solid line excluding initial point
40 - 47	(&28 - &2F)	Solid line excluding both end points
48 - 55	(&30 - &37)	Dotted line excluding initial point
56 - 63	(&38 - &3F)	Dotted line excluding both end points
64 - 71	(&40 - &47)	Point plot
72 - 79	(&48 - &4F)	Horizontal line fill (left & right) to non-background
80 - 87	(&50 - &57)	Triangle fill
88 - 95	(&58 - &5F)	Horizontal line fill (right only) to background
96 - 103	(&60 - &67)	Rectangle fill
104 - 111	(&68 - &6F)	Horizontal line fill (left & right) to foreground
112 - 119	(&70 - &77)	Parallelogram fill
120 - 127	(&78 - &7F)	Horizontal line fill (right only) to non-foreground
128 - 135	(&80 - &87)	Flood to background
136 - 143	(&88 - &8F)	Flood to foreground
144 - 151	(&90 - &97)	Circle outline
152 - 159	(&98 - &9F)	Circle fill
160 - 167	(&A0 - &A7)	Circular arc
168 - 175	(&A8 - &AF)	Segment
176 - 183	(&B0 - &B7)	Sector
184 - 191	(&B8 - &BF)	Block copy/move
192 - 199	(&C0 - &C7)	Ellipse outline
200 - 207	(&C8 - &CF)	Ellipse fill
208 - 215	(&D0 - &D7)	Graphics characters
216 - 223	(&D8 - &DF)	Reserved for Acorn expansion
224 - 231	(&E0 - &E7)	Reserved for Acorn expansion
232 - 239	(&E8 - &EF)	Sprite plot
240 - 247	(&F0 - &F7)	Reserved for user programs
248 - 255	(&F8 - &FF)	Reserved for user programs

Within each block of eight the offset from the base number has the following meaning:

0   Move cursor relative (to last graphics point visited)
1   Draw relative using current foreground colour
2   Draw relative using logical inverse colour
3   Draw relative using current background colour
4   Move cursor absolute (ie move to actual co-ordinate given)
5   Draw absolute using current foreground colour
6   Draw absolute using logical inverse colour
7   Draw absolute using current background colour

The above applies except for COPY and MOVE where the codes are as follows:

184 (&B8)   Move only, relative
185 (&B9)   Move rectangle relative
186 (&BA)   Copy rectangle relative
187 (&BB)   Copy rectangle relative
188 (&BC)   Move only, absolute
189 (&BD)   Move rectangle absolute
190 (&BE)   Copy rectangle absolute
191 (&BF)   Copy rectangle absolute

Appendix H – VDU variables

Name	No.	Meaning
ModeFlags	0	The bits of the result have the following meanings if set:

  Bit 0 Non-graphics mode
  Bit 1 Teletext mode
  Bit 2 Gap mode
  Bit 3 'BBC' gap mode (modes 3 and 6)
  Bit 4 Hi-resolution mono mode
  Bit 5 VDU characters are double height
  Bit 6 Hardware scroll disabled
  Bit 7 Full 256-entry palette
      (only valid if Log2BPP is 3)
     65536 colour RGB 5:6:5 mode
      (if Log2BPP is 4 and NColour is 65535)
  Bit 8 Interlaced mode using two framebuffers
  Bit 9 Greyscale palette
      (only valid in modes with a palette)
     Chroma sub-sampling mode
      (only valid if NColour is 420 or 422)
  Bits 10-11 Reserved
  Bits 12-15 Data format and colour space

Bits 12-13	Family	Bits 14-15	Meaning
0	RGB	0	TBGR
		1	TRGB
		2	ABGR
		3	ARGB
1	Misc	0	KYMC
		1-3	Reserved
2	YCbCr	0	BT.601, full
		1	BT.601, video
		2	BT.709, full
		3	BT.709, video
3	Reserved 0-3		Reserved

Name	No.	Meaning
ScrRCol	1	Maximum column number for printing text ie number of columns−1.
ScrBRow	2	Maximum row number for printing text ie number of rows−1.

Name	Number	Description
NColour	3	Maximum logical colour (for possible values see *Mode Variables* on page 479).
XEigFactor	4	This indicates the number of bits by which an X coordinate must be shifted right to convert to screen pixels. Thus if this value is n, then one screen pixel corresponds to 2^n external coordinates in the X direction.
YEigFactor	5	This indicates the number of bits by which a Y coordinate must be shifted right to convert to screen pixels. Thus if this value is n, then one screen pixel corresponds to 2^n external coordinates in the Y direction.
LineLength	6	Offset in bytes from a point on a pixel row to the same point on the pixel row below.
ScreenSize	7	Number of bytes one screen buffer occupies. This must be a multiple of 256 bytes.
YShftFactor	8	Scaling factor for start address of a screen row. This variable is kept for compatibility reasons and should not be used.
Log2BPP	9	LOG base 2 of the number of bits per pixel (for possible values see *Mode Variables* on page 479).
Log2BPC	10	LOG base 2 of the number of bytes per character. It is in fact the LOG base 2 of the number of bytes per character divided by eight. It would be exactly the same as Log2BPP, except for the 'double pixel' modes.
XWindLimit	11	Number of x pixels on screen–1.
YWindLimit	12	Number of y pixels on screen–1.
GWLCol	128	Left-hand column of the graphics window (ic)
GWBRow	129	Bottom row of the graphics window (ic)
GWRCol	130	Right-hand column of the graphics window (ic)
GWTRow	131	Top row of the graphics window (ic)
TWLCol	132	Left-hand column of the text window
TWBRow	133	Bottom row of the text window
TWRCol	134	Right-hand column of the text window
TWTRow	135	Top row of the text window
OrgX	136	x coordinate of the graphics origin (ec)
OrgY	137	Y coordinate of the graphics origin (ec)
GCsX	138	x coordinate of the graphics cursor (ec)
GCsY	139	Y coordinate of the graphics cursor (ec)
OlderCsX	140	x coordinate of oldest graphics cursor (ic)
OlderCsY	141	Y coordinate of oldest graphics cursor (ic)
OldCsX	142	x coordinate of previous graphics cursor (ic)
OldCsY	143	Y coordinate of previous graphics cursor (ic)
GCsIX	144	x coordinate of graphics cursor (ic)
GCsIY	145	Y coordinate of graphics cursor (ic)

Name	Number	Description
NewPtX	146	x coordinate of new point (ic)
NewPtY	147	Y coordinate of new point (ic)
ScreenStart	148	Address of the start of screen used by VDU drivers
DisplayStart	149	Address of the start of screen used by display hardware
TotalScreenSize	150	Amount of memory currently allocated to the screen
GPLFMD	151	GCOL action for foreground colour
GPLBMD	152	GCOL action for background colour
GFCOL	153	Graphics foreground colour
GBCOL	154	Graphics background colour
TForeCol	155	Text foreground colour
TBackCol	156	Text background colour
GFTint	157	Tint for graphics foreground colour
GBTint	158	Tint for graphics background colour
TFTint	159	Tint for text foreground colour
TBTint	160	Tint for text background colour
MaxMode	161	Highest mode number available
GCharSizeX	162	x size of VDU 5 chars (in pixels)
GCharSizeY	163	Y size of VDU 5 chars (in pixels)
GCharSpaceX	164	x spacing of VDU 5 chars (in pixels)
GCharSpaceY	165	Y spacing of VDU 5 chars (in pixels)
HLineAddr	166	Address of fast line-draw routine
TCharSizeX	167	x size of VDU 4 chars (in pixels)
TCharSizeY	168	Y size of VDU 4 chars (in pixels)
TCharSpaceX	169	x spacing of VDU 4 chars (in pixels)
TCharSpaceY	170	Y spacing of VDU 4 chars (in pixels)
GcolOraEorAddr	171	Address of colour blocks for current GCOLs
VIDCClockSpeed	172	VIDC clock speed in kHz (eg 24000 $\Rightarrow$ 24 MHz)
PixelRate	173	Pixel rate of the current mode in kHz
BorderL	174	Left border size (RISC OS 5.07 onwards)
BorderB	175	Bottom border size (RISC OS 5.07 onwards)
BorderR	176	Right border size (RISC OS 5.07 onwards)
BorderT	177	Top border size (RISC OS 5.07 onwards)
GraphicsVDriver	192	Current GraphicsV driver number (RISC OS 5.22 onwards)
WindowWidth	256	Characters that will fit on a row of the text window without a newline being generated
WindowHeight	257	Rows that will fit in the text window without scrolling it

- *ic* means internal coordinates, where (0,0) is always the bottom left of the screen. One unit is one pixel.

- *ec* means external coordinates, where (0,0) means the graphics origin, and the size of one unit depends on the resolution. The number of external units on a screen is dependent upon the video mode used and the EIG factors. The graphics origin is stored in external coordinate units, but is relative to the bottom left of the screen.

- *new point* is the internal form of the coordinates given in an unrecognised PLOT command, for use by claimants of the UKPlot vector.
- HLineAddr points to a fast horizontal line draw routine. It is called as follows:

    R0 = left x coordinate of end of line

    R1 = y coordinate of line

    R2 = right x coordinate of end of line

    R3 = 0   plot with no action (ie do nothing)
          1   plot using foreground colour and action
          2   invert current screen colour
          3   plot using background colour and action
          ≥ 4   pointer to colour block (on 64-byte boundary):

Offset	Value
0	OR mask for top ECF line
4	exclusive OR mask for top ECF line
8	OR mask for next ECF line
12	exclusive OR mask for next ECF line
...	
56	OR mask for bottom ECF line
60	exclusive OR mask for bottom ECF line

    R14 = return address

    Must be entered in SVC mode

    All registers are preserved on exit

    All coordinates are in terms of pixels from the bottom left of the screen. The line is clipped to the graphics window, and is plotted using the colour action specified by R3. The caller must have previously called OS_RemoveCursors and call OS_RestoreCursors afterwards.

- GcolOraEorAddr points to colour blocks for current GCOLs. If the value returned is n, then:

    n+&00–n+&3F is a colour block for the foreground colour + action

    n+&40–n+&7F is a colour block for the background colour + action

    n+&80–n+&BF is a colour block for the background colour with store action

    Each colour block is as described above. These are updated whenever a GCOL or TINT is issued or the ECF origin is changed. They are intended for programs which want to access screen memory directly and have access to the current colour/action settings.

Appendix I – BBC BASIC's history

This appendix is designed to pinpoint the variations found among the dialects of BBC BASIC. You can use it to determine whether a given feature of the language is present in a particular version. You should also refer to *Appendix B – Minimum abbreviations* on page 459. This gives the version number of the first appearance of each keyword. For example, OSCLI has II in the version column, as the OSCLI statement was first introduced in BASIC II.

There have been six major releases of BBC BASIC, the latest being BASIC VI, and a number of subsequent improvements. The complete list is:

BASIC I

The original version supplied with early BBC Microcomputers, models A and B. BBC BASIC is in turn descended from Atom BASIC, a fast integer-only BASIC supplied with the Acorn Atom.

BASIC II

This was an update to BASIC I. It also ran on the BBC models A and B. It incorporated various bug fixes to BASIC I, and added the OPENUP and OSCLI keywords, and offset assembly. Version II is the principal BBC Microcomputer version of BBC BASIC.

BASIC III

This was supplied on the BBC Microcomputer model B+. It was substantially unchanged from version II. There were one or two bug fixes, and a new keyword: the American spelling of the COLOR statement.

BASIC IV

Also known as CMOS BASIC, this version was a major development from BASIC III. It was designed for use on the BBC Master series and 65C12 Second Processors. Both these used a slightly more powerful version of the 6502 processor than the one used in the original BBC. This allowed several major enhancements to be squeezed into the ROM, such as LIST IF, EXT# as a statement, EDIT, TIME$, ON ... PROC, | in VDU statements and faster floating point. Some bugs were also corrected.

BASIC V, version 1.04

Developed for Acorn RISC computers. BASIC V built on the foundations provided by BASIC IV. However, because of the lack of restrictions such as 16 kBytes total code size, the enhancements made were far greater than those that appeared previously. The interpreter was by now about 61 kBytes long, including comprehensive built-in help text, and was probably the most powerful BASIC found on any computer. It was certainly the fastest interpreted BASIC in the world.

BASIC V, version 1.05

This upgrade of the version 1.04 interpreter gave BBC BASIC more speed and power. New commands were introduced. The interpreter had grown to 64kBytes to accommodate the improvements.

BASIC VI, version 1.05

BASIC VI runs on the Acorn RISC computers. Improved floating point handling means it now performs floating point arithmetic to IEEE standard 754, using 8-byte real representation.

Because BASIC V is still a useful language, you are given the option to invoke either BASIC V (using the *BASIC command) or BASIC VI (using the new *BASIC64 command). The interpreter is now only 57 kBytes long, although the value of PAGE is higher.

This version of BASIC is built into the RISC OS 3.10, 3.11 and 3.19 ROM.

BASIC V & VI, version 1.06

Version 1.06 of BASIC is built into the RISC OS 3.50 ROM. It extends the GCOL, COLOUR, POINT and MODE keywords.

BASIC V & VI, version 1.14

This version is built into the RISC OS 3.60 ROM. There are no functional changes to the BASIC language.

BASIC V & VI, version 1.16

Version 1.16 adds support for the StrongARM processor and is included in the RISC OS 3.70 and 3.71 ROM.

BASIC V & VI, version 1.34

Version 1.34 of BASIC is included in the RISC OS 5.01 and 5.02 ROM. It includes a substantial number of improvements and bug fixes, described in more detail in the next section.

BASIC V & VI, version 1.35

This version fixes some bugs and is included in the RISC OS 5.03 ROM.

BASIC V & VI, version 1.39

Version 1.39 of BASIC, included in the RISC OS 5.14 ROM fixes some bugs and adds a new variant of the COLOUR keyword.

BASIC V & VI, version 1.44

This version, included in the RISC OS 5.16 ROM, adds support for ARMv6 architecture processors.

BASIC V & VI, version 1.48

Version 1.48 of BASIC, included in RISC OS 5.18, adds some performance improvements for ARMv5 and ARMv6 processor, and changes TEXTLOAD so that programs with more than 6527 lines can be loaded.

BASIC V & VI, version 1.54

This version, included in RISC OS 5.20, adds support for VFP/NEON instructions to the BASIC assembler. It also changes the SYS keyword so that it treats null pointers returned by SWIs as null strings, updates the EDIT keyword so that it attempts to automatically load the ARMBE module if it is not present, and improves error handling when calls to code outside BASIC result in an abort.

BASIC V & VI, version 1.59

Version 1.59 of BASIC, included in RISC OS 5.22, fixes some problems in the VFP/NEON assembler support and some problems with tokenisation. It also changes the way BASIC manages its message resources, making it easier to softload a newer version of BASIC than the one in the RISC OS ROM.

BASIC V & VI, version 1.73

This is the latest version of BASIC at the time of writing, and is the version described in this manual. This adds the VFP version of BASIC VI, improves the conversion of floating point numbers to strings, and enhances the MODE keyword. It also adds support for ARMv6, ARMv7 and ARMv8 instructions to the assembler, as well as fixing an error in the assembler introduced in version 1.59.

BASIC II improvements

New keywords and features

OSCLI. This passes a string to the command line interpreter for execution. It is more powerful than simple * commands, as these cannot contain general string expressions.

OPENUP. This does an OSFIND with reason code &C0, i.e. open an existing file for update. This was the action of OPENIN in BASIC I. OPENIN now does an OSFIND &40, i.e. open for input only. OPENOUT still does an OSFIND &80, i.e. create and open for update.

Numeric printing has been improved to allow numbers to be printed to ten digits accuracy. This allows integers up to 2^{33} to be printed without resorting to 'E' notation.

The MODE statement now resets the COUNT function to zero.

A semi-colon (;) is allowed in place of a comma (,) in the INPUT statement.

Fatal errors are introduced. These have error number 0, and cause an automatic ON ERROR OFF. This means that the default error handler is always used for these errors. The STOP statement now causes a fatal error, as does the No room condition. Additionally, the standard error handler no longer uses stack space, so spurious No room errors are not produced.

A new error, number 45, Missing # is given if any of the keywords PTR, EOF, BGET, BPUT, EXT is not followed by a #.

String allocation has been improved. A string which was the last one created on the heap can be extended without discarding the old storage. This stops No room errors from being generated in certain situations.

Bit 2 of the assembler OPT expression is used to control offset assembly. If this bit is set, P% holds the run-time location counter, and O% holds the assembly-time counter where bytes are actually assembled to. If bit 2 is clear, P% holds both the run-time and assembly-time counters.

Four new assembler directives are introduced: EQUB, EQUW, EQUD, EQUS. These allow one-, two-, four- and multiple-byte (string) quantities to be embedded into the code.

Bug fixes

ELSE in an ON ... GOTO/GOSUB no longer leaves a byte on the 6502 stack. This prevented ELSE from being used in ON statements in BASIC I.

INSTR no longer leaves the main string on the software stack when it is shorter than the substring. This caused ENDPROC and =*expression* to crash when INSTR was used inside a PROC or FN under the above-mentioned condition.

The argument of EVAL is now tokenised correctly so that EVAL"TIME" (or any other pseudo-variable) works. Previously the statement versions of pseudo-variables were used, resulting in a `No such variable` error when BASIC tried to evaluate the expression.

The ABS function can now cope with non-negative integers without returning a string type. Previously, ABS1 appeared to yield a string so a statement like PRINT -ABS1 would give a type-mismatch error.

The LN and LOG functions have been re-written. This makes them more accurate and avoids a problem when BASIC tried to evaluate LN(2E–39). Other changes to the arithmetic package are a fix to a bug which caused INT1E39 to fail and the re-coding of the SIN/COS routine to make it more accurate.

A bug associated with ON ERROR GOTO 9999 (and other line numbers) has been fixed.

DIM *var n* where *n* is an expression less than –1 now gives a `Bad DIM` error instead of lowering the value of the free space pointer. This former action could result in the corruption of variables or the program.

BASIC III improvements

The COLOUR keyword may now be spelt COLOR, to aid the porting of programs from American dialects of BASIC. In programs, the keyword always lists as COLOUR, except in the American version of BASIC III, which always lists it as COLOR. This is the only difference between the two versions.

A string expression in a SAVE command works correctly now, so you can say, for example, SAVE A$+B$ without error.

The indirection operators ? and ! may be used as formal parameters without problems. For example, you could have a procedure DEF PROCa(!&70), where the contents of locations &70..&73 act as a local integer variable.

BASIC IV improvements

The ON ... GOTO/GOSUB statement has been extended to include PROCs. The syntax is ON *expression* PROC*a*, PROC*b*, PROC*c*... [ELSE *statement*]. The *n*th PROC in the list is called, where *n* is the value of *expression*.

The EDIT command converts the program to text and then calls the editor with a *EDIT command. The program can be edited then re-tokenised by returning to BASIC. A No room error will be given if there is not enough room to store both the tokenised and textual version of the program during conversion to text.

The TIME$ pseudo-variable can be used to display and alter the time held in the CMOS battery-backed clock.

The delimiter | may be used in VDU statements to send nine 0 bytes after the last expression. This can be used to ensure that, for example, VDU 23 commands which require many trailing zeros are correctly terminated.

LISTO bits 1 and 2 (which cause loops to be indented) now work correctly, inasmuch as the NEXT lines up with its FOR and UNTIL with its REPEAT. If LISTO is non-zero, leading spaces are stripped from input lines (i.e. between the line-number and first statement). Trailing spaces are always stripped.

LIST has been extended by adding the IF part to it. LIST IF*text* will only list lines which contain text.

The function EXT# returning the length of the file may now also be used as a statement to set the length of a file (EXT#*chan*=*expr*). It relies for its operation on an OSARGS call supported by ADFS and ANFS.

AUTO no longer prints a space after the line number, as this wasn't part of the input line anyway.

The assembler supports the full 65C12 instruction set, and now accepts lower case in all circumstances (e.g. the x in lda &70,x which previously had to be in upper case).

RENUMBER and LIST no longer get confused by the presence of an &8D Teletext control character in REM statements. (&8D is used in internal-format line numbers by BASIC).

In previous versions, a FOR loop which used an FN in the start, end or step expressions, where the FN itself contained a FOR loop would not work properly. This has been fixed.

The random number generator gives different results from previous versions for RND(1) and RND(*n*). This is to avoid certain statistical problems.

A bug whereby it was possible to RESTORE to a line which had no DATA statement but a comma present has been fixed.

Appendix I – BBC BASIC's history

BASIC V version 1.04 improvements

BASIC V introduces a large number of enhancements. Because the major part of this guide is concerned with the documentation of BASIC V, this section only mentions the new keywords and features in very terse terms. You are directed to the *Keywords* chapters for detailed descriptions of all BASIC keywords. The index also gives you the page reference for the main discussion of topics mentioned below.

The new constructs WHILE ... ENDWHILE, IF ... THEN ... ELSE ... ENDIF, CASE ... OF... WHEN ... OTHERWISE ... ENDCASE have been introduced. This makes readable, GOTO-less programming much easier to attain than previously.

Procedure and function calls have been enhanced in the following ways: value and result parameters (RETURN parameters), array parameters and local arrays, procedure libraries (LIBRARY, INSTALL and OVERLAY), LOCAL DATA and LOCAL ERROR handlers, a relative RESTORE statement which does not require the use of line numbers.

Many array operations have been introduced. These include: local arrays and array reference parameters, whole arrays operations such as assignment, four-function arithmetic, matrix and vector multiplication, SUM of array elements, the DIM function to find information on array parameters, array element initialisation, MOD (square root of the sum of the squares of a numeric array).

Several new operators have been introduced: << (left shift), >> (arithmetic right shift), >>> (logical right shift), | (floating point indirection), += (increment assignment, including all the elements of an array), -= (decrement assignment). The character % introduces binary constants as & introduces hexadecimal ones.

TRACE has been enhanced to allow single stepping and the tracing of procedure and function calls. Example: TRACE STEP PROC.

Line numbers may now be in the range 0-&FEFF, i.e. 0-65279. On line entry, BASIC checks for mismatched quotes and parentheses and attempts to reference line numbers greater than 65279. An error is reported if a mismatch is detected.

Attempts to set PAGE, LOMEM or HIMEM to incorrect values will result in an error message being printed, but execution will continue.

Many new statements have been introduced. The relevant keywords are: BEATS, BPUT#, CIRCLE, COLOUR, ELLIPSE, END, ERROR, EXT, FILL, GCOL, LINE, INPUT, LEFT$, MID$, RIGHT$, MOUSE, ON, OFF, ORIGIN, POINT, QUIT, RECTANGLE, SOUND, STEREO, SWAP, SYS, TEMPO, VOICE, VOICES, WAIT.

Several new functions have also been introduced. The keywords are: BEAT, BEATS, DIM, END, GET$#, LEFT$, MODE, REPORT$, RIGHT$, SUM, SUMLEN, TEMPO.

Some new commands have been introduced. They are: APPEND, HELP, LISTO (enhanced), LVAR, SAVE (enhanced), TWIN, TWINO. Additionally, the *BASIC command itself now supports several command-line options and arguments.

All error messages have been made more useful, and many new error messages have been introduced.

The assembler accepts the full ARM instruction set. Full details of the assembler are given in the chapter entitled ARM *assembler* on page 441.

CALL and USR may be used to call ARM assembler routines, or to emulate 6502-based MOS routine when supplied with the appropriate addresses. Access to many internal BASIC routines is (legally) available to writers of CALL, USR and OSCLI routines. SYS can be used to access operating system SWI routines.

The default error handler sets @% to a value which ensures that the line number will be printed as an integer. It restores @% at the end.

COUNT and WIDTH are now stored as 32-bit wide quantities. This means that tabulation using commas is more reliable. (Strange effects used to occur after 255 characters had been printed.)

The pseudo-variables may now be used as statements after an IF even when the THEN is omitted. That is, `IF relocate% PAGE=PAGE+&10000` will work, even though it didn't previously.

Integer FOR statements that would overflow will be ignored. (Basically this means that if limit+step−1 / &7FFFFFFF, the loop will terminate at the NEXT.)

BASIC V version 1.05 improvements

This uses version 1.05 of the BASIC interpreter. It is an upgrade of BASIC V version 1.04, and includes new commands as well as bug fixes.

The new CRUNCH command strips various spaces from a program. Its argument is a 5–bit binary word. Each bit in the word has a different meaning (for instance bit 0 controls the stripping of spaces before statements; bit 2 controls the stripping out of REM statements).

END= can now be used almost anywhere, with the following exceptions: nested within EVAL or LOCAL ERROR; nested within assignments to local arrays; within nested local arrays.

The @% print formatter now uses ANSI G, E or F formats. If you use the 1.04 interpreter, you can achieve the same results using the method given in the description of the PRINT command.

The new TEXTLOAD command can load a file that is either a BASIC program, or a BASIC program that was saved as a text file. In the latter case, TEXTLOAD automatically renumbers the program. TEXTSAVE stores a BASIC program as a text file, and strips out the line numbers.

The TRACE command is now more versatile. Output from a TRACE command can now be sent to a file, using TRACE TO *filename*. TRACE can also be used as a function, to enable output other than line numbers to be sent to the trace file.

The speed of the following array statements has been increased:

```
foo()=<expression>
foo%()=<expression>
foo()=fie()
DIM foo(, foo(, foo%
```

The interpreter now tags error messages with the name of the library which caused the error message (found from the REM statement on the first line of the library).

The interpreter can now handle such things as TAN1E-5.

PRINT -1^-10 will now print the value 1, instead of causing a crash.

There is now no difference between IF THEN ELSE and IF THENELSE.

BASIC VI version 1.05 improvements

This also uses version 1.05 of the BASIC interpreter. The major change for BASIC VI is that it now supports real numbers in 8–byte format (according to IEEE standard 754). This means greater precision and accuracy in floating point arithmetic.

BASIC VI can still understand 5–byte reals, but will only print numbers in the 8–byte real format.

BASIC VI is invoked using the new *BASIC64 command. BASIC V can still be invoked, by using the old *BASIC command. Both commands take the same command line options and arguments.

The interface of the CALL statement has changed to accommodate 8–byte reals. There are additions to the list of l–values to which R9 points.

INPUT# can now read variables in both 5–byte real format and 8–byte real format. PRINT# only prints numbers in 8–byte real format.

BASIC V & VI version 1.06 improvements

The GCOL statement has been extended to support GCOL *r,g,b* and GCOL *action,r,g,b* using ColourTrans_SetGCOL, and the COLOUR statement now supports COLOUR *r,g,b* using ColourTrans_SetColour.

The MODE *n* statement now calls OS_ScreenMode 0 when *n* is greater than 255, allowing *n* to be a pointer to a *mode selector* block. It has also been extended to accept a string parameter and call *WimpMode, although as well as changing the current mode this has the side-effect of changing the desktop mode.

BASIC V & VI version 1.34 improvements

The assembler now supports FPA, ARMv4 and ARMv5TE opcodes and defines the special variables SP (13) and LR (14).

The assembler directives DCFS/DCFD/DCFE and EQUFS/EQUFD/EQUFE for defining floating point values have been added.

ALIGN will now force any unused bytes to zero when assembling at both P% and O%. This is better than leaving possibly uninitialised memory behind, potentially resulting in different binary output each time code is assembled.

TRACE PROC (and the identical TRACE FN) now flushes the VCACHE when it is encountered. This is important, because procedure and function calls are normally cached to avoid looking-up the name and searching for the location of the DEF. When tracing is active, procedure or function calls are not added to the cache, because the name must be parsed in order for it to be sent to the trace output. By flushing the VCACHE at the start of PROC/FN tracing all calls are reported (before, any cached ones would not appear in the trace output).

TRACE ENDPROC has been implemented to allow the output of 'ENDPROC' and 'ENDFN' in the trace output whenever a procedure or function is exited. This complements the TRACE PROC/FN functionality.

QUIT *expression* has been added to allow a return code to be passed back when BASIC exits. This is the only sensible way for a BASIC program to set Sys$ReturnCode on exit (it will otherwise get changed when BASIC removes its environment handlers).

A new syntax for MODE has been added: MODE *width,height,bpp*[*,framerate*]. This uses OS_ScreenMode 0, and *bpp* may be 1,2,4,6,8,16 or 32 where 8 selects a full palette 256-colour mode and 6 a VIDC1-style one.

COLOUR and GCOL have been enhanced to allow colour numbers rather than old-style colours and to allow background colours can be set with R,G,B forms:

COLOUR [OF *f*] [ON *b*]
COLOUR [[OF] *r,g,b*] [ON *r,g,b*]
GCOL [OF [*action*],*f*] [ON [*action*],*b*]
GCOL [[OF] [*action*,]*r,g,b*] [ON [*action*,]*r,g,b*]

For COLOUR *r,g,b*, the OF is unnecessary, but provided for uniformity. For GCOL *r,g,b*, OF tightens up the usage of *action* – without it *action* is passed in to both R3 and R4 of ColourTrans_SetGCOL for backwards compatibility (some programs may have used GCOL 128,*r,g,b* to set the background colour, although this ends up setting reserved flags in the ColourTrans_SetGCOL call).

Used as a function VDU *n* now returns the value of the specified VDU variable.

BASIC will now surrender application space if possible at certain moments: during SYS calls (as long as no string parameters are passed in), MODE changes, OSCLI and * commands. Also, it will not refuse requests to grow application space (although it will not expand into the extra space). Application space is only surrendered if no library is INSTALLed, HIMEM is set to the top of BASIC's memory, and BASIC's memory extends to the top of the application slot. This permits easy MODE changes etc outside the desktop. Note the effect that now outside the desktop, with screen memory at <300K and no free pool, MODE 28 will work, while VDU 22,28 will not.

The new DIM *var* LOCAL *expr* syntax allows blocks to be claimed local to a procedure or function that are automatically released on exit or error. In addition DIM *var* LOCAL -1 can be used to obtain the value of SP at the time of request.

Performance on StrongARM and later processors has been slightly improved.

Expression evaluation for the WHEN statement has been improved so that syntax errors such as WHEN (R%>>25) AND 1)=1 are not incorrectly evaluated.

Problems that would occur when using memory addresses above 64M have been resolved.

An issue that meant untokenised programs could not be loaded via the *BASIC command on XScale and later processors has been fixed.

Performance has been improved when BASIC copies data from unaligned addresses.

BASIC V & VI version 1.35 improvements

In BASIC VI, A()=B()/C now works. Previously this specific case failed due to a stack imbalance.

Keywords that take tokenised line numbers no longer cause number tokenisation if they appear on the right. This fixes `BPUT#TRACE,32` but unfortunately breaks statements such as `IF F% THEN 30`.

In the assembler STRT/LDRT now enforce post-indexing. `LDRT R0,[R1]` generates correct code, and `LDRT R0,[R1,#0]` will be faulted.

BASIC V & VI version 1.39 improvements

The COLOUR *n,r,,g,b* form of the COLOUR keyword, which sets a palette entry, has been extended to take an optional fifth parameter specifying the supremacy bits for this palette entry.

The tokenisation of `IF F% THEN 30`, broken in version 1.35, has been fixed, but statements without a THEN such as `IF F% GOTO 30` are still handled incorrectly.

Out of range checks for the B and BL instructions have been added to the assembler.

BASIC V & VI version 1.44 improvements

BASIC now supports ARMv6 architecture processors.

BASIC V & VI version 1.48 improvements

Performance has been improved for ARMv5 and ARMv6 processors.

TEXTLOAD will now do RENUMBER 10,1 when renumbering is needed which means that programs with more than 6527 lines can now be loaded

BASIC V & VI version 1.54 improvements

Support for VFP/NEON instructions has been added to the BASIC assembler.

The SYS keyword now treats null pointers returned by SWIs as null strings. This protects against a crash if the user expects a SWI to return a string but it decides not to (e.g. due to an error).

The EDIT keyword will now attempt to automatically load the ARMBE module if it is not present.

BASIC will now correctly report ERL after an external abort. Previously when external code was called using CALL, USR, SYS, or a *command (either directly or using OSCLI), and that code failed with a Data Transfer, Undefined Instruction or Instruction Fetch abort, ERL was often set to the last line of the program, rather than the line containing the CALL, USR, SYS or *command.

BASIC V & VI version 1.59 improvements

Some problems in the VFP/NEON assembler support have been fixed.

The BASIC and BASIC64 modules now manage their own message resources instead of using the separate BasicTrans module. This makes it straightforward to softload a newer version of BASIC than the one in the RISC OS ROM. See the section entitled BASIC *versions* on page 6 for further details.

BASIC error messages (e.g. "Syntax error") are now passed via Service_Error for information. As with OSCLI, some extra registers are set with BASIC's internal state, which could be useful for debuggers.

The tokenisation problems introduced in version 1.35 for statements such as IF F% GOTO 30 have now been fully resolved.

The BASIC assembler now only considers SP, LR, PC or Rn to be references to register names if used in isolation and not as part of another word. This allows variables beginning with these letters such as speed or r9len to be used within assembler code.

BASIC V & VI version 1.73 improvements

A problem introduced in version 1.59 which meant the assembler would report a bad register error for statements like LDR Rn, [R1] or LDMIA Rn, {R1} has been fixed.

Support for ARMv6, ARMv7 and ARMv8 processors has been added to the assembler, and the VFP/NEON assembler support has been improved by adding VNMLA, VNMLS, VNMUL and VDUP.

Compatibility with RISC OS 3.10 has been improved.

The conversion of floating point numbers to strings has been improved to give increased accuracy in BASIC V and to ensure that BASIC V and BASIC VI format numbers in the same way.

A new version of BASIC VI has been added which uses the VFP instruction set found on modern ARM processors. The *BASIC64 command will now automatically start either the VFP or FPA version of BASIC VI as appropriate for the current CPU, and the new *BASICVFP and *BASICFPA commands allow each variant to be started explicitly.

MODE *string* now uses OS_ScreenMode 15 rather than *WimpMode, to avoid programs which use it altering the Wimp mode or having to worry about preserving it. If OS_ScreenMode 15 isn't supported internal mode string parsing code that provides a similar level of functionality to the host system's *WimpMode is used.

All MODE variants which use OS_ScreenMode now detect any "SWI not known" error and replace it with "Bad MODE" (under the assumption the user is running a version of RISC OS older than 3.50).

MODE *x,y,ModeFlags,NColour,Log2bpp|,framerate|* has been added to allow specification of the three parameters necessary for selecting the new screen modes introduced by RISC OS 5.

The HELP keyword no longer returns help for the obsolete TWIN and TWINO keywords.

Index

Symbols
^ 32
! 32, 166
? 32, 166
. (matrix multiplication) 51
" 39
(32
) 32
@% 57, 367
* 32
* Commands 435
/ 32
& 33
% 33
+ 32
+ (string concatenation) 40
+= 31
+= (string lengthen) 40
+= (with arrays) 49
< 32, 74
<< 32, 34
<= 32, 74
<> 32, 74
- 32
-= 31
= 30, 32, 74
= (assembler directive) 446
-= (with arrays) 49
=expression 87
> 24, 32, 74
>= 32, 74
>> 32, 35
>>> 32, 35
| 32, 167
~ 45, 56
$ 32, 167

Numerics
256-colour modes 110, 113

A
ABS 219
absolute coordinates 124
ACS 220
actual parameter 88
ADVAL 221
ALIGN directive 446
amplitude, sound 161
AND 32, 36, 75, 223
APPEND 25, 224
arc plot 134
arithmetic operator 31
array 47
array operations 49
ASC 43, 225
ASCII 43
ASN 226
assembler
    format of language statements 446-447
    implementing passes 443-444
    memory pointers 442-443
    OPT directive 444-445
    reserving memory for machine code 442
    using BASIC variables 442
assembly language, calling subroutines 234
assignment 29, 30
ATN 227
AUTO 21, 228
automatic line numbering 21

B

background colour 111, 122
    teletext 154
bases 33
    base 16 33
    base 2 33
*BASIC 436
BASIC assembler *see* assembler
BASIC interpreter 5
BASIC screen editor 191, 193-211
    altering text 195
    block copy 200
    block move 200
    cursor movement 195
    deleting lines 200
    deleting text 196
    EDIT 193
    errors 208
    insert/overtype 203
    inserting text 195
    keys 205
    line commands 199
    loading programs 196
    marking lines 199
    mode 204
    renumbering 198
    saving programs 196
    searching 202
    status line 194
    wildcards 203
    windows 205
*BASIC64 438
*BASICFPA 439
*BASICVFP 440
BEAT 163, 229
beat counter 162
BEATS 163, 230
BGET# 102, 231
binary 33
block structured IF 75
BPUT# 102, 103, 232
BY 124, 233
byte DIM 165
byte indirection 166

C

CALL 234
CASE 82, 248
CHAIN 249
changing colour 111
changing text size 110
channel number 101
channel, sound 161
*CHANNELVOICE 427
character input 65
CHR$ 43, 250
CIRCLE 121, 251
circle
    outline 121, 132
    solid 121, 132
CIRCLE FILL 14, 121
CLEAR 252
CLG 253
CLOSE# 102, 254
CLS 14, 255
COLOR 256
COLOUR 111, 256
colour
    changing 111
    modes 110, 481
    palette 112
    pattern 139
    teletext 153
command mode 12
comments 22
comparison operators 74
concatenation, string 40
conditional structures 73
control variable 77
conversions 43
Copy key 17
copying rectangles 137
COS 259

COUNT 260
CRUNCH 261
cursor
    appearance 182
    editing 17
    keys 68
    moving 185
    start line 182
cursor movement, in editor 195

D

DATA 66, 262
data files 101
DCB/W/D/S/FS/FD/FE assembler directives 446
debugging 174
DEF 88, 263
default
    colours 112
    error handler 171
    patterns 139
    viewports 149
defining
    colour patterns 140
    functions 95
    procedures 87
DEG 264
DELETE 18, 265
deleting programs 19
DIM 47, 266
    as a function 49
    reserving memory 165
dimension 47
disabling error trapping 171
displaying text 55
DIV 32, 269
division, in BASIC 13
dot-dash pattern 129
double-height characters 110
    in teletext 154
DRAW 124, 270
duration, sound 162

E

EDIT 271
Edit 191
    editing BASIC programs 191
    Options submenu
        Line number increment 192
        Strip line numbers 192
    printing a BASIC program 192
    tokenised files 192
editing a program 16
ELLIPSE 121, 272
ELLIPSE FILL 121
ellipse plot 133
ELSE 73, 76, 273
    (in ON) 85
END 274
End key 17
ENDCASE 82, 276
ENDIF 76, 277
ENDPROC 88, 278
ENDWHILE 81, 279
entering a program 15
entering BASIC 11
ENVELOPE 280
EOF# 102, 282
EOR 32, 36, 75, 283
EQUB/W/D/S/FS/FD/FE assembler directives 446
ERL 170, 284
ERR 170, 285
ERROR 171, 286
ERROR EXT 171, 286
errors 169
    external 171
    handling 169
    trapping 169
EVAL 44, 287
*EXEC 104
executing a command file 104
EXP 288
expression 216
EXT# 289

F

factor 217
FALSE 37, 290
files 101
    creating 101
    executing 104
    input 102
    output 101
FILL 137, 291
fixed point numbers 451
flashing colours 184
flashing, teletext 154
floating point coprocessor 455
floating point emulator (FPE) 455
floating point instruction set 455
floating point numbers 451
floating point variable 27, 29
    indirection 167
flood-fill 136
FN 32, 87, 95, 292
FOR 77, 293
foreground colour 111, 122
formal parameter 88
function keys 71
    programming 71
    special characters 72
function library 95
functions 87
*FX 15 68
*FX 219 68
*FX 4 68

G

GCOL 111, 122, 294
GET 65, 297
GET$ 65, 299
GET$# 103, 298
giant patterns 144
GOSUB 84, 300
GOTO 84, 301

graphics 117
    cursor 124
    horizontal line draw routine 488
    resolution 107
    screen 117
    teletext 155
    units 117
    viewport 147, 149

H

HELP 302
hexadecimal 33
HIMEM 303

I

IF 304
    multi-line 75
    single line 73
    THEN, ELSE 75
immediate mode 12
indirection
    byte 166
    floating point 167
    string 167
    word 166
INKEY 65, 306
    values 469
INKEY$ 65, 308
INPUT 15, 63, 309
INPUT LINE 64, 310
INPUT# 102, 311
INSTALL 96, 312
INSTR 42, 313
INT 314
integer 27, 451
    variable 29
interactive mode 12
interlace 181
ISO-8859 43

K

*KEY 71
keyboard
    buffer 67
    input 63
    programming 67
keywords 215

L

left shift 34
LEFT$ 40, 315
LEN 42, 316
LET 13, 30, 317
libraries
    function 95
    loading 95
    procedure 95
LIBRARY 96, 261, 318
LINE 119, 319
LINE INPUT 64, 320
line number 15
LIST 16, 21, 321
LISTO 73, 323
LN 324
LOAD 24, 325
LOCAL 89, 326
LOCAL DATA 92, 326
LOCAL ERROR 173
local error handling 172
LOG 328
logical operator 31, 37
LOMEM 329
loop structures 73
LVAR 28, 99, 174, 330

M

machine code, calling subroutines 234
matrix multiplication 53

MID$ 40, 331
MOD 32, 54, 333
MODE 107, 109, 334
mode 12, 107
MOUSE 338
mouse 69
MOVE 124, 340
moving rectangles 137
multiplication, in BASIC 13

N

negative INKEY 69
    values 469
NEW 341
NEXT 77, 342
NOT 32, 75, 343
note synchronisation 162, 164
null string 39
numeric types 451

O

*OBEY 104
octave 161
OF 83, 344
OFF 345
offset assembly 443
OLD 346
ON 347
ON ... GOSUB 86, 300
ON ... GOTO 85, 301
ON ... PROC 92, 371
ON ERROR 169, 348
ON ERROR LOCAL 172
ON ERROR OFF 171
OPENIN 102, 350
OPENOUT 101, 351
OPENUP 352
operators 74
    arithmetic 31

logical 31, 74
    precedence 32
    relational 74
OPT directive 444-445
OR 32, 36, 75, 353
ORIGIN 354
OSCLI 355
OTHERWISE 357
OVERLAY 98, 261, 358

P

PAGE 360
paged mode 180
palette 112
parallelogram plot 131
parameter 89
pathname 218
pattern fill 140
PI 361
pitch, sound 161
pixel 118
PLOT 127, 362
    codes 483
POINT 118
    function 364
    statement 363
pointer 70
POS 365
precedence, of operators 32
PRINT 12, 55, 366
PRINT# 101, 370
printer 178
PROC 87
procedure library 95
procedures 87
program 15
    data 65
    deleting 19
    editing 16
    entering 15
    inserting comments 22

    listing 21
    loading 24
    multiple statements 23
    numbering lines in 20
    running 15
    saving 24
    window managed 7
prompt 64
PTR# 372

Q

QUIT 12, 172, 373

R

RAD 374
READ 65, 375
reading from a file 102
reading text 63
RECTANGLE 120, 376
RECTANGLE ... TO 137
RECTANGLE FILL 120
RECTANGLE FILL ... TO 137
rectangle plot 130
recursion 93
relational 217
relative coordinates 124
REM 22, 378
RENUMBER 20, 379
REPEAT 80, 380
REPORT 170, 381
REPORT$ 382
resequencing programs 20
resident integer variable 31
resolution 107, 117
RESTORE 66, 383
RESTORE DATA 92, 383
RESTORE ERROR 173, 383
RESTORE+ 99
RETURN 84, 385

parameter 91
right shift
    arithmetic 35
    logical 35
RIGHT$ 40, 386
RND 387
RUN 15, 388
running a program 15

S

SAVE 24, 389
scaled characters 185
screen display 107
screen editor *see* BASIC screen editor
scrolling 182
sector plot 135
segment plot 136
*SETTYPE 104
SGN 390
shadow mode 109
shift operator 34
simple patterns 145
SIN 391
single-byte file i/o 102
single-character input 65
SOUND 159, 392
sound 159
    after parameter 164
    amplitude 161
    channel 161
    duration 162
    pitch 161
    scheduling 164
    synchronisation 164
    volume 161
SPC 394
sprites 151-??, 187
    loading 151
    plotting 152
SQR 395
statements 217

STEP 77, 396
STEREO 160, 397
STOP 174, 398
STR$ 44, 399
STR$~ 45
string array 49
string file I/O 103
string indirection 167
string variable 27, 39
    converting to numbers 43
    joining strings together 40
    splitting strings 40
STRING$ 42, 400
subroutines
    assembly language 234
    machine code 234
subscript 47
substring 40
SUM 54, 401
SUMLEN 54, 402
SWAP 403
synchronisation, sound 162, 164
syntax descriptions 216
SYS 404

T

TAB 59, 406
Tab key 68
TAN 407
teletext mode 153
TEMPO 163, 408
text
    cursor 58
    defining characters 60
    direction 184
    input 63
    output 55
    reading 63
    size 110
    viewports 147
TEXTLOAD 409

TEXTSAVE 410
THEN 73, 76, 411
TIME 31, 412
TIME$ 413
timed input 65
TINT 114, 119, 414
tints 111
TO 77
TOP 417
TRACE 174, 418
trapping errors 169
triangle plot 130
TRUE 37, 420
TWIN 421
TWINO 421

U

UNTIL 80, 422
user-defined
    characters 60
    function 94
    procedure 87
USR 423

V

VAL 44, 424
variable 13, 27, 217
VDU 425
    commands 60, 177
    variables 485
VDU 5 mode 110, 125, 186, 365, 429
VFP 456
viewport 147
VOICE 159, 427
*VOICES 160, 427
VOICES 159, 428
volume, sound 161
VPOS 429

W

WAIT 430
WHEN 82, 431
WHILE 81, 432
WIDTH 433
window managed programs 7
word indirection 166
writing to a file 101

Reader's Comment Form

BBC Basic Reference Manual, Issue 2

We would greatly appreciate your comments about this Manual, which will be taken into account for the next issue:

Did you find the information you wanted?

Do you like the way the information is presented?

General comments:

If there is not enough room for your comments, please continue overleaf

How would you classify your experience with computers?

☐ Used computers before   ☐ Experienced User   ☐ Programmer   ☐ Experienced Programmer

Please send an e-mail with your comments to:
manuals@riscosopen.org

Your name and address:

This information will only be used to get in touch with you in case we wish to explore your comments further